Run, Mummy, Run

Cathy Glass

Run, Mummy, Run

A NOVEL INSPIRED BY A TRUE STORY

HARPER

This novel is entirely a work of fiction. The names, characters and incidents portrayed in it are the work of the author's imagination. Any resemblance to actual persons, living or dead, events or localities is entirely coincidental.

HARPER

An imprint of HarperCollins*Publishers*
77–85 Fulham Palace Road,
Hammersmith, London W6 8JB

www.harpercollins.co.uk

First published in Great Britain by HarperCollins*Publishers* 2011

1 3 5 7 9 10 8 6 4 2

A catalogue record for this book is
available from the British Library

ISBN 978-0-00-729928-7

Printed and bound in Great Britain by
Clays Ltd, St Ives plc

Mixed Sources
Product group from well-managed forests and other controlled sources
www.fsc.org   Cert no. SW-COC-001806
© 1996 Forest Stewardship Council

FSC is a non-profit international organisation established to promote the responsible management of the world's forests. Products carrying the FSC label are independently certified to assure consumers that they come from forests that are managed to meet the social, economic and ecological needs of present and future generations.

Find out more about HarperCollins and the environment at
www.harpercollins.co.uk/green

Acknowledgements

M any thanks to my editors – Clare and Rochelle; my agent – Andrew Lownie; Carole and all the team at HarperCollins.

It is said that the eyes are the windows of the soul – an opening, a gateway, to the person within. But what happens when the glass is cracked? Do we see the distortion, or wanting desperately to believe, ignore it, until it's too late?

To Aisha, the kindest, most gentle person I have ever known. Your only crime was to be too trusting, for having no wickedness in your own soul, how were you supposed to see it in others?

One

Aisha touched the photograph and then moved it slightly to the right, trying to find its correct position. It had to sit at exactly the right angle, with the light streaming onto her face so that it showed her at her best. Mark liked it that way, he said it reminded him of the day when they had posed for the photograph – on the bench beneath the large oak tree. The sun had filtered through the leaves of the branches overhead, casting little diamond patterns onto the material of her dress. The two of them, with their arms entwined, taking their eyes from each other just long enough to smile into the lens. Mark had stopped a passer-by and had asked him if he would mind taking their photograph, then he'd given Aisha a framed copy, as a token of his undying love, he said.

Aisha inched the photograph left and right again and then saw a smudge, a fingerprint, on the glass. She picked it up and rubbed it hard with the sleeve of her cardigan until all trace of it had gone. She knew how Mark hated dirt, how angry he would become if he saw it. Mark said dirt was a sign of a slovenly and untidy mind, and that it was the inside of a person coming out and couldn't be tolerated. It wasn't Aisha's fingerprint on the glass; oh no, she would never have been so careless. It must have been the inspector when he'd picked up the photograph and examined it, as though a clue might be concealed within, and then returned it to the bureau, only in the wrong position and leaving his fingerprint.

Aisha silently cursed the inspector for his thoughtlessness – she was going to have to go through the whole of the downstairs of the house, making sure he hadn't touched and sullied anything else. She resented it as much as she resented the inspector's intrusion in the first place – his self-assumed right to ring on the doorbell and then stand there with his WPC expecting to be admitted. It was a liberty, that's what it was! Apart from which, didn't he know she wasn't allowed visitors when Mark was out? Didn't he know the consequences for her if she was found out? He was playing roulette with her life.

Aisha moved away from the photograph and crossed the lounge to the armchair, which was backed hard up against the wall. She'd sat in that chair every night since the accident, every night watching and waiting, on guard for her life. She flopped down into the chair and rested her head back. She was exhausted. Everything seemed such an effort – walking, eating, washing, even thinking tired her to the point of collapse. She closed her eyes and tried to block out the inspector's questions; so many questions with so few answers, they ran on and on like a tape recorder set on continuous, with no pause or stop button.

Where exactly had you been on the night of the accident, Mrs Williams? Where were you going? Was your husband away much on business? Would you describe your marriage as happy, Mrs Williams? On and on, making her head spin and her stomach cramp, nauseous with fear. And she'd seen their furtive glances when she'd taken time to answer a question, or stumbled, or repeated herself. She saw. Did they think she wouldn't notice? That she was so blinded by grief that she couldn't see? Or perhaps they thought the colour of her skin prevented her interpreting their looks and silence, as Mark had done.

Of course she had lied. There was nothing else she could have done, because to tell the truth would have sent her to prison and the children into care. And what would have been the point in that? It would have all been for nothing and they would be better off dead. Which might still be an option if the inspector persisted, and she couldn't answer his questions, or sort out the chaos running through her head.

'But what could I have told you, Inspector?' she said out loud into the empty room. 'What could I have told you that would have justified what I did? That I cried for so long and so hard that my tears fell like ice, and my heart crystallized, just like in the story of the Snow Queen that my father used to read to me as a child? And from my heart's cold dense mass came a determination, a single-minded purpose – the will to survive – so that when I saw the opportunity I was able to seize it as the only escape. That is the truth, Inspector, honestly. Not that it's going to do me any good.'

Two

A isha had always been destined to achieve. It was her father's philosophy – to carve a small notch in the world, fuelled by purpose and ambition.

'Set your sights high, Aisha,' he often said, 'and you can have whatever your heart desires. I am the living proof. I came to this country with nothing, now look at me.'

He was right, of course, it was there for all to see, an example to follow – something to aspire to. Aisha remembered how, when she was a child, he would shut himself away in the box room he called a study, and there, bent over his books, he had followed a correspondence course in accountancy. Night after night, weekends and bank holidays, with his meals brought to him on a tray, for five years until he had qualified. Occasionally she'd been allowed to take his supper up to him, a privilege she yearned for, but then doubted she was up to.

'Don't go in until he tells you,' her mother warned each and every time she carried the wooden tray covered with its fine lace tablecloth up the creaking stairs. 'Put the tray down while you open the door. Use both hands, and don't rattle the door or you'll disturb his train of thought.'

Aisha did as she was told; she followed her mother's instructions exactly, bursting with childish pride but at the same time almost recoiling from the responsibility. Once, the door had stuck, and no matter how hard she'd turned and twisted the knob it wouldn't open. She panicked and did what her mother had forbidden and rattled the door, then waited, hot and fretting, for her father to open it. She had disturbed his train of thought, he would be annoyed, and she would never be asked to take his tea up again.

But he hadn't been annoyed. He'd smiled as he opened the door, his tired and bloodshot eyes saying he understood and she was forgiven. Aisha mumbled a child's apology and passed up the tray. 'Don't worry,' he said. 'I'm pleased for the chance to stretch my legs.' But the door had immediately closed again and she'd turned and fled, bitterly disappointed. For not only had she failed in the task, but she'd also missed the opportunity of going into the study, and the rare glimpse of the Aladdin's cave: the huge oak desk which dominated most of the small room and was piled high with papers and books; the spotlamp which her mother had bargained for at a bring-and-buy sale, its beam of light concentrating on the exact spot where he worked, the rest of the room falling into its shadow. And Aisha had known for as long as she could remember that in that room lay the secret of success, and one day she would follow in her father's footsteps and make him as proud of her as she was of him.

When she won a scholarship to the best girls' school in the area, her father had built her a desk of her own. He constructed it from nothing, just planks of wood, jars of nails, and a drawing he'd sketched on an old envelope. Aisha thought it was incredible, marvellous, the way he created it. She and her mother had sat in the lounge, night after night, listening to the sawing and hammering coming from the conservatory where he worked. Night after night for weeks and weeks before the final stage came – the gluing, sanding and varnishing, the acrid smell and fine dust floating into the house, despite him keeping the door to the conservatory closed. He toiled away week after week, every evening and weekend; for when her father set his mind to something he did it with complete determination.

He'd had to take the desk up to her bedroom in pieces and assemble it in situ, as it was too large and heavy for the three of them to carry up the stairs and then make the tight right turn at the top of the landing and into Aisha's bedroom. Once in place there was some final sanding and varnishing – touching up – before her mother vacuumed her bedroom and she was finally allowed to see in. He told Aisha not to look and she placed her hands, palms down, over her eyes as he led her up the stairs and into her room, her mother following. The three of them were quiet and she felt her heart racing as the tension built and her excitement mounted. She wouldn't peep; she knew better than to peep and spoil the surprise. Only when he had positioned her directly in front of the desk was she allowed to take her hands away and look.

'Well?' he asked tentatively. 'What do you think? We can make some changes if you like. I know it's not perfect.' He laughed nervously and waited for her comment, suddenly small and vulnerable in seeking her approval.

'It's beautiful,' Aisha cried. 'Of course it's perfect. Thank you so much.' She kissed his cheek before rushing over to explore the magnificent desk.

It was made of dark mahogany wood with an inlaid pattern of lighter wood around the edge. There was a carved well for pens and pencils, and three drawers either side. She looked at the little brass locks and turned one of the keys.

'For your personal papers,' her father said. 'It was tricky fitting those locks. They were so small, I kept dropping them. I must be getting old.'

Aisha kissed him again and saw how he grew with pride for they all knew that the desk was far more than a table for studying; it was a symbol of achievement, and everything she could and would accomplish.

'You've made your mother and me very proud, Aisha,' he said. 'Very proud indeed. And I know you will continue to do so in the future.'

They'd had to buy her school uniform during the summer holiday before Aisha started at the girls' school in September. The uniform was navy with a bright logo on the blazer pocket; instantly recognizable, and signalling the wearer as someone who was clever enough to go to St Martha's. The uniform was only available from one leading London store and the three of them had made a special trip into the city, with her father visiting the building society on the way; he preferred to pay in cash, rarely used a chequebook, and refused all offers of credit cards.

'What we can afford, we will buy,' he said. 'And what we can't, we'll save for.' Which seemed to Aisha most sensible and something else she should remember for the future.

After they'd bought the uniform, they had lunch in the store's restaurant on the top floor. Her mother had hesitated as they walked in and a waiter in a black suit and bow tie greeted them. 'It's not for us, Ranjith,' she whispered, holding back. 'Let's find somewhere else.'

Her father insisted. 'It most certainly is,' he said, drawing himself up to his full height. 'This is to celebrate our daughter's achievement. It will make the day complete.'

But they had sat quietly at the table with its starched white tablecloth and crystal centrepiece; quiet and stiffly upright, with their bags and packages tied with the store's ribbon tucked well under their chairs. Aisha had felt as conspicuous as her mother obviously did, and wished they'd gone somewhere less grand. When she finally dared to raise her head and steal a glance around, she saw that those seated at the tables nearby were far more at ease than she and her parents were. Others spoke loudly, rested their elbows on the tables, and talked as they ate, all of which was strictly forbidden at the dinner table in her house. It seemed to Aisha that if you were confident enough, then your surroundings were there for your convenience and not the other way around. Only those who were unsure of themselves adhered strictly to the rules of etiquette and convention and worried about what others would think. So she allowed one elbow to rest lightly on the table, looked the waiter in the eye, and pretended to enjoy what her father had ordered – the delicate pink fish with a peculiarly sharp sauce and the neat bundles of thin vege-tables arranged along one side of the plate. The three of them had eaten carefully, with her mother repeatedly dabbing the napkin at the corner of her mouth, their silence broken only by her father's occasional comment about the high standard of the place. Aisha ate and feigned enjoyment for her father's sake but was grateful when he finally called for the bill and they could leave.

Her mother had taken her to school on her first day to show her the way on the tube; then after that she'd gone by herself with her books in a large bag on her shoulder. Aisha was surprised by how easily she adapted to the new school. While her classmates forgot things and missed their friends from their junior schools, she met the challenge head-on and relished it. After all, this was what she'd been aiming for – the first step along the road to success. And although she wasn't the most popular girl in her year, which seemed to rely on being an extrovert, she was loyal and quietly confident and would always help a friend who was struggling with her homework.

Each and every evening after dinner Aisha went up to her bedroom and studied at her desk beneath the spotlamp her father had given her. The beam of light seemed to focus her attention as though diffusing the knowledge into her, so that she had only to read something once, with complete concentration, and she remembered it.

'You've made a good start,' her father said when she presented him with her first end-of-year report. 'Well done, keep it up. Don't be lulled into complacency. There's a long way to go yet.'

Aisha continued following the doctrine of hard work and determination and won a place at Nottingham University, where she allowed herself only one day off a week to socialize. It was usually a Saturday, and she and a few like-minded friends went to the theatre, cinema, or for a walk along the river to a local bistro. Among this group of friends was a young man called Rowan whose parents were plantation owners in Sri Lanka. Rowan had been sent to England to study, and once he graduated he would take his education home for the benefit of the family business. Aisha never mentioned Rowan to her parents when she phoned, instead she told them of all the little details of college life which her father loved, having never had the opportunity to go to university himself. Why she never told them, she wasn't sure; it was just something she left out. She and Rowan remained good friends – but only friends, nothing more – throughout the three years. Coming from similar backgrounds, they both recognized the privilege of education, and made sure their parents' money didn't go to waste. When they graduated, both with first class honours, Rowan packed, ready to leave as soon as the results were published.

'I've done what I set out to do,' he said stoically. 'Now it is time for me to go.' If he had any regrets, he certainly didn't say.

Aisha went with him to Birmingham Airport and waited until his flight was called. They wouldn't write, they had agreed there was no point. He was returning to his homeland where he was promised in marriage to a girl from a good Tamil family. Aisha watched him go into the departure lounge and waved as the smoky-grey doors closed and he was lost from view. She admired his tenacity and his single-mindedness: they were qualities her father would have approved of if he'd known about their friendship and things had been different. The following day Aisha also packed, she too was expected to return home. She had secured a graduate trainee position with a bank in the City which offered a very good promotion ladder.

With her first month's wages, to say thank you for all the sacrifices her parents had made that had allowed her to go to university, she bought them a holiday in India; it would be their first visit in twenty-five years. 'I owe you both so much,' she said. 'It's a small gift in comparison to what you have given me.'

Her father's eyes moistened as he accepted the tickets. 'You've made us very proud, Aisha, very proud indeed. I only wish you could come with us and meet your cousins, they too will be proud of you.'

'Next time, maybe,' she said. 'There's so much to learn at work and I want to make a success of it. You know how it is.'

Three

*A*isha's hard work, commitment and determination to succeed continued at work. She stayed late at the office most evenings, took home files the night before important meetings, attended weekend seminars and read banking journals from cover to cover. She upgraded her computer at home so it was compatible with those at work; it was important to keep abreast of change in the fast-moving IT field. And the hard work and commitment paid off; the bank saw her worth and rewarded it. By the age of twenty-nine, she was a bank manager, with an office and personal assistant of her own.

'There's no need to work yourself so hard now,' her father said. 'You've got where you wanted to be. Relax and allow yourself some leisure time. You deserve it.'

'There's still a job at head office,' Aisha laughed, trying to deflect him from the real problem – the reason why she was still so absorbed in work. 'Second best will never do – for either of us. Will it, Dad?'

Her father smiled and nodded agreement, though it seemed to Aisha that he might suspect: that in concentrating with such purpose on one aim – a successful career – she had neglected another equally important aspect in her life. If they had lived in India or had had a large family network in England, Aisha knew it wouldn't have been an issue. Her aunt's children in Gujarat had all been found suitors as soon as they'd come of age, some had

Cathy Glass

even been promised in marriage as children, their union taking place when they were eighteen. For here lay the problem, the reason why Aisha still immersed herself so totally in work. It was the loose thread in an otherwise perfect garment. For in spite of everything she'd achieved, Aisha had no one to share it with; no husband or partner. So it seemed to her that all her commitment and hard work had been for nothing, although she'd never have admitted it to her father.

It made Aisha feel irritable and unsettled, though she knew it shouldn't. She knew she had much to be grateful for and that it was wrong to dwell on this one aspect of her life, considering everything else. She reminded herself that many women today remained single through choice, and willingly concentrated on a career to the exclusion of marriage and children. *But I never made that decision*, she thought. *It's crept up on me without warning, and now there's nothing I can do about it.*

She knew, of course, that there were ways of meeting people her own age: singles clubs and bars, dances for the divorced and separated, dating sites on the Internet. But the very idea of putting herself on the market as though she were goods for sale filled her with dread and horror. *Here I am, single and alone, not quite desperate, but getting very close. Please take me before it's too late!* No, she couldn't, not with the intention so crudely obvious. Apart from which, with no knowledge of his family or background, how would you know you weren't talking to some kind of pervert or an axe murderer?

On Sundays, after dinner, Aisha always read the Sunday paper. It made a change from the tomes of high finance, and the glossy *Style* colour supplement gave her an insight into a startlingly different world. The preening and pampering some people

12

indulged in was incredible, and it wasn't only the women: £840 for a man's suit; £75 for a pot of face cream; £350 for a handbag, and some of the handbags were for men! It was amazing what some people spent their money on. One of the colour supplements ended with a page entitled *ENCOUNTERS*, and contained advertisements for those seeking partners. As usual, Aisha skimmed down the page, marvelling at the abbreviated descriptions some people used to describe their qualities and what they were looking for in a partner. How, for example, could anyone describe themselves as a 'buxom blonde' as though that was her only asset, the one she was marketing and with which she hoped to catch a mate? Aisha's gaze slid down the page to the boxed agency advertisements, then stopped. Here was one she hadn't seen before and the wording caught her eye.

'*Too busy being successful to meet people? I understand. A personal introductory service for professionals. The crème de la crème from London and the Home Counties. Not a dating agency.*'

Aisha glanced up at her father who was still immersed in the sports section of the paper, the one section Aisha never read. His glasses were perched on the end of his nose and he looked like a wise old owl. She tilted the magazine towards her and reread the agency advertisement. The sentiment was right; it was strange she hadn't seen it before. Perhaps it was a new agency? But no, it said they were established. *Perhaps I could just telephone*, she thought, *a general enquiry asking for a few more details? They must have hundreds of calls that are never followed up. I could phone from the office tomorrow lunchtime, just to satisfy my curiosity; there would be no harm in that.* Later she slipped the magazine into her briefcase ready for Monday.

Knowing it was there, awaiting her attention, caused her a little surge of anticipation, a flutter of excitement, which she hadn't felt in a long time.

At one o'clock on Monday, with her office door closed and her secretary at lunch, Aisha carefully dialled the agency's number. A staccato voice, which sounded as though it had been activated by the trill of the phone, answered. 'Hello, Connections, Belinda speaking, how can we help you?'

Aisha replied that she only wanted some details, a leaflet in the post please, something she could look at at home. But Belinda clearly had to say her piece, and continued: 'We pride ourselves on our very personal approach, and we are highly selective. I prefer to talk through the literature with my clients at the interview.'

'Interview?' Aisha said, taken aback.

'Well, more of a friendly chat really. I always see all our prospective clients personally, preferably in their own homes. It gives me a clearer picture of the type of person I am helping and who would be most suitable for them. You can tell a lot by a person's home environment. Well, *I* can, after so many years in the business.' She gave a little laugh.

Aisha heard the words 'friendly chat' and 'own home' and inwardly cringed. She nearly hung up – the very thought of this woman interviewing her at home: her parents' house, furnished and run by her mother. It offered no clue to her own identity or hopes for the future.

'But we can arrange an office interview if you prefer,' Belinda added quickly.

'Yes, I would prefer it,' Aisha said. 'I live with my parents and I'd rather they weren't inconvenienced.'

Aisha heard the little silence, the small hesitation, and knew what Belinda must be thinking: *Still living with her parents and wanting to keep it secret, how quaint.*

'I quite understand,' Belinda said diplomatically. 'My office it is then. When would suit you? I'm here Monday to Friday until eight in the evening.'

Aisha found herself reaching into her handbag for her diary and opening it to the week ahead. 'You realize I probably won't go ahead with this,' she warned. 'I mean, I don't want you to be under any misapprehension. I don't want to waste your time.'

Belinda gave another little laugh. 'Don't worry. Most people say that to begin with, but there's no harm in us having a chat. If you decide not to go ahead, then there is nothing lost other than half an hour of your time, is there?'

Aisha liked Belinda's approach and warmed to her slightly. This was no hard sell or pressure meeting, and she of all people could afford to wager thirty minutes of her time.

'Now, when would suit you?' Belinda asked.

'An evening after work would be best.'

'Of course, no problem. How about Wednesday? Is six thirty convenient?'

'Yes, that's perfect,' Aisha said. She gave her name and then wrote the appointment very quickly in her diary before she had time to change her mind.

Four

*P*erhaps *I could look upon it as similar to the arrangement my father would have made had we been living in India,* Aisha thought by way of justification as she climbed the stairs to Belinda's office after work that Wednesday. *Belinda is finding me a suitor, vetting him, and then introducing us. Belinda is in place of my father and her fee is in lieu of the dowry. If I view it like that,* she thought, *it might seem more acceptable.* Might. But the Western notion of romantic love kept getting in the way; she wasn't in India, but England.

Alone on the landing, Aisha rang the bell to Belinda's office. A brass plaque on the lilac glossed door boldly announced 'CONNECTIONS'. Her office was over an antique shop in SW1, where rents were horrendous, so Aisha guessed Belinda must be doing very well for herself. Aisha knew exactly what Belinda would look like – she could picture her from their brief conversation on the phone: tall, blonde and willowy; with an effusive yet slightly reserved manner that girls in this part of London seemed to acquire.

The door opened. 'Aisha? So sorry to have kept you, I was on the phone.' Belinda smiled and shook Aisha's hand. 'Do come in.'

She wasn't at all how Aisha had imagined: petite, mid-thirties, with brown hair, and a navy suit, Belinda wouldn't have looked out of place at the bank.

'Well done,' Belinda said, leading Aisha down the short hall. 'That's the worst part over with. Now you've made it this far, the rest is easy.' Aisha liked Belinda's appreciation of just how much it had taken to get her here.

The room Belinda showed her into was furnished more like a flat than an office, with two beige sofas either side of a long, low coffee table. The flowing beige drapes at the windows matched the thick pile carpet, and the light terracotta walls were dotted with modern watercolours. A massive fig tree stood in the bay window which looked out over the street.

'Do sit down,' Belinda said, waving to the sofas. 'What can I get you to drink? Tea, coffee, fruit juice? Or something stronger perhaps?'

'A fruit juice would be nice, thank you.'

Aisha sat self-consciously in the middle of one of the sofas while Belinda crossed to a small fridge discreetly placed in a recess at one end of the room. Belinda's shinning bobbed hair swung as she bent forwards to open the fridge door. *She's only a few years older than me,* Aisha thought, *but she's so vibrant and sophisticated. How dowdy I must seem beside her.* And Belinda had such good taste. Aisha looked around the room with its minimalist style, and decided that if ever she was lucky enough to have a home of her own, she would furnish it just like this. Plain and simple, no clutter, and certainly none of the gaudy memorabilia her parents had collected from India.

Belinda returned with two glasses of orange juice which she placed on the coffee table, then sat on the sofa opposite Aisha. She smiled reassuringly and took a large white folder from the shelf beneath the table and passed it across. 'I usually start by letting my clients take a look at these,' she said. 'They are testimonials from some of my satisfied clients. They're not all there, of course – as you can imagine, there are hundreds – but it will give you some idea.'

Aisha took a sip of her juice and then opened the album to the first page; it was a large photograph album that had been adapted for its present purpose. On the first page, under the cellophane, was a handwritten letter from a Susan, thanking Belinda for introducing her to Steven. On the page opposite was a photograph of the couple, raising champagne glasses, with the caption: 'Engagement Party. Susan and Steven. February 2000.'

'That was my first success,' Belinda said.

Aisha glanced up, smiled, and turned the page.

'While you're looking at those,' Belinda said, 'let me give you some background about how I got started, so you know where I'm coming from.'

Aisha nodded and studied the next page, which showed an Asian couple at their wedding reception with some of their family members in the background.

'Twelve years ago,' Belinda began, 'I arrived in London from the Cotswolds to take up a job as a PA with a large firm of solicitors. I enjoyed my job immensely, but I returned every evening to an empty flat, with only the television to look forward to. The only people I met were my colleagues at work, and they were either married, not my type, or too busy with their own social lives to notice me. Months passed and nothing changed, and I began to wonder how many other people were in the same position as me, isolated in the big city, surrounded by entertainment, but with no one to go with. Out of curiosity more than anything, I placed an advertisement in the *Evening Standard*, asking if anyone else was too busy being successful to meet people. I was astounded at the response. I had over a hundred and fifty replies! So I picked a few for myself, compiled a register of the rest, and started introducing them on the basis of their interests. It was so successful that a year later I left my job at the solicitors to turn it into a full-time business. And here I am now, still going from strength to strength!'

Aisha looked up, impressed. 'You've certainly done very well,' she said.

'Thank you. I always stress this is not, and never will be, a dating agency. It's a way of bringing like-minded people together, without all the time-consuming and tacky business of hanging around in bars and clubs, waiting to be picked up. I'm highly selective, Aisha. I only take professional, interesting and well-rounded people. I screen out anybody with emotional baggage.'

Aisha paused in turning the pages and briefly wondered if she was guilty of having 'emotional baggage', but decided she hadn't had enough experience to acquire baggage of any sort.

'So,' Belinda continued, 'that's how it all started, and I've continued in much the same vein ever since. I always work one-to-one with my clients. Once I have met them and have a clearer understanding of the type of person they are, and I know they're suitable for my books, I spend quite a bit of time talking to them, then complete a short questionnaire. From that I know what qualities they are looking for in a partner and who would be most suitable for them. I always have a large number of clients on my books, but I only select one at a time for introduction. That's why I say we are not a dating agency. I'm meticulous and only introduce a couple when I'm completely sure they are suited to each other.'

Aisha flicked through the last few pages of the portfolio which contained photographs of more recent weddings and engagements and returned it to the coffee table. 'But supposing the couple aren't suited?' she dared to say. 'I mean, you're obviously very good at your job, but supposing they're not right for each other and don't get along after all?'

'Absolutely no problem,' Belinda reassured her. 'In that case, I select again. Then a third, fourth, and even fifth time if necessary. After that I'm more likely to suggest they wait for a week or so as new clients join daily. But it rarely happens, Aisha. Usually the next thing I receive is a telephone call saying they won't be needing my services anymore.' Belinda gave a small laugh. 'By then the couples are saying they met through a mutual friend and don't want anything to do with me. Strange, isn't it? Nowadays we happily discuss everything else, but finding a partner through an introductory agency is still taboo.'

Aisha nodded and smiled weakly. She met Belinda's gaze. 'I wouldn't want anyone to know either. I mean, if I went ahead, I wouldn't want you phoning me at home, for example.'

'I completely understand,' Belinda said. 'Your wishes are paramount. I could call your mobile or work number at a pre-arranged time. Whatever my client asks for I respect. After all, without you I wouldn't be in business.'

Aisha nodded again. 'My work at lunchtime would be best,' she found herself saying. 'My mobile is off during the day. I eat at my desk and I'm usually alone between one and two o'clock.'

'Good. And you're happy with what I have told you so far? It's important you are able to put your trust in me.'

'Yes.' Aisha nodded. She was trying to adopt the same objectivity to what Belinda was telling her as she used at work, but something kept getting in the way. 'And you vet all your clients?' she asked.

'Absolutely. I wouldn't take anyone on if I had any doubts. I've been in this job so long I form an immediate impression and I haven't been wrong yet. Is there anything else you would like to ask before I take your details?'

All the questions Aisha should have been asking – the exact nature of the client vetting, for example – flew easily and happily out of reach. And in their place stood the obvious and irrefutable: Belinda was good at her job and may even be able to give her what Aisha so desperately needed; assuming, of course, she was to be included among Belinda's very select clientele.

'I can't think of anything else at present,' Aisha said. 'From what you've seen of me so far, would you say I was the type of person you would accept?'

Belinda leant forwards in earnest. 'Most definitely. You are a professional and well-qualified person, with an open and honest nature. I have no doubt you are sincere in your wish to be in a long-term committed relationship. I'd say you were exactly right. Shall we start on the questionnaire then?'

Aisha took a deep breath and told herself that if she ever did one thing that could be described as self-centred and impulsive, it had to be this and it had to be now. 'Yes, please, I'd like to go ahead; I haven't got anything to lose.'

'Excellent,' Belinda said, picking up her pen. 'But let's make it a bit more positive and say you have everything to gain.'

An hour later, when Aisha had answered all Belinda's questions, and the receipt for the fee of £475 was safely tucked in her purse, she congratulated herself; not only had she made a possibly life-changing decision, but in talking to Belinda she had discovered her likes and dislikes, attitudes and preferences, a personality, which had somehow become lost along the road to success, and which Belinda had approved of.

'It's been lovely meeting you,' Belinda enthused, seeing Aisha to the door. 'I'll phone you as soon as I've done my homework; Monday at the latest.'

Aisha thanked her again and said goodbye; then went back down the stairs, past the antique shop, which was now closed and night-lit, and out onto the street. Her shoes clipped a newfound confidence on the pavement as she headed towards the tube, a lightness, a little risqué freedom, which hadn't been there on the inward journey. Before she went down into the tunnels and lost the signal on her mobile, she phoned her mother. 'Sorry, I was held up in a meeting. I'll be home in an hour.' Which was all she intended saying now or in the future, to save them all embarrassment, and her parents the futile job of trying to dissuade her from going ahead.

Five

'It's a Miss Mayhew,' Aisha's PA said, her hand covering the mouthpiece of the phone.

Aisha glanced up from the printout she was studying. 'From which company?'

'She said it was personal.'

Aisha frowned, puzzled, and took the phone from Grace. 'Hello,' she said, and was surprised to hear Belinda's voice. She hadn't known Belinda's surname, and it was not her lunch hour yet, and only the day after the interview. 'Just a moment,' she said into the phone. Then to Grace: 'Can you give me five minutes, please?'

She waited until Grace had left her office and closed the door behind her. 'Hello Belinda. What can I do for you?'

'I'll be quick because I know you're busy, but I just had to tell you. I have an introduction for you! Already!'

Aisha heard the excitement in Belinda's voice and knew she should have felt it too. 'Yes?' she asked tentatively.

'Let me explain. By the time you left yesterday evening I already had three gentlemen in mind. All absolutely charming and meeting your criteria. So, in keeping with my usual policy, I telephoned each of them with a few details about yourself, and from that I was able to proceed and select one. He's so right, Aisha, so absolutely right! Perfect. You're very lucky indeed.'

Aisha admired the diplomatic way Belinda passed off the rejection of her details by the other two; they were probably looking for someone younger, she thought, or more vibrant, or both.

'Now, before I go any further,' Belinda continued, 'there's something I need to clarify with you first. I am right in thinking you are happy meeting someone from a different ethnic background? That is what you said, isn't it?'

'It is.'

'Good. I wanted to be certain because it's obviously important.'

'It could be to some,' Aisha said, and felt the familiar niggle of irritation. 'Is he white?'

'Yes. Now let me tell you a bit about him. He's thirty-six, a bit older than you, as you requested. He's a graduate engineer, and tall – you said you like tall men. He works for a large multinational in the City, in fact not far from where you work. He sometimes travels on business, but he's more than happy to take his partner whenever possible. Don't worry though, I've already explained it would be difficult for you with your career. He has his own house. His car is a BMW, which he changes every year. Without doubt he's completely sincere in his wish to have someone important in his life again, and is over the break-up of his marriage, which I understand wasn't his fault. He loves what I've told him about you and hopes you will allow him to telephone you. This will be his first introduction, Aisha. Like you, he's very particular about the type of person he is looking for.'

Belinda stopped and Aisha latched on to the one sentence she would rather not have heard: the break-up of his marriage. 'He's been married before then?' she asked.

'A long while ago, when he was young. Too young, he told me. As I said yesterday, Aisha, men of his age will have either been married or have cohabited in a long-term relationship, and

24

if they haven't, I would hear alarm bells ringing. It could suggest commitment issues.'

Aisha wound the telephone wire around her little finger as she pictured the look on her parents' faces if she were to introduce a divorcee, regardless of how long ago it was, or whose fault it had been. Divorce didn't happen in her family in India, and given the choice, her parents would have doubtless preferred a never-married doctor or accountant from Gujarat, but her father no longer had those connections so that wasn't an option.

'Does he have children?' Aisha asked.

'Two, but he doesn't see them. His wife remarried straight after the divorce and encouraged the children to look on her new husband as their father. He told me he didn't want the children upset by a court battle so he left them in peace. Which I think was highly commendable, don't you?'

'I suppose so,' Aisha said and let the telephone wire go with a twang. 'Why did the marriage break up? Did he tell you?'

'He said he would like to discuss that with you personally, but I understand his wife was having an affair.' Belinda seemed to hear Aisha's hesitation. 'Aisha, you can't possibly make a decision until you have met him. And when you do, I'm sure you'll be as impressed as I was. He's charming, absolutely charming. In fact, if I wasn't happily married I'd be quite tempted myself.' She gave a little giggle.

Aisha hadn't thought of Belinda as married, and it was heartening to have this first-hand example of a woman combining a career and marriage so successfully; no one at her level at the bank seemed to have managed it.

'Well? What do you say?' Belinda asked. 'I've put a lot of work into this, Aisha, and I wouldn't have suggested him if I didn't think he was absolutely right.'

'Yes, I'm sorry. I understand. So, what happens now?'

'I'll give him your phone number and he'll call for a chat.'

'And he won't mind if we don't go ahead and meet?' Aisha asked, needing a get-out clause.

'No, of course not. But you must give it a chance.'

'All right then,' Aisha said. 'There's no harm in us having a chat.'

'Excellent. His name is Mark. I'll tell him to phone your office. Tomorrow lunchtime?'

'Yes, between one and two o'clock, please.'

They said goodbye and she hung up. *Mark,* she thought. No surnames at this stage, only first names. Mark. She tried to picture him, but beyond him being tall and white it was impossible, for in truth Belinda had given her very few details.

The rest of the day was very busy and that evening she had a report to write for a meeting the following morning so there was little time for worrying or idle speculation. It was only when she was alone in bed and drifting off to sleep that her thoughts turned to Belinda and Mark, and with it came the inherent worry of what she had committed to. *Oh well, I can always wind up the conversation with an excuse,* she thought; *that's assuming he phones at all.* And the more she considered the chances of him phoning the less likely it seemed he would.

The following day her morning meeting overran and by the time she arrived back at her desk it was one fifteen. She asked Grace if there had been any phone calls; Grace said there had been four, but when Aisha looked at the note Grace handed her she saw they were all business calls. She wasn't sure if she was relieved or disappointed. Aisha asked Grace to switch the phone line through to her office while she went to lunch as she usually did. She then sat at her desk, took her sandwich box from her bag, opened the carton of orange juice, and tried to concentrate on the correspondence Grace had left for her. The phone rang almost immediately and she sprang to answer it, but it was a disgruntled customer who had asked to speak to the manager. Eager to clear the line Aisha apologized profusely for the banking error and promised to look into it personally. With the customer pacified she replaced the receiver. Two minutes later the phone rang again with another unhappy customer. Aisha again apologized and said she would look into it. Ten minutes passed before the phone rang again and when Aisha answered she knew straight away it was different. A friendly warm male voice, not complaining – far from it, a little hesitant, she thought. 'Is it possible to speak to Aisha, please?'

'Speaking.'

'Hello Aisha, this is Mark. I hope you're expecting my call?'

'Yes, I am, Mark. Hello.'

She heard his small sigh of relief and the pause before he said: 'Good. Excellent. Now, where do I go from here? I don't know about you, but all this is new to me. Maybe I should start by telling you a bit about myself? That's what Belinda said I should do.'

'Yes, please do,' Aisha said, and smiled to herself at the image of this grown man taking his instructions from Belinda.

'Well, I'm six foot one, so you won't lose me in a crowd,' he joked, 'and I like the usual things – theatre, cinema, travelling, a drink in a country pub. I enjoy my work and it takes up a lot of my time. But when I can, I play squash, and I swim. I'm a member of my local gym, but I don't use it as much as I should. Occasionally I watch television, the late-night films mainly – they help me to unwind. I like most food, but I'm particularly partial to Italian and Indian. There are some excellent restaurants close to where I live and they're not helping my waistline at all.'

He gave a little laugh then paused, and Aisha knew it was her turn. Her heart thumped and her mouth went dry. How to make it snappy and interesting as he had done?

'Well,' she began, twiddling the phone wire, 'I expect Belinda has told you I'm also busy with my work, but when I have free time I like to read, or go for a walk in the country. I find a country walk quite relaxing. I go to the theatre every so often, and eat out, but not as much as I'd like to. Sometimes I take my parents to the cinema.' She stopped. *Don't get too cosy and domestic,* she told herself. *He won't want to know that.* 'But more often I take work home,' she added, 'which I do while listening to music. Mozart and Tchaikovsky are among my favourites, but I like some jazz as well as some modern music.'

'I have eclectic tastes in music too,' Mark said. 'What about country and western, do you like that?'

'Yes, some, the old favourites – Patsy Cline, Johnny Cash, Tammy Wynette.'

As the exchange of information continued and then developed into a conversation, Aisha found it wasn't as difficult as she had thought and indeed she was quite enjoying herself; she wondered what she had been afraid of. Mark took the lead in the conversation, steered it, and filled in any gaps. Fifteen minutes later when he finally broke off and said, 'I'm sorry, I'm going to have to go. I'm due in a meeting soon,' she felt a pang of disappointment. Then he added: 'Shall we continue this in person and meet?'

'Yes, I'd like that,' she replied without hesitation.

'How about Friday? After work? We could go for a bite to eat perhaps?'

'That would be lovely. I usually finish about six on a Friday.'

'OK. I'll have my car with me but we can use the tube if you prefer. Can I suggest you wait near the main entrance of Harrods? Say six thirty? I'll collect you and we'll take it from there?'

'Yes, that's fine with me.'

'Good. I drive a metallic silver BMW with personalized number plates. If you've got a pen handy, I'll give you the registration. I don't want you running off with the wrong man.'

Aisha laughed easily and reached for her notepad and pen.

'MAR K12,' he said and she wrote it down. 'I'll be wearing a navy suit. The jacket will be hanging in the rear window of the car. I always hang it there when I'm driving. But don't worry, I'll recognize you first because Belinda has told me you've got the most amazingly long black hair. Is it true you haven't cut it since you were a child?'

Unused to personal compliments, Aisha felt herself blush and was pleased Mark couldn't see her. 'I have it trimmed, but my mother believes it brings bad luck for a girl to cut off her long hair before she's married.' Immediately she could have kicked herself for introducing such a personal note so soon; it sounded as though marriage was the only thing on her mind and she was desperate.

'I can't wait to see it,' Mark said. 'Until Friday then. Have a good week.'

'And you. Thank you for phoning.'

'My pleasure.'

That evening after dinner, Aisha went straight to her bedroom, shut the door and sat at her dressing table mirror. The face that looked back at her had hardly changed since she was a teenager and, Aisha thought, was as plain and unsophisticated now as it had been then. There was nothing interesting in it, no intrigue, no signs of having lived, no experience; in fact nothing to distinguish it from that of countless other women her age, apart from maybe the colour, and that hardly singled her out in London. But it was the face Mark was going to see outside Harrods and then later across a table in a restaurant. The one that he would either want to see again for another meeting or politely reject.

Perhaps I could start by wearing some make-up, she thought, *something that would define my features. That might help.* She opened the top drawer of her dressing table and found a kohl pencil and lipstick which she'd bought a year or so ago but had never used. Widening her eyes, she drew a thin line with the kohl pencil under the bottom lids; then placing the pencil to one side, unscrewed the lipstick. Tightening her lips, she ran the lipstick lightly over her lips and to the corner of her mouth and looked in the mirror. The result she had to admit was more the expression of a surprised clown than an attractive woman. Aisha sat back in the chair and scrutinized her head and shoulders. Perhaps it was her hair that made her so plain? Although it was in good condition and shone she always wore it drawn straight back off her face in a plait.

Aisha undid the plait and shook her hair free; it fell to her waist. It was certainly long and black as Belinda had told Mark but Aisha wasn't sure about the 'amazing'. Taking her hairbrush from the drawer she gave her hair a good brush and then arranged it loosely around her shoulders. But the sheer length and volume made her look more like a woman possessed than attractive or even seductive. Stoically, Aisha re-plaited her hair and wiped off the kohl and lipstick. She was naturally plain, that was all there was to it, and if Mark didn't like it, well, he simply wouldn't ask to see her again, which in many ways would be something of a relief.

Standing, she moved away from the dressing table and picked up the banking journal that was on her beside table. Propping herself on the bed she buried herself in the comparative safety of the London Stock Exchange. At least here graphs predicted outcomes and a negative forecast could be acted on to minimize loss. Pity life wasn't as controlled and predictable, she thought. But then again hers probably had been, which was why at nearly thirty she was living at home with her parents with nothing beyond work to look forward to.

Six

It was raining hard on Friday evening so Aisha sheltered in the doorway of Harrods. Other shoppers and tourists were doing the same, hoping the rain would ease. It hadn't been raining when she'd left home that morning and she wished she'd thought to bring an umbrella just in case. Trying to stay dry under the canopy of the store she leaned forwards and, peering out, surveyed the traffic for any sign of Mark. She then checked her watch again – it was nearly six twenty-five; she'd arrived early, there was still time for him to come.

A few minutes later at exactly six thirty she began to think that Mark wouldn't be coming. There were all sorts of reasons that could have stopped him from meeting her: the rain, the traffic, an unexpected appointment, or more simply he'd just changed his mind. She'd just decided she would give him until six forty and then head for home when she saw what she thought could be his car and her heart lurched. Half a dozen cars back, there was a metallic silver BMW, shimmering with rain in the street lamps. Was it him? She couldn't be certain until it drew closer. She moved further forwards for a better view, careful to stay under the store's canopy and out of the rain. She watched and waited, peered out through the drizzle and round the heads of passers-by, monitoring the car's painfully slow progress in the bumper-to-bumper traffic. Then she saw the silhouette of the driver, male and large, and yes, there was a jacket swinging in the nearside rear window. Her heart set up a queer little rhythm as the car drew close enough for her to read the number plate – MAR K12 – yes, it was definitely him.

Aisha stayed where she was as the car pulled in to the kerb. She saw him lean over and peer through the passenger window, looking across the pavement, searching for her. Then the driver's door opened and he got out. He was tall, yes; she could easily see him looking over the roof of the car towards the store, scanning the pavement. Umbrellas got in the way as Aisha moved out onto the pavement and into the rain. She gave a little wave, her hand flicking nervously from her side and back again. For a moment she thought he hadn't seen her as his gaze continued past her, and she stood there feeling foolishly exposed. Then his eyes returned to her, and with a small nod of recognition he moved towards her, his large strides bringing him easily onto the pavement and up to her.

'Aisha?'

'Yes, hello Mark.' She smiled.

'I'm so very pleased to meet you, very pleased.' He shook her hand. 'The traffic is appalling, I hope you haven't been waiting long?'

'No, not long.' She smiled again and noticed how blue his eyes were and how they sparkled as he spoke, and that he seemed genuinely pleased to see her.

'Good. Come on, get in or you'll be drenched.'

He cupped her elbow and steered her protectively across the crowded pavement to his car. She felt pleasantly conspicuous as he opened the passenger door and then waited while she got in. He unhooked her seat belt and draped it over her shoulder and into her lap; then closed the door. Aisha watched as he crossed in front of the bonnet – took in his well-defined features: the firm angular jaw suggesting confidence; his upright manner; his slightly thinning fair hair. He wasn't handsome in the traditional sense, she thought, more rugged: a man with presence who was at ease with himself. A man's man, she thought.

The driver's door opened with a rush of cold air and the interior light flickered on as Mark got in. 'What a dreadful night,' he said. 'I do hope you haven't got wet.'

'No,' she said, and ran her hands over her plaited hair, which was only slightly damp.

She glanced sideways at him and saw the little patches of rain on his shirt and a few beads of rain glistening on his forehead. He smiled and, reaching behind her for his jacket, took a freshly laundered and pressed cotton handkerchief from the pocket and dabbed the moisture from his face. She watched, transfixed – the act appearing intimate and magnified in the confines of the car. Briefly checking the result in the interior mirror he stretched out his legs and pushed the handkerchief into his trouser pocket. A car horn sounded behind them.

'Patience,' Mark said evenly. 'A little patience goes a long way.'

Which, Aisha realized, was exactly the type of thing her father would have said; he had a maxim for every occasion.

Mark clicked on the indicator, but before pulling out suddenly turned to her, concerned. 'Aisha, you are happy about using my car, aren't you? Say if you're not, and I'll park and we can get a taxi.'

She smiled, and dispelling any reservation she may or should have felt said, 'Yes, Belinda said it was OK, although I would like to know where you're taking me.'

He laughed. 'I'm sorry, I should have said. I thought we'd get out of the city. Do you know The Crooked Chimney, just off the

A1? Coming from North London, I thought you might. It's had some excellent write-ups.'

'Yes, I do,' she said, and felt comfortable that they were going somewhere she knew. 'It's not so far from where I live. I've never eaten there though.' Another horn sounded and Mark looked over his shoulder and began to pull out.

'I used to go there regularly, a while back,' he said, straightening the wheel. 'The menu's a bit conservative, but not at all bad.' He glanced at her. 'You do like English food, don't you? You know, meat and veg?'

'Yes, I was born here,' she said. And she knew straight away she shouldn't have said it – that quick retort her father chided her about: 'You're so sharp you'll cut yourself one day, Aisha,' he said.

'I didn't mean—' Mark began.

'No, neither did I. Sorry. It's just that I'm used to the question, and often put a lot less subtly. I love English food, and Italian, and Indian. In fact, I eat almost anything.'

'Great! That's settled then,' Mark said and then fell silent as he concentrated on manoeuvring across the two lanes of traffic to turn right. 'Now,' he said after a moment. 'Belinda suggested we should talk about our childhoods as a safe topic to begin with. Best not disappoint her?'

'No, indeed,' Aisha laughed, and glanced sideways at him again. 'But you go first, Mark, I'm sure your childhood was a lot more interesting than mine.'

'I doubt it, but if you insist … Stop me when you've had enough, I don't want to bore you to death on our first date.'

First date, she thought, suggesting he was already thinking of more. She settled herself back in her seat and looked through the windscreen. The wipers continued their steady, almost hypnotic rhythm as she listened to Mark's rich, mellow voice. He told her about his early years in Perth with his parents and younger brother, their move south of the border, and eventually to London. She was pleased he'd suggested using the car, with just the two of them cocooned in the semi-darkness, and Mark having to concentrate on his driving. It gave her time to adjust and relax rather than suddenly being on display in the stark illumination of the underground, or opposite him in a restaurant close to where they worked. When Mark reached his teenage years in his life story, they were on the A1. He stopped talking and glanced at her. 'I'm sure you've heard plenty now. I could go on all night. Your turn.'

Aisha smiled and briefly met his eyes. 'My childhood was very different from yours, a world away. It might help if I tell you a bit about my parents first.'

Mark nodded. 'Yes, I'd like that. I'd be very interested.'

'They were born in Gujarat,' she began, 'which is on the west coast of India, in a village not far from the port of Okha. Their families were poor but my father had his sights set on coming to England, right from an early age. He had a very menial job first, working in one of the government's offices, but he worked his way up in their accounts department. Much of his money went to supporting his younger brothers and sisters but eventually he managed to save enough for the plane ticket here. He tells how he arrived with all his belongings in one bag and trekked the streets until he found a job as a clerk with a firm of accountants. He studied in his spare time, and once he had a decent income and a permanent address, he sent for my mother. They were married in a registry office and I was born a year later. My father made a lot of sacrifices to get where he is now and he is a very proud man. He's strict with me and so is my mother – she wants me to do the right thing. My father would give my mother and me anything, but he's frugal. I suppose it comes from knowing what real poverty is. He won't ever buy anything unless he has the money.'

'There's nothing wrong in that,' Mark said. 'I know too many people sinking under the debt of credit cards. We live in a gotta have-it-now culture. Never mind if you can afford it. I think your father's attitude is right.'

It pleased Aisha considerably that Mark agreed with and upheld her father's principles, and it gave her the confidence to continue.

Presently they turned off the A1 and Mark braked as a sudden squall sheeted against the windscreen and momentarily blocked their vision. He upped the wiper speed. Aisha looked out of the side window at the trees bending over in the wind.

'I'm glad I'm not driving,' she confessed. 'My car is old and doesn't like the rain. I'm always worried about being stranded with a breakdown or flat tyre.'

'Don't worry, you're safe with me,' Mark said. 'She hasn't let me down yet.'

And, yes, Aisha felt safe sitting beside Mark, his broad shoulders squared into the seat, his large hands covering the steering wheel, she felt very safe indeed. Mark emanated a confidence, an assurance, that whatever befell them he could deal with it. He was someone, she decided, who'd had enough experience of life to be in control of it rather than at its mercy, as she sometimes felt.

The sign for The Crooked Chimney presently appeared out of the trees, swinging in the wind and rain. It had always reminded Aisha of the signboard for The Jamaica Inn – the pub on the edge of Bodmin Moor: the oil painting of the old inn sign creaking as it swung from its tall metal stand. Mark made the left turn then drove a little further along the B road and pulled into the restaurant's car park. The car's tyres crunched over the gravel to one of the few remaining spaces on the far side.

'Stay put and I'll get the umbrella from the boot,' he said, cutting the engine, 'I'll impress you with my chivalry. And don't forget to tell Belinda.'

Aisha laughed easily, she felt far more relaxed now. Mark reached behind her, unhooked his jacket from the rear, slipped it on, and threw open his door. The wind and rain sprang to seek refuge inside the car before he slammed the door shut. Aisha heard the boot open and close, and then he was at her window, shaking out a large golfing umbrella, which he pointed into the wind. He opened her door and she got out and stood beside him, close, but not quite touching. With Mark holding the umbrella like a shield into the wind, they began across the car park. Aisha looked down and concentrated on trying to avoid the little potholes that were quickly filling up with water.

'Who would ever live in this country?' Mark shouted against the wind. 'It's a wonder any of us survive in this climate.'

'My father would,' she shouted back. 'He wouldn't live anywhere else.'

'He must be mad!' he said. 'But I'm glad for my sake he is, otherwise you wouldn't be here now.'

The door to the restaurant was opened from inside as they approached and to Aisha's small surprise she found that not only was the maitre d' waiting for them, but that he knew Mark. 'Nice to see you again, Mr Williams,' he said with a small nod. They shook hands. 'It's been a while. I hope you've been keeping well?'

'Yes, and yourself?'

'Very well, thank you.'

Mark passed him the umbrella, and then helped Aisha out of her coat.

'Your table is ready,' the maitre d' said. 'Or would you and your guest like a drink first?'

Mark turned to Aisha. 'I don't know about you, but I'm famished. Shall we go straight through and order a drink at the table?'

She nodded and ran her hands over her skirt, wishing she'd changed out of her office suit. Now she was inside, the restaurant seemed very grand and she felt underdressed. The maitre d' led the way from reception, down a small carpeted hall and into the dinning room, which was full and buzzed with conversation and the chink of cutlery. A huge inglenook fire roared orange and yellow and above it rose the crooked redbrick chimney from which the inn had taken its name. To their right a large party of a dozen or more were opening champagne for a birthday celebration, while the other tables, nestled between the exposed oak pillars, were occupied by small groups and couples. The room was warm and cosy and not as formal as Aisha thought it might be. The maitre d' led them down the centre aisle, between the tables with their single candles and flowers. Aisha noticed that the other diners, men and women, looked up as Mark passed, their gaze lingering. It wasn't just Mark's stature, she thought, although it was true he didn't stoop as some tall men do, but he had that unmistakable quality – that presence of being – that drew people's attention. Aisha felt proud that she was with him for she also noticed that as a diner's gaze left Mark, it went to her, as though some of his charisma was rubbing off.

The maitre d' removed a reserved sign from a table in a secluded alcove and drew out a chair for Aisha. He eased it under her as she sat, while Mark took the chair opposite. The maitre d' handed each of them a large leather-bound menu. 'Would you like a drink now, sir?' he asked as a waiter appeared and hovered, ready to take their order.

Mark looked at Aisha. 'A mineral water, please,' she said.

'And a gin and tonic for me, with ice and lemon,' Mark added.

'Very good, sir,' the maitre d' said and, with another slight nod, left, followed by the drinks waiter.

Aisha opened the menu and propped it between the table and her lap. She began studying the extensive list of dishes presented in flourishing italics.

'Well?' Mark asked after a moment. 'What do you think?'

'I'm not sure yet. There's so much to choose from.'

'No, I mean the restaurant. Do you like it?'

She looked up with a nervous little laugh. 'Oh, yes, it's very nice. I'm so pleased you suggested it.'

'Good. Although I can't take all the credit. I ran it past Belinda first.'

Aisha laughed again. 'Belinda has very good taste.'

'Absolutely,' Mark said, and his eyes lingered admiringly until she looked away embarrassed. 'Anyway, Michael Winner reviewed it once in his column,' he continued. 'Do you read the *Sunday Times*?'

She looked up again. 'I do. But the arrogance of the man! It's a wonder restaurateurs let him in. I'm sure I wouldn't.'

'I suppose any publicity is better than none.' Mark laughed.

The starters arrived and as they ate and talked of work – a subject which came easily to them both – it crossed Aisha's mind how proud her father would be to see her sitting here now, in this very nice restaurant, as confident and relaxed as Mark and the other diners. She thought that one day she would treat her parents to dinner here: book the table, order the food, and call for the bill at the end, to show them just how self-assured she could be, how at home she was in these surroundings.

'I'm incredibly well organized,' Mark said by way of confession as her chicken and his steak arrived. Aisha nodded and helped herself to the vegetables from the dishes the waiter had placed in the centre of the table. 'It can be seen as a fault,' he said. 'Angela certainly thought it was.' Aisha looked up and met his gaze. 'Belinda told you about Angela, didn't she?' Mark asked, slightly concerned.

'Not really, she mentioned that you had been married before, but that was all.'

'I see.' Mark looked down and sliced into his rare steak. 'OK, it's probably a good idea if I tell you now and then we'll get it out of the way.' He chewed and swallowed before continuing as Aisha sipped her mineral water, waiting. 'It was the classic tale of marrying too young really,' he began, 'and then spending too much time at work. I was in my first position with the company and wanted to do well. My career has always been important to me, as I know yours is to you.' Aisha nodded. 'You don't get a second chance in my line of work – if you haven't made it by the time you're thirty, you can forget it. With hindsight, I can see how isolated Angela must have felt, alone in the house all day with only the children for company. She became very depressed and was prescribed Valium. It turned out to be the worst thing that could have happened. We might have ridden out the rough patch had it not been for that drug. It affected her moods and she became a different person.' Mark suddenly stopped talking. He held his cutlery still and looked carefully at Aisha. 'You don't mind me going into this detail, do you? Only I feel it's important we're honest with each other right from the beginning.'

'No, not at all,' Aisha said. 'I'm pleased you can.' She latched on to the word 'beginning' as proof there could be more: another meeting, another date, which meant Mark was finding her company acceptable and possibly even enjoying it.

'Angela cited unreasonable behaviour as grounds for the divorce,' Mark continued. 'The little time I spent at home, my neglect of her and the children, and something she called my obsessive attention to detail. I wasn't going to sign the divorce petition to begin with – it made me sound like a nut case, when all I had been doing was working my socks off to try and provide the best for my wife and family. But my solicitor said I should sign it, that it was the easiest way out, and it would be expensive to defend a divorce, so I did. I signed the papers and gave Angela the house and everything in it. She moved her new bloke in the same day I moved out. I'd no idea she was seeing someone. I was gutted.'

Aisha gasped and set down her cutlery. 'But that's dreadful,' she said, genuinely shocked.

Mark nodded. 'My parents were devastated. They lost their grandchildren, and to a certain extent they blamed me. We're still not fully reconciled, even now.'

Aisha looked at Mark with heartfelt pity; to have a family torn from you and not see them was the worst thing she could imagine. It could never happen to her. How she would have liked to have reached out and touched Mark's hand, to have lightly squeezed it and reassured him. To have told him that she understood and felt ashamed that a woman had behaved so despicably, and that never in a million years would she behave so badly. That she had waited so long for the chance to show love and commitment and knew its worth and would cherish it forever.

'Anyway,' Mark said, suddenly returning his hand to his fork, 'enough. I'll ruin the evening with my tales of woe. Tell me about your relationships and I hope you'll be as honest as I have been.'

Aisha gave a little shrug and looked down. 'There's nothing to tell really,' she said quietly. 'I had a good male friend at university, but that was a long time ago. There's been no one since.'

'Oh, I can't believe that,' Mark teased. 'You're far too lovely to have been saving yourself for me. Come on, out with it. I'm a man of the world, I can take it.'

He laughed again, but stopped himself when he saw her face for that was exactly what she had been doing: saving herself.

He leaned forwards in earnest and, laying his hand on hers, said, 'I feel very privileged that you agreed to meet me, and while the evening isn't over yet, I'm already planning our next date. Now, let's call for that sweet trolley. Tonight's a special night and we should treat ourselves.'

When Mark took her home after their meal he drove slowly as though the didn't want the evening to end. The conversation flowed easily now they were used to each other's company. He pulled up outside her house and cutting the engine gently asked, 'I hope you enjoyed this evening, Aisha? I'd like to think it's the first of many.'

'Yes, I have,' she breathed. 'I've enjoyed it very much, thank you.' Then added shyly, 'I'd like to meet again too.'

'Terrific!' he exclaimed with the uninhibited enthusiasm of a little boy and she laughed. 'Shall I phone you on Monday to arrange something for next week?' he asked.

'Yes, please.' She smiled; then her eyes left his as she looked past him, through the windscreen and up to her parents' bedroom window. The light was still on, they were awake. She wondered if they'd heard the car draw up. She'd told them she was meeting a friend after work and not to wait up, but she knew they would.

'It's late,' she said. 'I'd better go in. Thank you again for a lovely evening.'

'There's no need to thank me,' Mark said. 'The pleasure is all mine. I'll walk you to the door.'

Aisha remained in her seat while Mark got out and went round and opened her door. She already knew he liked to do this, it was one of his many little acts of chivalry which made her feel so special. He offered her his arm as she stepped out and onto the pavement.

'At least it's stopped raining,' he said, cupping her elbow and guiding her the few steps to the front gate. She waited while he undid the latch and opened the gate; then they walked side by side up the path to the front door.

He turned to face her. 'Until Monday then,' he said. 'I'm already counting the hours. Have a good weekend.' Then without warning he leant forwards and lightly kissed her cheek. 'Goodnight, Aisha. Take care.'

'Goodnight,' she said and quickly turned and fumbled her key into the lock.

'Goodnight,' he called again from the path as she opened the door. She stepped inside and paused before closing the door. She watched him as he fastened the latch on the gate; the street lamp above him threw a faint aura of light around his head and shoulders. He looked up, 'Monday,' he mouthed and blew her a silent kiss before returning to the car.

Aisha quietly closed the front door, took off her shoes, and crept up the stairs and past her parents' bedroom. She hoped her mother wouldn't hear her, for if she did, she would call out and ask her if she'd had a nice time. Aisha didn't want to have to answer – to talk would break the spell; tonight she wanted it all to herself, to savour and remember.

She went silently into the bathroom and quickly washed and brushed her teeth, then crept across the landing into her bedroom. Slipping out of her clothes, she left them where they fell, then pulled on her nightdress and eased herself into bed. Nestled beneath the soft, warm duvet, she ran over the evening in her head, scene by scene, reliving every detail from that first glimpse of Mark, to the journey in the car, and the restaurant. She could picture the way he had looked at her across the table, attentive and interested in what she had to say. She could hear the little compliments he had slipped in at every opportunity. She could see his face, his clear blue eyes and neatly clipped fair almost blond hair. She caught the faintest breath of his aftershave, and as her eyes finally closed, heavy with sleep, she felt the light touch of his lips on her cheek, a feeling so intense she shivered with desire. 'Until Monday,' she whispered.

Seven

'Isn't he exactly as I said?' Belinda enthused when she phoned at nine fifty on Monday morning. 'Absolutely charming! You've made a real impression. He's asked me to find out.'

'Find out what?' Aisha asked, not best pleased by Belinda's early call. 'I'm sorry, I haven't got much time this morning.'

'Yes, I apologize. I know it's not your lunch hour, but Mark needs to know if you feel the same. He telephoned me first thing this morning, like a dog with two tails. He's besotted with you, Aisha, but he doesn't want to make a fool of himself. I always give my clients feedback if they ask for it, and he's worried he might have scared you off. I told him I didn't think he had.'

Aisha pressed the phone closer to her ear and watched the door to her PA's office. 'I like Mark,' she said. 'But we *have* only just met.'

'And what's wrong with love at first sight?' Belinda intoned, her voice rising. 'You can tell a lot by first impressions, and I've got a sixth sense for this one. It feels right, so very right. I'm excited for you both. I'll tell Mark you feel the same then and—'

'Belinda,' Aisha interrupted, 'will you please tell Mark that I enjoyed Friday evening very much, and I am looking forward to him phoning.'

46

'OK, playing it cool is fine by me, but be careful you don't lose him.'

Aisha's Monday morning at the bank passed with the usual fall-out from new Saturday opening plus analysing the sales figures from the previous week, readjusting the staffing rota for the week ahead allowing for absences, and a meeting with the area manager. Then the ATM broke and it was two hours before the replacement arrived, and another hour before it was fitted and fully functioning, which put an additional strain on the already depleted staff of cashiers, all of which Aisha had to oversee because her deputy was on leave.

At one forty-five she was at her desk, surrounded by piles of papers and folders, with the outside line switched through while Grace took her lunch. Aisha's sandwiches lay in their box beside the phone, and her computer was on, but she did nothing with either. She sat watching the movement of the hands on the wall clock, as they gradually inched towards two o'clock. Mark hadn't phoned and he said he would. *I'm like an adolescent schoolgirl,* she thought, *unable to settle to anything, waiting for him to call.* She chided herself for having been so cool with him, as Belinda had put it, and for not giving her the encouragement she had wanted to take back to Mark. *Perhaps I should phone Belinda,* Aisha thought, *and apologize for not being more forthcoming; explain that it's just my nature, that I'm naturally reserved, that I really do want to see Mark again, and am as besotted with him as he is with me.* Then she wondered if 'besotted' was his word or Belinda's exaggeration.

At five past two, when Aisha had almost given up hope, the phone rang and she snatched it up. 'Aisha Hussein,' she said.

'Aisha, it's Mark.' *Thank goodness,* she thought. His voice was exactly as she remembered it – as she had continuously recalled it since Friday. 'I'm sorry I've left it so late,' he said. 'I got held up. Is it still OK to talk?'

'Yes, but I might get interrupted.'

'Me too. Sorry,' he said again. 'We'll have to have a code word to alert each other when we're not alone. Something we wouldn't normally use like "sausages" or "wellington boot".'

Aisha laughed. 'Wellington boot. We could have done with them on Friday.'

'Too right,' he said, then paused and lowered his voice in intimacy. 'It was a lovely evening, Aisha. I've thought about nothing else all weekend. I hope you didn't mind Belinda calling?'

'Not at all. The go-between.'

'Yes. But it's no longer necessary now, I hope. I just needed the reassurance, after everything I've been through. You do understand, don't you?'

'Of course.'

'I was beginning to think I was having an early mid-life crisis,' Mark said. 'I took work home and brought it back again, untouched, I couldn't concentrate on anything. Aisha, it really was a lovely evening. Damn,' he said and stopped. She heard a noise at his end that sounded like a door opening and closing. 'Wellington boot coming soon,' he laughed. 'Let's arrange to meet quickly before I get interrupted again. Are you free tomorrow?'

'Yes, I am.'

'Great. I could pick up some tickets for the theatre. We could eat first, if you're coming straight from work.'

'That would be lovely.' She paused as Grace knocked on the door; then poked her head round, signalling her two o'clock appointment had arrived. 'I have a wellington boot here too,' she said.

He laughed. 'It must be very muddy out there. Look, I'll collect you from work at six. Is that all right with you?'

'Yes, fine. I'll wait outside the office.'

'Until tomorrow then. Take care. You're already very special, Aisha. I can't believe how lucky I am – an old geezer like me.'

And so it began, his courtship, her romance. Whirlwind, yes, but given their ages and circumstances that wasn't so very strange. For, as Mark said and Aisha agreed, they had both lost too much time already in going down the wrong path, and had a lot of catching up to do. Mark always managed to say and do the right thing; he was always the perfect gentleman, and wholly attentive to her needs.

In the six months that followed, they spent every available minute together and Aisha felt that all her dreams had come true. She and Mark talked endlessly about anything and everything – the myriad of little incidents that shape us and make us who we are. Mark met her parents and, although he still wasn't close to them, she met his. He introduced her to his work colleagues and friends, of which there were many, for with his sympathetic ear and ready wit Mark attracted people like bees around a honeypot. By the time Aisha told her parents that Mark was divorced, carefully explaining the circumstances – how he had worked hard and had been badly deceived – they were so impressed with him, and he had become so much a part of their family that other than a couple of questions from her father about his children, it wasn't an issue.

* * *

'So did I miss something?' she asked herself later, when she sat night after night, alone in her armchair, answering the inspector's questions, trying to get it right in her mind. 'Did I miss something in the headiness of it all, when Mark literally swept me off my feet? Something that a different person might have seen? A seed of doubt, borne on the wind of chance that should have been harvested and grown to fruition? Would a different person have said, Now stop, wait a minute, that doesn't quite add up. Would they? Was there a clue?'

And looking back, with the benefit of hindsight, she could see that there might have been: one clue, one crack in the otherwise unblemished china. A fine line of repair where the glue had been applied too liberally, and had set prominent over the join. So had she been more worldly-wise, she might have looked more closely, and then asked how it had been broken in the first place. But the clue, if it was one, came immediately before Mark proposed, and you don't question the man who's just asked you to marry him. Of course you don't, not if you're as much in love as Aisha was.

Eight

It was a clear, cold day in late October, when the autumn sun shone through the trees and sent little shafts of sunlight onto the hard earth. Hand in hand, Aisha and Mark made their way along the edge of the field, stopping every so often to pick up pine cones. They examined them, discarded the mildewed ones and, keeping only the best, dropped them into the carrier bag that swung from Aisha's arm. A little childish rivalry had developed between them, a competition to see who could discover the biggest, the most perfect pine cone: the one that would be used in the centrepiece on their dinner table on Christmas Day.

Aisha had collected pine cones every year for as long as she could remember, spending an afternoon foraging in the country-side with her parents. Once they had collected enough cones, they would return home for her mother's piping hot *dhal*, which she'd prepared the night before and said would 'warm their bones'. After they'd eaten, Aisha would carefully wash the pine cones and spread them on newspaper to dry in the airing cupboard. Once dry, they were put away until December, when she painted them silver and gold, and used them as Christmas decorations, fresh ones every year.

Only this year, Aisha wasn't doing it with her parents. She was doing it with Mark, who had fitted so perfectly and completely into her life, it was as though he had always been there.

51

'Your house must look beautiful at Christmas,' Mark said, brushing off the dirt from yet another find. 'I confess, I haven't put up decorations in recent years, there didn't seem much point.'

'And is there one now?' Aisha teased, sure of his response.

'Oh, without doubt. But I'm glad I'm coming to your house just the same. It will be a proper family Christmas. My first in ages.'

He put his arm around her shoulders, and drawing her to him, kissed her lightly on the cheek. He often did this – in the street, out shopping, meeting her from work, and when they were alone. It was a little statement of affection that said they were together, a couple, and she was his.

'Our Christmases are very quiet,' Aisha said, glancing up, a little concerned. 'I hope it's not too quiet for you. There's just my parents and a few friends who drop by. I'll make sure we have some decent wine in for you though. No one else drinks.'

Mark laughed good-humouredly and gently squeezed her shoulder. 'Never mind the wine. I'll be with you, that's what counts. It will be my best Christmas ever, decent wine or not.'

He dropped his arm from her shoulders as they left the edge of the field, and then climbed over the stile into the wood. Mark led the way along the narrow, untrodden path, for only he knew where they were going. It had been his suggestion that they came here, when Aisha had told him of her proposed outing, and had asked him if he would like to join her.

'I know just the place,' he said, matching her enthusiasm. 'Plenty of pine trees and very few people. It's quite a walk as I remember, you can only take the car so far. It's well off the beaten track.'

Aisha said she didn't mind a walk, in fact she enjoyed one. And going somewhere different would make it all the more exciting, particularly as this year it was with him.

'Now if I'm right,' Mark called over his shoulder as they continued in single file, 'there's a stream just up here. My brother and I used to play there for hours as boys. He fell in once and I got a right bollocking, being the eldest.'

'Don't worry, I won't fall in,' she laughed.

'Good. I don't want a telling-off from your mother. I'm still trying to impress her.'

Further up, the trees thinned out and a makeshift wooden bridge appeared. 'I was right!' Mark cried, stopping. 'It hasn't changed at all in all these years! Now, do be careful and use the rail. I'll go first; if it takes my weight, it will certainly take yours.'

Aisha waited as Mark took hold of the gnarled branch that acted as a handrail and tentatively tested the planks of wood with his foot, then started gingerly across. 'It's OK,' he called. 'But mind how you go.'

She followed, running her hand along the rough wooden rail. She looked down into the small gully only a few feet below and saw the trickle of a stream running at the bottom. Even if the bridge were to give way, she thought, and they fell in, they wouldn't do themselves much damage. They were like children really, alone in the countryside and imagining an awfully big adventure.

'Your brother couldn't have got very wet falling in that,' she called, laughing.

'No, it's deeper further up. I'll show you in a moment.'

On the other side of the bridge, the bank rose sharply and was heavily overgrown. Thick, brown, waist-height briars protruded menacingly from the undergrowth. Mark went ahead, forging a path, holding back the vines so they didn't spring up and scratch her. It cleared again at the top and Aisha heard the sudden rush of water, unseen and close by. Mark took her arm and led her slowly to the edge of the clearing and they looked down. She gasped in awe and steadied herself against him, for what had been a trickle of a stream beneath the bridge was now a rushing waterfall in a steep and narrow gully.

'It's beautiful,' she cried. 'Absolutely beautiful! And to think I've lived not far from here all these years and didn't know it existed.'

'Not many people do,' he said. 'Which is why it's remained so unspoiled.'

She stood beside him, gazing down into the clear pure water as it crashed between the narrow banks before bouncing into a whirlpool and disappearing underground. It looked so fresh and pure she could almost taste the droplets rising in the fine spray. The steady hypnotic flow was so constant and unfaltering it seemed as if there was no movement at all.

'My brother and I used to make little boats out of sticks and leaves,' Mark said, after a moment. 'We would drop them here, at the top, and see whose survived the longest. It kept us amused for hours.'

'And who won?' Aisha asked, happy at the shared memory.

'Me, of course,' he laughed. 'I was the eldest. It had to be me!'

Mark bent down and picked up a large leaf and, curling up the edges so it looked like a small boat, dropped it into the torrent. Aisha linked his arm and they watched together as the makeshift boat rose high on the current of spray, twisting and turning, holding its own, before being sucked into the water and disappearing into the whirlpool at the bottom.

'Oh well, you can't win them all,' he shrugged, straightening.

Aisha continued looking down, gazing into the swirling pool and hoping against the odds that their little boat might yet reappear. But there was no sign of the leaf, it had gone for good, sucked under to decay at the bottom of the riverbed.

'My father has a saying,' she said shortly, 'one of many. He says brooks become crooked by taking the path of least resistance, and people do too. I sometimes wonder if that's what I've done – taken the path of least resistance. The easiest, the most acceptable.'

Mark looked sideways at her with a mixture of humour and indulgence. 'You say the quaintest things sometimes, Aisha. How could you possibly think that, with everything you've achieved?'

She looked up and met his gaze. 'I've conformed though, haven't I? I've always done what was expected of me. The way I met you was the one and only exception.'

'And what's wrong with conforming?' he said. 'If it's made you the person you are? You're perfect, absolutely perfect, as I keep telling you. Though I must confess that makes me feel a certain responsibility sometimes.'

'For me?' she asked, surprised. 'Why should you feel responsible for me? You didn't make me what I am.'

'No, but you're so untouched, unscathed. Vulnerable, almost. I worry that I might harm you in some way.'

She looked at him and then spoke with uncharacteristic sharpness. 'I'm not an ornament, Mark. I won't break. Please don't treat me as if I will.'

He fell silent for a moment. Then, with a small start, he turned squarely to face her. Taking hold of her shoulders, he drew her gently away from the edge of the gully, then placed his fingers lightly under her chin and tenderly tilted her face up towards his. His parted lips came down on hers and Aisha closed her eyes, and felt his mouth, firm and insistent with desire. She felt his body pressing against hers, his tongue exploring her mouth as he clasped her to him. She looped her hands round his neck and clung to him, buried her fingers into his hair, and returned the passion in his kiss. How she loved him, how close she felt to him, how she now yearned for him. She wanted Mark to know that – that if his passion continued and grew, and he wanted her, then she was at last ready to give herself to him, completely. For Mark had always said it must be her decision; that there was no pressure, no rush, and that he would wait until she was ready. Now she was, and she wanted him to know.

His lips left her mouth and moved slowly across her cheek and to her neck; kissing, sucking, gently taking the skin between his teeth. Her body trembled with desire and anticipation. 'I need you,' she breathed. 'I want you, Mark.'

What could be more natural, she thought, than making love for the first time in this beautiful woodland setting, with the sky as their canopy, and the undergrowth flattened to a makeshift bed. It would be perfect, she knew, and he would be gentle in this as he was in all things. He wouldn't laugh at her inexperience or clumsiness, he would guide her, she knew. But he would have to be certain that she was ready to give herself to him because he had said he would never take advantage of her.

'Mark, I want you,' she breathed against his cheek. 'I want you now.' She pressed herself harder against him and felt the desire overpower her and the willingness to give herself up to him completely.

His hands were rubbing the small of her back and his lips were buried in her neck. Then gradually he became very still. His body was close but losing some of its pressure now as the firm embrace of his arms eased. Her hands were still around his neck and her eyes were closed as she felt him pull slightly away. Aisha thought he was going to take off his coat and spread it on the ground, then ease her slowly down and onto it. And she yearned for him now, as she never had before; she wanted him, she was ready. But there was no other movement or sound beyond the distant waterfall and a bird fluttering nearby. She felt Mark close but very still. Slowly she opened her eyes and looked into his as his hands dropped away. It took her a moment to realize that he wasn't taking off his coat, but was standing still looking at her. Then he spoke, and his voice was flat and empty. 'We'd better go, Aisha,' was all he said.

He turned and started walking towards the undergrowth that led to the hill they had climbed together. Aisha went after him, not knowing what was happening. He swiped an overhanging branch as he went and his speed increased.

'Mark! Wait for me,' she called. He was walking fast, too fast, she was having to run to keep up and nearly tripped. 'Mark!' she called again. 'Wait for me!' But he didn't; he didn't stop or turn, but kept on walking, gaining distance: through the undergrowth, then out of the thicket and down the hill towards the bridge at the bottom. 'Mark! Stop! I can't keep up!' she cried and ran after him, the bag of cones banging awkwardly against her leg. 'Mark? Wait! What's the matter?'

There was no reply. Fear gripped her. He strode on as she slipped and slid down the grassy bank, frantically trying to catch up with him. She went to grab hold of the passing twigs and brambles to steady herself, but the grass was wet and her feet kept slithering from under her. 'Mark! Please wait!' she shouted louder, but he ignored her.

Down to the bottom of the hill, his back was towards her, receding, moving further away as he continued, putting more distance between them. The bridge came into sight and he marched straight onto it with no concern for the rotting planks. He stalked across and off the other side. Aisha's heart pounded as she arrived at the bottom of the hill and ran onto the bridge, trying to keep him in sight. Off the other side of the bridge the gap between them widened as he began along the track that led to the stile.

'Mark, stop!' she yelled, out of breath and consumed by panic. 'For goodness' sake stop! Tell me what I've done!'

She heard the hysteria in her voice and perhaps he heard it too, because he cleared the stile with a leap, then took another step and stopped. His back was towards her, his head was held stiff and erect. She ran to the stile, her breath catching in her throat, and clambered over, scratching her leg as she went. Mark was standing just in front of her now, still turned away, but not moving. She went round to face him. His face was deathly white and the fine lines of his forehead were furrowed deep. He looked past her; focusing on some distant point straight ahead.

'Mark,' she said again. 'Mark, please. What is it? Tell me. What have I done?'

He shrugged, a silent gesture of despair, then slowly brought his gaze to meet hers; his expression saying it was impossible, futile even to begin.

'Mark?' she implored. But no, he stepped round her and continued at a slower pace towards the field.

She followed him along the edge of the ploughed field and then into the wood where they had previously sauntered hand in hand, enjoying the peace and tranquillity. And whereas before the isolation had added to her pleasure – just the two of them alone in the countryside – it now made her nervous and afraid. As she followed him, her mind frantically searched for an explanation, something that would give her a clue, a handle on what had happened. A small voice from her past said that it was her fault and she was to blame, that she had thrown herself at a man like some cheap hussy as her mother had warned against, and he had rejected her. Aisha felt bitterly ashamed.

The sky ahead burst fiery orange as the winter sun began its descent. Aisha saw its beauty and felt it bittersweet. Mark would have normally stopped and commented on it – he loved the perfection in nature as much as she. But now they continued separate and in silence, the artwork overhead an unacknowledged witness to their isolation.

A few minutes later, the car came into view and Mark quickened his pace again, delving into his coat pocket for the key fob. She heard the click, and watched as he opened the passenger door and stood aside to let her in. Her stomach tightened as she brushed passed him, his little act of chivalry now seeming ludicrous.

She watched him cross in front of the bonnet, his face set and expressionless as she'd never seen it before. She continued to look straight ahead as he climbed in and slammed the door. She could feel her pulse beating wildly in her chest and could hear his breath, fast and shallow. He threw the car keys onto the dashboard, jammed his hands into this coat pockets and, lowering his head, stared into his lap.

'Well?' she said at last, still not looking at him and only just managing to fight back the tears. 'What have I done, Mark? What could I have possibly done to make you behave like that?' Again her conscience said it must have been her fault, and fear rose up and engulfed her – if this was the end of their relationship, then she only had herself to blame.

He was silent for what seemed an eternity; a silence that seemed to condemn her; then slowly he took his hands out of his pockets and gripped the steering wheel. She saw his knuckles, clenched and white.

'*You* haven't done anything,' he said tightly. 'It's me. I should have told you sooner. Now it's too late.'

She turned to look at him, even more confused. 'Told me what? What do you mean?'

He paused and drew a muted breath. 'About me. My past. Choosing the wrong partner. I should have told you, but I knew you wouldn't understand.' .

She stared at him and found no comfort in his words. Clearly whatever had happened, she hadn't understood. 'You did tell me – about Angela?' she said at last.

He paused again, then clenched and unclenched his hands on the wheel. 'But I haven't told you all of it. There was someone else before you.'

She stared at him. 'So, you went out with someone else, before me. That's not so awful. It doesn't explain—'

'No,' he interrupted roughly. 'It was more than that. I *lived* with someone – for five years. I wanted to tell you, but I never found the right moment and then it was too late. I knew that if I did tell you there was a chance I would lose you, and I couldn't bear the thought of that.' A muscle twitched nervously at the corner of his mouth. Aisha heard the words individually before understanding their full implication.

'You lived with someone?' she said slowly. 'For five years? So you were married really, only without the piece of paper.'

He laughed, cynical and biting. 'There! I *knew* you wouldn't understand. How could you, with your upbringing?'

She was quiet, feeling the accusation, the condemnation of her culture and naivety. 'I don't think I have ever judged you, Mark,' she said quietly.

'Until now!'

She turned away and looked through the windscreen, concentrating on the darkening skyline as the sun continued its descent. 'So what's changed?' she asked after a moment. 'Why tell me now?'

He sighed. 'Your passion. It made me realize how far our relationship had come. I knew I couldn't continue without you knowing. I'm sorry, I don't expect you to understand. I'll take you home.'

'No!' she cried, panicking at the finality of what he'd said. 'If you try talking to me instead of shutting me out, I might. I can't possibly understand anything unless you tell me, Mark.'

He flexed his shoulders and looked around as though scouring the air for the right words. Releasing the wheel, he sat back and took a deep breath. Aisha looked ahead and tried to calm the nausea rising in her throat.

'When my marriage to Angela ended I moved out, as you know,' he said in a dead-beat voice. 'I lived alone in a rented bedsit. It was squalid, but it was all I could afford what with having to pay maintenance. I was alone, with nothing to think about but the children and what I'd lost. I became very depressed. I couldn't see any point in anything anymore. I know that must seem strange to you, seeing the person I am now. I really had reached rock bottom. Then I met Christine. She was younger than me and full of energy and fun. She picked me up and brushed me down, gave me a new lease of life. I didn't stop to consider what I was doing, I was just grateful for her company. Within a few months, we had set up home together, and it was only then I found out.'

He paused, but Aisha didn't say anything, she looked ahead and waited for him to continue.

'Christine was fun all right, the life and soul of the party, but she needed a drink to do it. In fact, she needed a drink for everything – she was an alcoholic. I'd had my suspicions early on but I hadn't realized the implications until we'd been together for nearly two years. She was very clever at hiding it; they are, alcoholics. I enjoy a drink as much as the next person, but I'd never known anyone dependent on it like she was. It was a drug to her. The most important thing in the world. She used to live for the next drink. When I finally realized, I confronted her and there was a dreadful scene. She accused me of spying on her, but I was only trying to help. From then on it went from bad to worse. She no longer hid her drinking and drank openly, all the time. She lost her job, then didn't have to sober up at all. She began staying in bed, just getting up to go out for more booze. I threw the bottles away, time and time again, but that always led to another ugly scene. She paid with her credit card; it didn't bother her that she couldn't afford it. I would come home from work to find her drunk or unconscious and lying in a pool of vomit.

'I stood it for as long as I could and I tried to help, believe me, I did. I didn't want another relationship to fail. Then, one night, she wasn't there when I came home from work. I was relieved to begin with, but when it got to midnight I started to worry. I thought she could be unconscious somewhere, in a gutter, freezing to death. I didn't know where to look so I sat up all night, waiting. She finally staggered in at four o'clock in the morning, completely paralytic. God knows where she'd been; she looked dreadful and stank of piss.'

He paused for a moment, struggling to find the words.

'She wanted sex. We hadn't made love for months; I hadn't wanted to, not in the state she was in. It was disgusting, I couldn't possibly. But she wouldn't take no for an answer and kept coming up and pressing herself against me. I could smell the sick and booze. In the end I pushed her away ... I didn't know what I was doing ... I pushed her too hard, she fell and hit her head. That was the end for me. The following day I packed and left. I never saw her again. It was all so humiliating and ugly, Aisha. I just wanted to forget it. But when I felt the depth of your love today – your passion – I knew I should have told you sooner.'

He fell silent and Aisha heard his breathing soften and felt her own heart settle. He had told her his darkest secret, the worst had been said and it wasn't so bad, not really; she was just sorry he hadn't told her sooner. She hadn't realized she was so unapproachable, so perhaps it *was* her fault after all. She reached out and touched his arm. 'Mark, I'm glad you've told me now. Thank you.'

He turned to look at her, his face still pale, his expression tight. 'Can you ever forgive me, Aisha? I'm sorry. I've hated myself these past six months for not telling you. And I'm sorry I overreacted back there, it's not like me at all.'

She moved closer to him and slid her arms around his neck. 'There's nothing to forgive. I only wish you felt you could have told earlier. You've no idea how much you frightened me just now. I thought I'd done something awful.'

He pulled her to him and buried his face in her hair. 'Oh, my little love! You could never do that. You're perfect, so very special. I'd die rather than hurt you.'

He kissed her hair, then her face and neck, and she clung to him as relief flooded through her. It was his conscience that had made him react as he had and the depth of his love for her.

'Can you ever forgive me?' he breathed into her hair, holding her tight, so tight, as if he would never let go.

'Of course I forgive you,' Aisha said gently. 'I understand why you behaved as you did.'

'Do you? Really?' Mark asked slightly surprised.

'Yes, I do.'

'Aisha, can you ever trust me ...' His voice faltered. 'Can you ever love me again? Can it be the same as before?'

'Yes I can, Mark. It will be.'

'Can you trust and love me enough to be my wife? Aisha, will you marry me?'

Aisha gasped. Love flooded her heart as all fear of him vanished. It was going to be all right after all. She turned to him, took one of his hands in hers and kissed it gently. 'Yes, Mark. I will.'

Nine

Mark and Aisha were married on the anniversary of their first date, exactly one year to the day after Mark had met her outside Harrods and taken her to The Crooked Chimney to eat. The date had been Mark's idea, it was part of his happy knack of saying and doing the most romantic things, wanting above all to please her. He asked her father formally for his daughter's hand in marriage, knowing he would appreciate the traditional approach.

'I shall always regret my divorce prohibits us having a church wedding,' Mark said. 'I know how much you and Mrs Hussein would have liked it. I am so very sorry.'

'We are all entitled to one mistake,' her father replied convivially. 'I was fortunate in being found the wife I was. I am pleased you've decided to follow the ceremony with a church blessing. You know that means a lot to us, as practising Christians.'

Aisha had said nothing to her parents about Mark's 'second mistake' – his dreadful ordeal with Christine – only about his marriage to Angela. Why upset them with what they didn't need to know? she reasoned. Why complicate the past, or detract from the present, when there was no need to? And perhaps part of Aisha knew that her father might have questioned her further about the circumstances of the break-up of Mark's relationship with Christine, or cast doubt about his culpability, or disapproved

65

of Mark having lived in sin, or disapproved completely. For there was a gap between her generation and her parents', and indeed their cultures, which, since meeting Mark, seemed to Aisha to have widened. She had come to realize that while she was a true Westerner, her parents were not and would never be, even though they had tried and so wanted to be.

Aisha's father shook Mark's hand after he had given his consent and then congratulated them both, while her mother kissed their cheeks and dabbed at her eyes with a little lace hand-kerchief she kept tucked in the waistband of her sari. Then Aisha's father had presented Mark with a cheque for ten thousand pounds. 'Towards the cost of setting up home,' he said. 'It's not a dowry.' And they all laughed.

Mark hadn't wanted to accept the money to begin with, but Aisha nodded to him that he should. It was a matter of pride and family honour, and to have refused her father, even for the right motives, would have been unforgivable.

'It costs a lot to get started nowadays,' her father said, 'and it's no more than I would have spent on a full white wedding had my daughter had one.'

Aisha's heart went out to her father as he handed over his hard-earned money. He seemed so small and humble beside Mark's worldly sophistication. But Mark's gratitude was heartfelt and sincere and her father seemed to grow from his response. Aisha thought then, as she had done countless times before, that she was the luckiest woman alive, both to have found Mark, and to have his love. She couldn't have been happier.

The wedding was a small, simple affair with twenty guests including Mark's parents, brother, an aunt and uncle, Aisha's parents, and a few close friends of Mark's from work. Aisha had invited Grace, the only person from work she wanted to ask, but unfortunately she had been taken ill two days before and wasn't able to attend. Aisha's relatives in India were sent invitations, but for protocol only as there was no possibility of them coming – they couldn't afford it. As her father had said, 'If I offer to pay for some, the others will take it as a personal slight.' Including cousins and their children, there were over sixty members of the extended family so they decided it was better to send the invitation only, and then post wedding photographs to all of them after the day.

Aisha wore a very simple beige silk two-piece suit made by a dressmaker in London who Mark knew. It cost nearly as much as a full-length wedding dress, but Mark said it was more refined and in keeping with their maturity and a registry office wedding than something more flamboyant, and Aisha agreed. She carried a bouquet of lilies which her mother had arranged and wired together herself. Mark's brother, whom he hadn't seen in three years, was the best man, and naturally Aisha's father gave her away. Aisha didn't have a bridesmaid – with no sisters or relatives in England there wasn't anyone she felt close enough to have comfortably asked. She had lost contact with her university friends, and since moving back home had been so busy with work she hadn't had time to make new ones.

As Aisha repeated the words of the marriage service that she'd had so many years to practise, she said a silent prayer of thanks. *Thank you God for sending me my perfect partner. You have made me very happy, and my parents unbelievably proud.*

After the blessing, they were driven to the reception in a white Rolls-Royce – their one real extravagance of the day which Mark had insisted on. The reception was a five-course meal at The Crooked Chimney. The restaurant had been Mark's suggestion although her father had paid for it. The sentiment of the venue was obvious, and Mark made it the focal point of his speech. He stood tall and proud and so very handsome in his suit as he spoke and pointed to the table where they'd sat on their first date, and where there was now a huge spray of flowers in the shape of a heart which he'd ordered secretly as a surprise for Aisha. He reminisced how he had gazed at Aisha across that candlelit table, and had been unable to eat because of his nerves. Aisha laughed for his nerves hadn't been obvious and were nothing compared to how she had felt. Mark described how his first glimpse of Aisha had been sheltering from the rain and that he'd been immediately struck by her natural and unassuming beauty. He said he'd known from that moment on that one day he would make her his wife. He proposed a toast to Aisha's parents, and thanked them for giving him their most cherished possession, and promised to look after Aisha as well as they had done. He said he would strive to live up to the honour of being their son-in-law and make them as proud of him as they were of their daughter. Aisha saw the look on her parents' faces and those of the other guests as they raised their glasses for the toast, and felt a burst of pride. They obviously thought as she did, that to be loved and adored so much would create as near a perfect union as it was possible to get.

That evening, after the reception, they left for a week's holiday in Dubai. They had purposely not called it a honeymoon – they felt that would have sounded frivolous at their age, a 'short holiday' was better Mark said. The destination was Mark's choice, he had visited Dubai on business a number of times and wanted to share the splendour of its modern architecture with Aisha. As they waved goodbye through the rear window of the Rolls and the photographer took his last picture, Mark sat back in the car and sighed with relief. 'Thank goodness that's over with,' he said. 'It's been the longest day of my life.'

Aisha laughed and poked him playfully in the ribs. 'It wasn't that bad! In fact, I quite enjoyed myself once I got over my nerves.'

'So did I,' he said. 'But I had a nightmare last night that you would change your mind and call it off. It was so real I woke up in a cold sweat.'

'Did you?' she asked laughing. 'But you know me better than that. I would never change my mind about you, ever.' Little did she know how wrong she would be, for fate can be very cruel sometimes.

Ten

I t was soon, very soon, of that Aisha was sure, for she remembered thinking, *Isn't it a little early? Why the rush?* Indeed, if she thought hard enough, she could remember saying it.

On their return from Dubai – which had been everything it had promised to be, and more – Aisha moved into Mark's house. Mark had said it made sense for them to use her father's money towards paying off the mortgage on his house rather than sell it and buy another jointly. Aisha had agreed. Mark hired a van and moved all her belongings in the weekend they returned from holiday. Now, on Monday morning they were in their bedroom getting ready for their first day back at work as a married couple. Aisha was zipping up the skirt of her grey office suit while practising her new surname.

'Mrs Williams. Mrs Williams, some letters for you to sign,' she said out loud and laughed. 'It still sounds so strange,' she said. 'I won't know who they're talking to.'

'Oh, you'll soon get used to it,' Mark said. 'Then it will be time for you to leave.'

'Leave?' She paused. She was now hunting through the boxes that they hadn't yet unpacked for a file she needed for work and was only half-listening to Mark.

'Yes, to start a family,' he said. 'You surely haven't forgotten?'

She straightened. 'No, of course not. But I'll have enough time to learn my name. We've only been married two weeks. There's no rush, is there?' She moved to the next box.

'True,' he said, watching her. 'But we can't leave it too long. A woman is at her fertility peak during her early twenties. After that there's a steady decline. It would be dreadful if we missed the opportunity.'

'Yes, it would,' she said absently. 'You haven't seen a blue A4 folder with the bank's emblem on the cover? I need it for a meeting this afternoon.'

He shook his head. 'No, it could be anywhere. Look, we need to go now or I'll be late, and that won't create a very good impression on my first day back at work as a married man.'

'Sorry,' she said, and quickly closed the box. She grabbed her jacket and briefcase and followed him out of the bedroom. There was always the possibility, she thought, that she'd left the file at the office.

She followed Mark down the still unfamiliar stairs and out of the front door. They were going together on the tube as far as Moorgate and then would separate – him going on to Gresham Street and her to Lombard Street. If they timed their return correctly, they would meet up again at Moorgate at the end of the day, otherwise they'd agreed the first one home would start the evening meal as they were both working. It really was all so new and exciting, Aisha thought, even the commute to work.

'Check you've got your keys,' Mark said as he Chubb-locked the front door. 'We don't want you being locked out.'

Aisha looked in her bag. 'Yes, they're here,' she said and smiled. It was nice and safe having Mark to look after her, after so long alone; it made her feel warm and secure.

On the pavement, she fell into step beside him. How proud she felt walking with her new husband. She wondered if the neighbours had noticed that Mark now had a wife. The street they lived in was mainly renovated Victorian houses, similar to the one her parents lived in four miles away. She hadn't seen or spoken to her parents since Mark had moved her belongings the previous weekend; there just hadn't been the time. Now she suddenly realized she was missing them after seeing them every day when she lived at home. She made a mental note to phone them as soon as she got to work, and invite them over for tea on Sunday. They hadn't seen the house yet, and she knew they would never just drop by now she was a married woman.

'You know, I've been looking into it and there are measures we can take to increase your chances of conceiving,' Mark said, returning to the previous conversation.

Aisha glanced up. 'Oh, yes?'

'A multivitamin supplement is a good start, apparently,' he said. 'It's important that you're in tip-top condition prior to conceiving, as well as during pregnancy.'

'Yes, I can see that's important,' she agreed.

'If we take your temperature every morning we can identify when you're ovulating. Apparently there is a small but perceptible rise in temperature just prior to ovulation. We don't want to leave anything to chance. Women ovulate mid-cycle – fourteen days after the first day of your last period. You are regular, aren't you, Aisha?'

She looked up at him slightly bemused by all this information, and embarrassed by his directness. Her father would never have talked of ovulation or periods to her or her mother; discussion of 'women's things' had always been considered for women only and was taboo in male company.

'Yes, I am, more or less,' she said in answer to his question.

'Good. And just in case you're wondering what I'll be doing in all this, I shall wear cotton boxer shorts and take a tepid shower night and morning. Apparently sperm thrive in a cool environment, which is why they're stored outside the body. Did you know that?'

She nodded and, laughing, linked his arm. 'It all sounds a bit clinical. I thought babies just happened naturally. Do you think other couples go to this trouble?'

'If they're well-informed, yes,' Mark said flatly. 'Which on reflection probably excludes the majority.'

She laughed again and affectionately squeezed his arm. Clearly her new husband was going to be as knowledgeable and disciplined in this as he was in all other aspects of his life. And while her initial reaction, when Mark had raised the subject of starting a family, had been to wonder why the rush, she could now see that there was very good reason not to delay.

So every morning Aisha was woken by the alarm clock at six o'clock, and Mark would pass her the thermometer he kept on his bedside cabinet. He'd carefully explained that it was critical she took her temperature before she moved; had she taken a sip from her glass of water or gone to the toilet, it would have altered her temperature slightly and rendered the reading void.

Mark produced graphs of the results: little black crosses joined by a pencil line, each labelled with the day of the month. It was like a schoolboy's maths project, neat and precise, as he plotted the rise and fall of her cycle for four months, so they came to know when she would ovulate to within twenty-four hours. Then, having abstained from making love for a week (to allow the sperm to multiply, Mark said), they had made love the next night. Mark withdrew straight away and then, with one swift movement pushed a pillow under her bottom and bent her knees up to her chest. Aisha cried out in alarm for he hadn't warned her or explained, and she had hoped she'd lie in his arms after.

'The angle is necessary,' he said, placing a gently restraining hand on her legs. 'To stop the sperm seeping out. They are too precious to be lost in the bed.'

Aisha pulled the duvet up to cover her and then lay there with her knees bent double, feeling exposed, for what seemed like hours but was only fifteen minutes. Fifteen minutes exactly – Mark timed it with his wristwatch which he also kept on the bedside cabinet for this very reason. When the fifteen minutes was up, Mark lowered her knees, kissed and petted her, then snuggled into the small of her back and went to sleep. And so the pattern of their lovemaking continued.

Aisha confessed each month to the four periods that followed in much the same way as a child admits to breaking a precious vase – its discovery inevitable and she weighed down by guilt. Mark accepted the first two confessions with resolve, had been openly disappointed by the third, and was ready to apportion blame by the fourth.

'I simply don't understand it,' he said, spreading the graphs out on the dining-room table and studying them. 'There's nothing wrong with my calculations. I can see exactly when you are ovulating. Here.' He prodded the graph with his finger. 'I think you had better go to the doctor for a check-up, Aisha, to make sure there's nothing wrong.'

'Perhaps if we stop trying so hard,' she suggested hesitantly. 'Perhaps if we just relax and forget about it for now. I think some things are beyond our control.'

Mark looked sideways at her with a scepticism she had seen on her father's face when, as a child, she had said something ridiculously naïve when she should have known better. 'You're surely not suggesting babies are made in heaven?' Mark said, raising an eyebrow in disbelief. 'That a quick turn in the confession box and a few Hail Marys will get you pregnant?'

'No, of course not,' she said quietly, chastened, 'and I'm not a Catholic. But I think all this is taking over. We talk about nothing else. We've got each other and have so much to be grateful for. I want us to enjoy our time together – our lovemaking – not rely on a calendar.'

Mark immediately softened and, folding away the graphs, drew her to him and held her close. He kissed the top of her head. 'I'm sorry, my little love, I didn't mean to upset you. Why don't we keep trying with this for another three months and if we still haven't had any luck we can consider something else? There's always artificial insemination or even IVF, private if the NHS won't fund it.'

It wasn't exactly what Aisha had meant and she was beginning to think that Mark hadn't fully appreciated her concerns. But she was also aware that no couple saw eye to eye on everything all of the time, and compromise was essential for a good marriage so she agreed to his suggestion. It was nice that Mark was so committed to having children.

Another month passed with its bloody reckoning and Aisha began to accept the possibility that it was her fault and she should go to the doctor. There was clearly nothing wrong with Mark – he had already proved his fertility by fathering two children, and his silence at her next admission seemed to confirm this. He didn't say a word, but with a slight shake of his head walked away and began tinkering in the garage.

A week into her next menstrual cycle, Aisha took an hour off work, telling Grace she was popping out and that if anyone phoned, to tell them she was with a customer. The 'anyone' Aisha referred to was more specifically Mark – she never knew when he was going to phone her at work, only that he would, at least twice a day and often more. Aisha wasn't going to tell Mark of the visit she was about to make, either now or in the future; it would remain her secret, probably the only one she would ever have from him. For so much did she love him, she was going to explore every avenue, and leave no stone unturned, even if it meant going behind his back and doing something she knew he wouldn't have approved of.

Slipping out of the side door of the bank, Aisha quickly crossed the road and turned the corner. The streets were relatively empty at three o'clock, with most of the City workers having returned from lunch to their offices. She passed wine and coffee bars, with their pavement tables and chairs, then went down a short alley where she turned right. A little further up, she stopped outside a heavy oak door which was blackened by car fumes and engraved with lovers' initials. She passed it every morning on her way to work and, until recently, had only given the notice on the sandwich board outside a cursory glance. Now she felt its message applied directly to her:

God's House.
All are Welcome.
He Hears our Prayers.

She turned the wrought-iron handle and slowly opened the creaking door. Once inside, she stood for a moment, allowing her eyes to adjust. It was cold and dank smelling, but it was also mercifully empty. *Not much call for God in the middle of the Square Mile*, she thought, which was probably what Mark would have said as well had he known where she was.

There was a small stained-glass window above a simple altar at the far end, the colours in the glass vivid in the gloom. The image showed Christ nailed to the cross in the last throes of his death agony, with Mary at his feet. The only other church she had been in recently was the one near her parents' house – the one they'd used for the blessing after their wedding. This one was much smaller, older and less prosperous than the church where her parents worshipped.

Keeping her eyes on the stained-glass image, Aisha went slowly down the centre aisle and to the front. She slid into a pew in the second row from the front and knelt on the threadbare cushioned kneeling pad. Clasping her hands together and with her eyes open and still concentrating on the stained-glass image, her lips began moving in silent prayer.

'I really don't know if I believe,' she said. 'My parents do, but I can't be sure. It's not out of selfishness I come, but for my husband. Well, for us both, really. You see, we love each other very much, and this is so important for us both. I'm not a hypocrite, I genuinely don't know what I believe. Please, God, put aside my doubt and hear my prayer. I'll be a good mother, I promise. I'll make you and Mark very proud of me. And my parents will be overjoyed. If it's within your power and you think it right, please grant me this. I promise I won't ever ask for anything again. Thank you.'

She stopped, her hands still clasped together, her lips becoming still. She didn't know what else to say. It seemed unsavoury to start talking about sperm and conception in a church. And if there was someone out there listening – she tried to minimize the 'if' – if there was an omnipresent being who saw and understood everything, then he would know what she wanted and understand her need.

She finished with the Lord's Prayer, which she had learnt by heart at school, then stood, slowly, moving into the aisle and crossed herself, just as her father always did. Looking at the image of Christ above the altar, she said out loud, 'Thank you, God, whoever you are. I've tried to be honest, which I'm sure you prefer.' Crossing herself again, she turned and walked back up the aisle, then paused at the offertory box by the door and dropped in a two-pound coin.

When she got back to the office, she found Grace taking a second call from Mark, who was asking exactly where Aisha was. Aisha motioned for Grace to switch the call through to her office. Taking a deep breath, she went in and, sitting at her desk, picked up the phone.

'I'm here, love,' she said. 'Sorry, I got called away.'

She heard his sigh of relief. 'Thank goodness, I was getting worried. You didn't say you had a meeting away from the bank.'

'No, it was last-minute. You shouldn't worry so much. I'm fine.'

'I can't help it, Aisha. You're so very precious. Oh, damn,' he laughed. 'Wellington boot coming.'

She laughed too at the phrase they still used for an interruption. 'OK, see you later.'

'Yes. The station at six. Take care. Love you.'

'Love you too, Mark, very much.'

Eleven

God, or whoever he was, must have been listening and smiling down on Aisha, and must have decided that her request was not too ambitious and well within his power to grant. The following month, her period was late which, combined with the vague feeling of nausea and her sudden aversion to strong smells such as coffee and garlic, made Aisha think she might be pregnant. She said nothing to Mark, but each night in bed before she went to sleep she said a silent prayer of hope and thanks which ended, *Please, God, let it be so.*

Mark, who knew exactly when Aisha's next period was due, said nothing either. The knowledge hung between them, palpable and duplicitous, until ten days had passed, when Mark arrived home from work with a pregnancy testing kit. He produced it with a little flurry from his briefcase, after the evening meal, and set it on the table between them. Aisha eyed the box suspiciously; it had some silly name like 'First to know'.

'Oh dear,' she said, finally looking at him. 'Do you think we should? There could be lots of reasons why I'm late. It's not been two weeks yet. Will it work so soon?'

Mark nodded. 'These tests are far more sophisticated now, Aisha. Ten days should be plenty of time. If we don't get a clear reading on this occasion, we can repeat it in a few days. We want to know as soon as possible, don't we?'

Aisha nodded, and then watched as Mark slowly removed the contents of the box. There was a folded instruction sheet, a small

Perspex bowl, and a litmus-tipped stick in cellophane. Aisha was surprised that was all there was, given the importance of its task. Mark placed the stick and bowl on the dining table, and unfolding the instruction sheet, began reading aloud, slowly, deliberately, as if she might otherwise fail to grasp it.

'The urine sample must be early morning, the first of the day,' Mark repeated, running his finger along the line for emphasis. 'The result must be read immediately. If the litmus stick changes to dark blue then the result is positive. See here.' He tapped the sheet. 'Any of these other shades means the result is inconclusive and the test has to be repeated a week later.' He glanced up. 'It doesn't necessarily mean you're not pregnant, Aisha, just that the hormone hasn't built up sufficiently in the urine to be detected. Women are different in the amount they produce, particularly in the early stages of pregnancy.'

Aisha nodded. 'It sounds pretty straightforward. I got an A for my Science GCSE, so it shouldn't cause me too much of a problem,' she said, trying to lighten their mood.

Mark threw her one of his stern paternal looks and refolded the leaflet. 'Good, I'll leave it in the bathroom tonight then, and we can do it first thing in the morning. And, Aisha, well done. I was beginning to wonder if we'd ever be doing this test.'

So had she. Her stomach contracted at the thought that there might be another reason for her late period – anxiety or stress – and Mark might yet be disappointed. He put his arms around her shoulders and kissed her tenderly.

'Let's just wait and see the result, shall we?' she said, drawing back. Then, silently, she added, *Please, God, make it so.*

They went to bed early that night for, as Mark said, once they were asleep the waiting wouldn't seem so long. Aisha remembered that that was exactly what her parents used to say on the eve of her birthday, Christmas, or a planned outing, when she had become overexcited and couldn't wait for the following day.

Aisha slept fitfully that night, plagued by a dream that she was back in the school science laboratory and her teacher was standing sternly over her, and she was unable to perform a simple experiment with a Bunsen burner and salt-water solution. She was wide awake before the alarm went off, acutely aware of what she had to do. Mark was still asleep on his side and facing away from her, breathing regularly. Careful not to disturb him, she eased back the duvet and, slipping out of bed, crept round to the bathroom where she silently slid the bolt on the door. The pregnancy testing kit was already neatly laid out on top of the toilet cistern. Mark must have done it before he had come to bed. The litmus stick had been removed from its cellophane wrapper and was balanced across the Perspex container. The instruction sheet with the salient points highlighted by a yellow marker pen was propped conspicuously in front of it. It was typical of Mark, she thought, to be so precise and practical.

Setting the litmus stick to one side, Aisha picked up the little Perspex bowl and sat on the toilet. She released just enough urine to fill the bowl to the marker, then carefully placed it on the side of the sink before emptying the rest of her bladder. Quietly lowering the toilet lid, she washed and dried her hands, but didn't flush the toilet as the noise would be sure to wake Mark.

She stood looking at the pale yellow liquid in the little bowl, momentarily overwhelmed by the significance of what she was about to do. It seemed more than just a test for pregnancy, but one which could confirm or deny her competence as a wife and her role as a woman. Silencing the rising wave of panic, Aisha picked up the litmus stick and, barely able to watch, dipped it into the urine sample. At the same time she heard the bedside alarm begin to bleep. Within seconds, Mark was at the door.

'Aisha? Are you all right?' he said, rattling the handle and then, finding it locked, knocking on the door. 'Aisha? What's the matter? Why's the door locked? Are you ill?'

'I'm fine. I'm just going to the loo,' she said steadily. 'Don't worry, I know what to do.'

He fell silent outside the door as she carefully removed the stick from the urine and tapped off the excess liquid. She brought the stick up to her line of vision and watched, barely able to breathe. It was changing colour, definitely losing its creamy, off-white appearance and slowly darkening. But how dark was it turning? How dark should it be? She carried the instruction sheet and litmus stick to the centre of the room and stood directly under the overhead light. The bar chart on the leaflet showed six subtly graded shades, ranging from the negative creamy-white to definitely positive dark blue. She ran the tip of the stick down from the top until she came to the best match and her heart skipped a beat. It matched the last and deepest shade of blue, and she stared, transfixed, unable to believe what she saw. There was no mistake, it matched perfectly – she was most definitely pregnant.

Returning to the toilet, she flushed it and, before opening the door, remembered to say a final prayer of thanks. 'Thank you, God, thank you so much. I shall never forget your generosity.'

Mark was ecstatic. He kissed and cuddled her and insisted on making breakfast that morning. He prepared it all while she showered and dressed, and when she came downstairs he led her to the breakfast bar and helped her onto the stool.

'What a lot!' she exclaimed. 'Is this all for me?'

He nodded, pleased. 'You're eating for two now.'

Run, Mummy, Run

There was a bowl full of bran flakes, two slices of toast and honey, a banana and a glass of freshly squeezed orange juice. Beside the glass of juice was the multivitamin and mineral pill, which she'd been taking each morning for the last six months. Mark poured the full-cream milk onto her cereal, then picked up her spoon and passed it to her. She smiled as she took it, and to please him, because his efforts couldn't go to waste, dipped in the spoon and began eating, although she would much rather have had a dry cracker to settle her early-morning nausea.

Mark perched on the other stool with his mug of black coffee and watched her eat, like a doting mother hen, she thought. 'Once you've stopped working,' he said, his excitement obvious, 'I'll be able to look after you properly. I'll bring you breakfast in bed every morning; then you'll be able to get up slowly, at your leisure. If you hand in your notice straight away, you'll be finished by ten weeks.'

She concentrated on the bowl of sickly cloying bran flakes and made a conscious effort to swallow each spoonful as Mark continued.

'The most dangerous time to miscarry is twelve weeks,' he said. 'That's when the placenta takes over from the ovaries. It's vital you finish work by then and get all the rest you can. I can't wait to have you home, my love, my precious one. What a clever girl you are.' He kissed her cheek again.

Aisha paused from eating and looked up. 'But, Mark, supposing, heaven forbid, I did miscarry and I had left work ... I wouldn't have a job. Shouldn't I take maternity leave so all my options are left open?'

Mark shook his head solemnly. 'No. You won't miscarry if you're sensible and rest. I know some women work until the

83

end, but that's because they need the money. Happily we're not in that position, so there's no point in taking risks.' He downed the last of his coffee – normally all she had for breakfast – then tore off a strip of kitchen towel, wiped his mouth and threw the tissue in the bin.

'I'm supposed to be meeting a new client at eight,' he said. 'Will you be all right going in on the tube alone? Or shall I cancel so I can come in with you?'

She smiled at his concern. 'No, I'll be fine. Please don't worry. I went in yesterday by myself and I'm just the same today.'

'If you're sure,' he said and hovered. 'It will be quite a feather in my cap if I win this contract. There's a lot of competition.'

'Yes, you go,' she said again. 'I'll be careful, I promise. And you always phone me when I get to work anyway.'

He was standing behind her now, and placing his hands on her shoulders he lightly massaged her neck. 'Have you any idea how special you are, Aisha? I've never been so happy in my life. I can't wait to have you home and all to myself. I'm going to spoil you something rotten. Both of you!' He laughed, and kissing the top of her head, said goodbye.

He called another goodbye before she heard the front door open and then close behind him.

Aisha remained where she was, the spoon hovering over the bowl of congealed bran flakes. Yes, she did feel special, very special indeed, and she could imagine how well Mark was going to take care of her and their newly conceived child. And if it crossed her mind what she was going to do all day after she had stopped work, and was waiting for the birth, it was only fleeting, for the alternative of ignoring Mark's advice and miscarrying was far too awful to even contemplate so she struck it from her mind. She would type a letter of resignation as soon as she got into the office. A month's notice from today meant that she would only be nine weeks pregnant when she left work, which would be well within the twelve weeks danger time Mark had said. She knew she couldn't afford to take any chances, she might never get a second opportunity.

With new resolve, Aisha plunged the spoon into the pulpy cereal and started eating again. If she could get used to this brown mush, she could get used to anything. She just needed to accept the fact that her life was going to be very different for seven months and would require planning to fill her days. Once the baby was born, she would be fully occupied, of that there was no doubt, and before then she could catch up on reading and seeing her parents, both of which had slipped, what with work and married life.

One month and two days later, the entire management team and departmental staff left their desks early on Friday afternoon and gathered in the conference room with drinks and savoury nibbles for Aisha's leaving presentation. Dave Trent, the area manager, spoke very highly of her in his speech – dedicated, loyal, committed and unfailingly conscientious. He said there would be a gap created by her departure which would be impossible to fill. Everyone clapped as he presented her with Mothercare vouchers worth £150, bought with a collection from all the staff.

When Aisha rose to her feet to thank them, she suddenly found she was overcome and had to swallow hard before she could speak. She said how much she'd enjoyed working for the company and being part of the team. She thanked her boss for his kind words and said she would miss them all dearly. She then recounted how, on her first day at the bank, as an overzealous and naïve graduate wanting to make a good first impression, she had signed all her colleagues' letters hoping to save them the trouble. They all laughed, hardly able to imagine that naïve graduate compared to the confident business woman who stood before them now. Dave Trent called out that at least she wouldn't have that problem in her new role and they laughed again.

But later, when she was alone in her office, as she packed away the last of her personal belongings and prepared to leave for the last time, Dave Trent came to find her. He closed the door and stood awkwardly, his hands thrust deep into his pockets. 'Any time, Aisha. If you find bottles and nappies aren't enough, there's always an opening for you here.'

She kept her head down and concentrated on clearing her desk. 'Thanks. I appreciate that, Dave, but you'll find a replacement soon enough. I've heard Bill Hutchings has applied. He's more than capable of doing my job.'

Dave took a couple of steps towards her. 'I dare say he'll get the post if you're definitely not coming back. But it takes more than business acumen to run an outfit like this; it requires diplomacy. Do you know that since you've been manager here we haven't had one disciplinary or head office complaint? That says a lot about you, Aisha. I hope that Mark appreciates just how lucky he is.'

She looked up. 'Thank you, Dave. He does, he really does.'

Of course Mark appreciated her, he told her every minute of the waking day. He fussed and worried, petted and waited on her, and wouldn't let her do anything that could be deemed detrimental to her or the unborn child. He telephoned Aisha from work, two, three, four times a day. 'Just to make sure you're not overdoing it,' he would say. 'You know how I worry. You are resting, aren't you?'

Aisha would immediately stop whatever she was doing and sit down. 'Yes, I'm resting,' she said.

If Aisha wasn't in when Mark phoned, if she had gone to the shops or simply for a short walk, Mark would leave a message on the landline answerphone, stating the time he'd called, and that he would call back in ten minutes, then he would ring her mobile. She found she didn't need her mobile so much now she wasn't at work so she didn't always have it with her charged and switched on. But if it was with her and Mark phoned he would ask her where she was, how far she'd walked, and when she was returning home. 'Please be careful, Aisha,' he said. 'I beg you, for all our sakes.'

After a few months, when she was twenty weeks pregnant and her belly had started to grow and she could feel the new life stir within her, Aisha began curtailing her outings to stop Mark from worrying and imagining the worst. It also silenced her conscience for she couldn't bear the thought of doing something he disapproved of, even though she was past the danger period for miscarrying. So she started going to the local grocery store in the High Street instead of the supermarket in the town, and began limiting her visits to her parents to one afternoon every third week, instead of a whole day every week. Eventually, she abandoned her little country walks altogether – Aisha never knew when Mark was going to phone, with his work commitments he couldn't say, she only knew that he would. 'Just grabbed the opportunity,' he would say. And often that was all he did say; the contact call to reassure him that she was safely at home.

Mark's care and concern knew no bounds and were well beyond what even Aisha had expected. He was a glowing example of the New Man, she thought, the father-to-be who wanted to be involved in every stage of the pregnancy. He bought books

Cathy Glass

on all aspects of pregnancy and parenthood. Aisha knew her body inside out and so too did Mark, in fact probably better than her obstetrician, she mused. He bought diet supplements, which she took as well as the daily multivitamin complex, and the iron tablet prescribed by the hospital. He visited the health shop during his lunch break and found a specially formulated gel which was guaranteed to stop stretch marks. The label said it contained a secret ingredient – an extract from a plant found only in a remote part of the Amazon. The leaflet inside said that the plant was harvested by a local tribe and its location was kept a closely guarded secret. Aisha gasped when she saw what Mark had paid for it: £29.99 for a tiny pot, and he had bought three!

'You're worth it,' Mark said when she expressed her concern. 'Some women worry their husbands will no longer find them attractive when they get big. But you needn't fear that with me. You are more beautiful than ever. Like my very own fertility goddess.' Aisha wasn't sure if this made her feel better or worse, but she knew it was well meant.

Mark smoothed the gel onto her swollen stomach every night when they were in bed. Slow, circular movements that covered every inch of her taut, dry skin, from just below her swollen breasts, over her bump and down to her pubic line. Round and round for fifteen minutes or more. She felt like a beached whale glistening in the moonlight. And towards the end of the pregnancy, when she was so tired that she longed only for sleep, Mark insisted in the nicest possible way that he cream her stomach. 'It's you I'm thinking of, my little love,' he said. 'You'll thank me later. When you're back to normal.'

After Mark had finished massaging in the gel, he snuggled into the small of her back and with his hands around her stomach they would drift off to sleep. He liked to put his hands on her

88

bump and feel the baby slowly move, or the muscles of her stomach suddenly contract as the baby kicked or sometimes hiccuped. It helped him bond, he said, made him feel part of the process, or as near as he could get.

Aisha liked to feel the baby's movements too, but she waited until she was alone during the day while Mark was at work. She walked around the house with one hand on her stomach and imagined Sarah's tiny hand reaching out to hold hers, just the other side of her stomach wall. Sarah was the name they'd chosen if it was a girl, James if it was a boy. Aisha instinctively knew it was a girl, she was sure of it, and she talked to Sarah constantly and told her all the things they would do once she was born. Talking to Sarah helped her bond too, apart from which there was no one else to talk to, she was alone in the house all day. There would be outings to the park, Aisha said, and walks in the country, they would join a mother-and-baby group, and visit her parents. She could visualize herself pushing the pram when Sarah was tiny, then the stroller as she grew, and later when Sarah began to walk, toddling contentedly beside her.

And if during the pregnancy Aisha didn't see as much of her parents as she would have liked, it was because Mark was taking such good care of her, catering for her every need and often anticipating them even before they had arisen. Now she was a married woman her parents would never have interfered in her life. They waited for her phone calls and invitations to visit but they grew increasingly infrequent. 'There's no need to bother your mother with that,' Mark would say when Aisha thought of something she wanted to ask her mother about childbirth or babies. 'You know how she worries. I'll find out. And please don't think of driving over there alone. I'd die if anything happened to you. We'll visit, just as soon as we have a free weekend.'

But the weekends seemed to come and go in a hive of activity, which wasn't surprising really, given the extent of the preparations. They decorated the nursery in pastel grey and white, and hung gaily patterned curtains, which matched the wall frieze of marching, coloured elephants. The colour scheme was carefully chosen to suit a boy or girl. And the Moses basket for the baby's first few weeks was already on its stand, next to the changing platform, with its drawers full of first-size Babygros, disposable nappies, baby wipes and lotions. The pram and cot were on order and would be delivered after the birth, because Mark said it was unlucky to have them before the baby was born and they certainly didn't want to tempt fate.

'Once the baby's here,' Aisha told her parents during one of her rare phone calls, 'I'll be over every week. We're going to buy a baby seat for the car so I can drive over during the day. You'll have plenty of time to spoil your grandchild, I promise.'

Her mother had to accept this and hid her disappointment at not being more involved now. She knew her husband Ranjith would chide her if he found her interfering and she would never go against him. Mark's parents lived in Birmingham and seemed to accept that the infrequent visits from their son would remain few and far between. Aisha wondered if they still held Mark responsible for losing their first grandchildren and if so she hoped the new grandchild would go some way to make recompense. What she didn't realize was that she was becoming ever more isolated.

The suitcase for her stay in hospital was packed, closed and ready in the spare room by the time Aisha was eight months pregnant. Mark had compiled the contents from the list given to them at the antenatal classes, ticking off the items as he bought and packed them, with extras to be sure.

'I don't think they provide much nowadays,' he said, adding another box of nappies, of which there were already twice the number suggested. 'If you do find you're short of something, you must phone the office and I'll bring it up straight away.'

'Yes. Or Mum can if you're busy,' Aisha said.

'Never too busy for you, my love,' he said. 'Besides, I'm a lot closer to the hospital than your parents are.'

There was absolutely nothing Mark hadn't thought of, nothing he had overlooked, so when, two days after Aisha's due date, the Braxton Hicks contractions grew harder and more frequent, Mark timed the intervals and monitored the result. Forty minutes. Thirty. Twenty-five. Twenty. Then the contractions began to take her breath away as the discomfort seared into pain, and she reached out to steady herself, trying to concentrate on her breathing. Mark waited, as the hospital had advised, until the contractions were coming at regular fifteen-minute intervals, then calmly fetched her suitcase, handbag and coat, and telephoned the hospital to say they were on their way.

'I'll call your parents just as soon as we've got you settled,' Mark said as he eased Aisha into the car.

Her body stiffened as another contraction gripped her. 'Yes, please,' she gasped. 'I promised Mum we'd tell her as soon as I went into labour.'

'I know. Now relax. And remember that deep breathing.'

And the labour, while long, wasn't as bad as she thought it would be, with Mark beside her, reassuring and encouraging her. The pain was manageable with him stroking her hair, repeating the midwife's instructions and telling her when to breathe and push, and wiping her forehead with a damp flannel. So that when the cervix was fully dilated, and the full force of the baby's head bore down and she thought she was being torn apart, she grabbed his hands, dug her nails in, and screamed into his shoulder. Yes, manageable, with him beside her knowing that very soon she would be a mother and he a father.

'A proper family at last,' Mark said, receiving the bundle into his arms. 'Sarah, my beautiful baby girl.'

Twelve

Aisha sat in the chair beside the hospital bed and gazed at Sarah. She was asleep in the Perspex crib, her little face just visible above the swaddled blanket. She slept so peacefully that only the occasional twitch of her bottom lip showed she was breathing at all. Aisha looked at her miniature features and marvelled. She was truly a miracle – so perfect and complete it was difficult to imagine where she'd come from – although the stitches were an uncomfortable reminder. Aisha shifted in her chair and tried to get more comfortable, never once taking her eyes from Sarah.

With Sarah's crop of jet-black hair, little turned-up nose and dimpled chin, Aisha could see the likeness her parents had spoken of. 'A chip off the old block,' her father had said, pleased as punch, for it had always been held that Aisha took after her father, and now without doubt Sarah took after her. Her parents had visited the previous afternoon when Sarah was barely nine hours old. Mark, as promised, had phoned them when they'd arrived at the hospital, and then again when the baby was born. 'Eight pounds two ounces,' he'd told them proudly. 'She's perfect. Fingers, toes, everything. I still can't believe it.' Aisha's mother had told her Mark had nearly cried on the phone, he was so overcome with emotion.

Her parents had arrived with flowers, fruit and containers of homemade food, enough for several weeks although Aisha was only going to be in hospital for forty-eight hours. Her mother had produced them one by one from her shopping basket, and stacked them on her bedside cabinet, pleased at last to be doing something. There were *samosas*, *bhajis* and *aloo bonda* – Aisha's favourites. 'I thought you'd be hungry,' her mother said. 'Hospital food is never that filling, and you need to keep up your strength if you're breastfeeding.'

They'd sat beside the crib as Aisha ate, and her mother had kept a watchful eye over Sarah while her father marvelled at the family likeness. 'Like two peas in a pod,' he said. 'Both so beautiful. Wait till they see the pictures back home.'

When Sarah had eventually woken for a feed, Aisha's parents had waited until she'd settled Sarah in her lap, then said their goodbyes and left. Aisha was grateful for their sensitivity for it would have been embarrassing if they had witnessed her fumbled attempts, the last of which had left Sarah annoyed, and Aisha with most of her chest exposed.

Mark had seen the family likeness too when he'd returned soon after her parents' departure. Sarah was losing that newborn red scrunched-up look and her colour was darkening.

'It's like seeing a little Aisha,' he said. 'A miniature replica. Yours must be the dominant gene.' He lifted Sarah from the crib and cradled her in the crook of his arm. Aisha looked at Mark with his daughter with pride and her eyes welled.

'I'm so very happy,' she said.

'Me too.'

Now Aisha sat in the chair beside the hospital bed, packed and waiting to go home. She was disappointed Mark wouldn't be coming to collect her and Sarah from the hospital. It was one of the pictures she'd carried in her mind and had looked forward to during her stay. She'd imagined them arriving home, with Mark carrying Sarah in the Moses basket up the path to the front door, the three of them entering their home for the first time as a family. But it was unavoidable. Mark had only known himself an hour before, when Aisha had been called to the phone at the nurses' station.

'I'm so sorry, my little love,' Mark had said. 'I'm so sorry to let you down. It's that Japanese client again. He's altered his schedule and I have to fit in. I've tried, but there's no way round it. If he'd told me sooner, I could have asked your parents to collect you, but there's no time now.'

Aisha had hidden her disappointment and told him not to worry, that she would be all right for an hour or two at home alone, and would ask a nurse to phone for a taxi.

'No need to, love,' Mark said. 'I've arranged for one of the company cars to collect you, with my driver, Tony. He will take very good care of you. I've told him to come up to the ward at two thirty.'

Aisha smiled to herself – even at short notice Mark was able to organize and find a solution. No wonder he was so successful at work.

'Now you take care, my little one,' he said. 'I'll be with you as soon as I can. I love you. Both of you. Kiss Sarah for me.'

'I will.'

It was disappointing, but unavoidable. Just one of those things, she thought as she waited for Tony. Aisha had already been formally discharged by the doctor, with an appointment for her postnatal check-up in six weeks' time. She had packed her belongings, thrown away the last of the food her mother had brought, and fed and changed Sarah ready for the journey. The Moses basket, which Mark had fortuitously brought in the night before, was tucked out of the way under the bed. She would wait until Tony arrived before moving Sarah into it, then if Sarah did wake up and cry there would only be a few minutes before they were off the ward. Aisha felt self-conscious tending to Sarah's needs surrounded by the nurses and the other, more competent, second-time mothers. Once they were home she knew she would be far more relaxed, and if it took all day to feed and change her, well, there was no one to see but Sarah, who fortunately didn't know any better.

At two twenty-five the doors at the far end of the ward swung open and a man appeared. Aisha watched as he stopped a nurse who pointed to her bed. He was a short, stocky man in his early forties with dark, wavy hair and pleasant, open features. He came towards her, smiling, his hand outstretched. 'Mrs Williams? The name's Tony. Mark sent me.'

She shook his hand. 'Hello Tony.'

'What a beauty,' he said, peering into the crib. 'The wife and I wanted a girl but we've settled for three boys now. Congratulations. You must be very proud.'

Aisha blushed, again feeling the surge of achievement that somehow she had produced this perfect beautiful creature. 'We are. Thank you.'

She bent down to retrieve the Moses basket from under the bed, but Tony intervened. 'No, let me. You shouldn't be bending and lifting yet.'

She stepped back as Tony pulled out the wicker basket and then laid it on the bed. Aisha went to the crib, and with one hand supporting Sarah's head and the other around her little body, she carefully transferred Sarah into the Moses basket. Sarah, still satiated from the feed of half an hour before, opened her eyes, yawned, then obligingly went back to sleep.

'Shall I carry the basket?' Tony asked.

'No, I'd like to, thanks. But if you could take the rest of my things, I'd be very grateful.'

Aisha looped her fingers through the wicker handles of the Moses basket and, with Tony watching ready to help if necessary, eased it off the bed. It was light, little more than the weight of Sarah, and she held it protectively to her side. 'I'm fine, really,' she reassured Tony.

Tony gathered together the rest of her belongings — suitcase, coat, handbag, and the flowers Mark had brought. 'Now, easy does it,' Tony said, stepping round her to lead the way. 'You're bound to feel a bit wobbly. No running on the ward.'

She laughed. 'I don't think I could yet.'

Aisha walked slowly as the stitches pulled, and followed Tony up the ward. As she went she said goodbye to another first-time mother she'd been talking to during her stay, and then stopped at the nurses' station to thank them.

'You've all been so kind,' she said. 'Please pass on my thanks to Irene. She was so helpful with the feeding.'

The nurses wished her well, then Tony opened the swing doors and Aisha carefully walked through making sure the sides of the Moses basket didn't catch the door. She vaguely remembered coming through reception when she'd been in labour, but it seemed a lifetime ago now, and she'd been so involved in concentrating on her breathing, that she really hadn't taken in her surroundings.

'You'll want your coat on,' Tony said protectively as they came to the outer doors. He set down the suitcase and flowers and shook out her coat. 'The first lesson of good parenting is to look after yourself.'

Aisha smiled as Tony helped her into her coat, he was indeed taking very good care of her, just as Mark had said he would.

Outside, she breathed in the fresh clear air; it felt good. The ward had been stiflingly hot, with the heating turned up and the double-glazed windows rarely opened for fear of the babies catching cold. An ambulance siren wailed as it drew into the hospital grounds, and Aisha looked anxiously down at Sarah, but she remained asleep, unaware of the noise or sudden change in temperature.

'It's the blue Toyota,' Tony said, pointing to one of three cars parked at the pick-up point. 'I'll get you and baby settled in first, then I'll see to the luggage.'

He opened the rear door and Aisha passed him her precious load then eased herself into the car. The stitches pulled again and she hoped Tony hadn't seen her grimace; she would have been embarrassed if he'd realized the cause of her pain. She fastened her belt as Tony slid the Moses basket onto the seat beside her, then looped the other seat belt around it.

'Keep your hand on the basket and I'll drive real slow,' he said. 'You'll need to get a car baby seat, they're safest.'

'Mark's ordered it,' Aisha said defensively. And she thought that if Mark had forgotten one thing, it was that they should really have had the seat now.

Testing the belt, and satisfied that he had done his best for his little passenger, Tony closed the rear door and then loaded the boot. He climbed in, and starting the engine, reversed out, and slowly pulled away. Aisha laid her right arm along the length of the basket to steady it.

'OK?' Tony called over his shoulder as they left the hospital grounds and gathered speed.

'Yes, fine. She's still asleep.'

He smiled at Aisha in the rear-view mirror. 'Long may it continue. It will give you a chance to rest.'

With fifteen minutes to home, Aisha settled back into her seat and glanced between Sarah and the scenery passing outside her window. Everything seemed fresh and vibrant outside after the blandness of the ward. She would have been happy to have sat quietly and taken it all in, but Tony wanted to chat.

'I expect you're looking forward to getting home,' he said. 'My missus was, with all of ours.'

Aisha nodded. 'I just hope I know what to do. There seems so much to learn and remember. It's all a bit over-whelming.'

'Do what comes naturally,' he said good-humouredly. 'Throw away all those books and pamphlets they give you. They're writ-ten by psychologists who've studied kids but never had them. You're Mum, you know best.'

Aisha smiled to herself as she thought of Mark and all his books, the most recent of which was *Practical Parentcraft*, which had come with a DVD.

Tony continued chatting, reminiscences about his own chil-dren, the youngest of whom was now eleven. Parenthood seemed to encourage these shared confidences, Aisha thought; it had been the same on the ward. Other mothers, nurses, and even her neighbour's visitor, had shared anecdotes and pieces of advice about child-rearing. It seemed to Aisha that, in having a baby, she had crossed a threshold, completed a rite of passage and she was now accepted into a new and exclusive club.

'He's a good chap, your Mark,' Tony said, suddenly changing the subject. 'He's caring. You don't always find that in manage-ment. I hear a lot being a driver, but I've never heard a bad word said against him. That's not to say he's a soft touch. Far from it.

He works like a trooper and expects others to do the same. But he's thoughtful with it.'

Aisha met his eyes in the rear-view mirror, and nodded. 'Yes, I know. I'm very lucky.'

'Now, you take my wife,' he continued. 'She had a big operation a while back. You know, women's stuff. Mark sent her a smashing bouquet of flowers with a card wishing her a speedy recovery. She's never forgotten it, neither have I.'

Aisha thought that that was exactly the type of thing Mark would do, the little touches that didn't take much but brought a smile to a person's face. 'I expect you've known each other quite a while,' she said. 'You do all his driving, don't you?'

'Since he joined the company, yes. Must be coming up for four years now.'

Aisha glanced at Sarah whose little fist had appeared over the blanket and was now resting on her chin. 'I think you'll find it's longer than that,' Aisha said. 'Mark's been with the company for over eight years.'

Tony hesitated as the car in front slowed and then suddenly pulled into the kerb without indicating. He tutted as he drew past. 'No, I'm sure. It was just before my wife's op and that's three and a half years ago. Mark had only known me for a few months, which was why the flowers were such a nice touch. Not many would do that for someone they hardly knew.'

Aisha didn't argue the point. Time flew, and Tony wouldn't be the first to miscalculate the passing years. She turned to the side window; they were in the High Street now and the area was typical of many Greater London streets with shops topped with flats. It was a melting pot of wares and cultures, where kebab houses and Indian takeaways rubbed shoulders with electrical stores and twenty-four hour pop-ins. She liked the cosmopolitan feel, it was similar to the area in which she had grown up. And since she'd been in hospital the High Street seemed to have been given a polish so the slightly rundown, dusty façades now seemed brighter. It's motherhood, she thought, for as her mother had said – a new baby makes you see life completely differently. New and afresh.

Tony drew into the kerb outside her house and Aisha noticed that the daffodils in their small front garden, which had been no more than green shoots before she'd gone into hospital, had now burst into flower. The garden was a mass of bright yellow blooms swaying in the breeze.

'Stay put,' Tony said, getting out. 'I'll see to the luggage first.'

She waited while he unloaded the boot and carried her belongings up the path, stacking them by the front door. She wondered if she should give him a tip, he'd been so kind and helpful. But she only had a couple of pounds in her purse and didn't want to embarrass him. Doubtless Mark would see to it if it was appropriate.

Tony opened the rear door and carefully slid out the Moses basket, then offered his arm as she got out. 'Front door key?' he asked as she straightened beside him.

'It's in my handbag,' she said nodding to her belongings at the door.

Aisha let Tony carry the Moses basket up the path while she took her keys from her bag and unlocked the porch door and then the inner door. Tony passed her the basket and then lifted her suitcase and flowers just inside the hall.

'Will you be all right alone?' he said, stepping back outside. 'They usually like you to have someone with you so soon after the birth. Shall I wait until Mark gets home?'

'No, I'll be fine, thanks. Mark will have made sure I have everything I need and he won't be long.'

'Well, if you're sure. Take care then, and give my regards to Mark.'

Aisha thanked him again and closed the doors. She stood for a few seconds taking in her surroundings. *Home at last,* she thought. This was the moment she'd been waiting for, had ticked off the hours to. And if it wasn't quite the homecoming with Mark she'd anticipated, at least the time to herself meant she would be able to get organized. She would shower and change, then start the preparations for the evening meal, so that when Mark came home from work it would be to a well-ordered house. She wanted to create a good first impression as a mother.

Setting down the Moses basket in the hall, Aisha glanced through the open lounge door. How bright and colourful it seemed after the drabness of the ward. Hospitals lacked colour, she thought. Why did they insist on painting everything light green? A little imagination would have done wonders, even on a tight budget.

Now the first thing to do was to settle Sarah in the nursery, then she could find some fresh clothes and shower. She and Mark had agreed that Sarah would use the nursery right from the beginning, thereby hopefully avoiding the pitfalls of separation some parents faced when they tried to move an older baby into a room of its own. The baby alarm was already in place so she would be able to hear Sarah from anywhere in the house and immediately answer her cry. Aisha knew she wasn't a hundred per cent well yet, but she would go carefully, and the basket was hardly heavy lifting. Sarah was still asleep, her loosely curled fist just showing above the blanket. She was going to be a good baby, Aisha thought, just as she had been in the hospital.

Aisha took one step up the stairs and then stopped. Strange, she thought she heard a noise. She paused and listened. Yes, there it was again. Distant, but definitely a noise. She brought her foot down from the stair and stood perfectly still, her ears straining for any sounds. A few seconds passed and then it was repeated, and again. It sounded like a click. A metallic click in a house that should have been empty.

Her fingers tightened around the handles of the basket and her pulse quickened as the distant noise repeated and then again. It seemed to be coming from the kitchen. Clink. Silence. Clink. Yes, she thought, it was travelling in from the kitchen and through the open door of the lounge. It was forming a regular pattern now of metal on metal, clink, pause, clink. Could it be an open window tapping in the breeze? No, Mark always closed windows; he was adamant about security, and it didn't sound like that type of noise either. Not a window tapping. As Aisha strained and listened the clink began to sound vaguely familiar. Clink, pause, clink. A noise of a routine, a part of everyday life in the house. Finally, she placed it. Of course! How could she have been so stupid? It *was* metal on metal, it was cutlery being dropped in the drawer. Someone was drying up and putting the knives and forks away. Relief flooded through her. Mark. He must have finished with his client early, but not early enough to collect her. He had obviously come straight home, rather than going to the hospital and risk crossing en route and possibly missing her. Now he was doing some last-minute clearing up, drying the cutlery, making everything spick and span the way he liked it, ready for her return. He couldn't have heard her come in, which was hardly surprising with her having been so quiet to avoid waking Sarah.

What a wonderful surprise, she thought, and how pleased he would be to see her. She knew what she would do, she would creep up and surprise him; they both would. She looked down at Sarah who, seeming to sense the excitement and change of plan, obligingly opened her eyes and yawned. 'You're awake,' Aisha whispered. 'Come on, Daddy's home. Let's go and find him. Won't he be surprised?'

Returning the basket to the floor, Aisha eased back the blanket and carefully lifted Sarah out. She cradled her in the crook of one arm and supported her bottom and legs with her other hand. It was going to take some getting used to, this carrying her around. They hadn't been allowed to carry their babies on the ward in case they tripped or fainted. And Sarah's tiny form, which had felt so robust and determined while inside her, now seemed unbelievably vulnerable and fragile.

'All right?' she whispered, lightly brushing her lips across Sarah's warm, smooth cheek. 'You wait until your daddy sees us. His face will be a picture.'

Aisha thought she saw the faintest flicker of a smile cross Sarah's face, although at two days old she knew this was more likely to be wind. Aisha went into the lounge, moving quietly across the carpet which seemed suddenly luxurious after the linoleum of the hospital ward. How tidy Mark had kept every-thing. Despite all his to-ing and fro-ing to the hospital and work, everything was in its place, apart from the newspapers, which he hadn't had time to read and were in a pile on the coffee table. She smiled to herself, not many women would have come home to a house so neat and clean. She was the luckiest person alive, in every possible way.

Creeping the last few steps, Aisha stopped outside the archway which led to the kitchen. She heard a drawer close as Mark finished putting away the cutlery. She imagined him folding the tea towel and hanging it precisely over the radiator to dry, the way he always did and the way he liked it. Aisha waited out of sight, just on the other side of the archway, and steadied her excitement. The next step would carry her and Sarah through into the kitchen, and both of them into his arms. She gave Sarah a little squeeze of anticipation and moved forwards, then stood quietly unseen at the end of the kitchen. Mark was in full view now, but he had his back to her, and was wiping the sink spotlessly clean.

She took another step. He must be very deep in thought not to have sensed her presence. He was probably wondering when she would be home, and if Tony was taking good care of her. He would see her soon out of the corner of his eye, then with a gasp of surprise he would throw the dishcloth in the bowl and rush over to embrace them – 'Oh, my little love. You're home! I didn't hear you come in,' followed by hugs and kisses, the joy of them all being together, a proper family at last. Then he would open the bottle of champagne, which he'd told her was already in the fridge, and maybe just this once, she would break her abstinence and have a glass. Mark had said it was tradition to wet the baby's head, for good luck and prosperity.

But he still hadn't seen her or sensed her presence. He must be really preoccupied, she thought. He was probably thinking about the client who had stopped him from collecting her; she hoped Mark had won the contract for she knew how much it meant to them both financially and for his career. She glanced down at Sarah who lay perfectly content, then up again.

'Mark,' she said quietly. 'Mark, we're home.'

She waited, in heightened expectation. Aisha waited for Mark to stop cleaning the sink, turn, and come to her. She waited in silent anticipation, her heart bursting with love and pride; she waited for him to turn and see her. Then, with a small sideways step, Mark stopped wiping the sink, but continued across to the Formica work surface beside it. Still cleaning, lots of little wipes, like a parody of her own cleaning when she was in a hurry and had more important things to do. Clearly he still hadn't heard her.

'Mark?' she said again, louder this time. 'Mark. Look! We're home!'

He was only a yard or so in front of her now, but was still turned away, and still rubbing the work surface, making it very clean. She hoped his preoccupation wasn't due to bad news at work. Then, suddenly, noticing it for the first time, she saw that he was wearing his dressing gown: the navy towelling one that he changed into briefly after his shower in the morning, before he got dressed. Odd, she thought, he never wore his dressing gown during the day. He said it was slovenly and it was impor- tant to keep up appearances, even when there was just the two of them. And why, she thought, why was he in his dressing gown if he had come straight from work? Shouldn't he be in his suit, or if he'd had time to change, his jeans and sweater? That was normally what he wore when he came home from work.

'Mark?' she asked, concern in her voice. 'Is everything all right? We're home.'

He stopped cleaning, but he still didn't turn to face her. She watched as he rested his hands on the work surface and then, raising his head, stared out through the window to the garden beyond.

'We're home,' she said again.

'I can see that,' he said flatly, still not looking at her.

He must be joking, she thought, teasing her, as he did some- times. 'Can't have you taking me for granted,' he would say, when he had left out the 'love and miss you' which ended each of his telephone calls. 'Haven't you forgotten something?' she would ask. 'Just teasing,' he'd say. 'Don't want you taking me for granted. Of course I love and miss you.'

Yes, that's what it was. He was teasing her before he came over and took her in his arms and hugged them both. But she knew what to do; she'd do what she normally did. She'd play him at his own game, which was part of their little ritual and showed their love was strong enough to bear teasing.

'Well,' she said, looking down at Sarah to share the joke, 'if you don't want your daughter I may as well go and take her back to the hospital.'

He was turning now, as she knew he would. It always worked, playing him at his own game. Mark liked a joke.

He dropped the dishcloth into the sink and looked at her, his shoulders drawn back, his feet slightly apart. She returned his gaze, smiling and proudly holding their daughter, waiting for the moment he would come over and encircle them.

But no. He wasn't coming towards her, and there was something else. Something she had never seen before and couldn't place. Something in his eyes, narrow and distant. And something in his voice, when he spoke. What was wrong with his voice? She barely recognized it, and what he was saying was impossible. She couldn't grasp the meaning and it was well beyond a joke.

'Yes,' he said. 'You do that! Go! But the baby stays with me.'

He drew himself up to his full height, a big man made even bigger in the confines of the kitchen. He stared at her, a cold, biting stare that pierced her soul and made her uncertainty turn to fear. 'Go on! Get out!' he said. 'Take your bag and go! But leave her. She's mine. She stays with me.'

He was shouting now. Impossible. Mark never shouted at her. He said everything was open to rational discussion and that they could sit down and talk out their differences sensibly. But they never had any differences, not really; they agreed on almost everything.

'You scheming bitch!' he yelled. 'You thought you'd got the better of me, didn't you! All that planning. You thought you'd got away with it. Oh, but I'm wiser now. Oh, yes! One step ahead.'

There was a tightness in her chest and she was finding it difficult to breathe. She opened her mouth but no sound came out. She clasped Sarah tightly to her and her arms jerked involuntarily.

'Stay where you are!' Mark yelled, his face contorted and deathly white. 'I'll phone your parents. You can go there – if they'll have you.'

Sarah began to cry. He was coming towards her now, towards the phone mounted on the wall behind her. He came right up to her and passed, brushing her shoulder. Aisha instinctively stepped back.

'Mark?' she stammered, her heart pounding and her breath catching in her throat. 'Mark?'

But he was reaching up, taking the phone from its cradle, ready to key in the numbers and call her parents.

'Mark! No. Don't do that,' she cried. 'Please don't. You'll upset them. Tell me first. Tell me what I've done.'

He paused, his hand resting on the phone and looked back at her over his shoulder. 'Upset?' he sneered. 'They'll be upset all right when I tell them what their precious fucking daughter has been up to.'

She stared in disbelief. The room tilted and swayed. If she didn't sit down soon, she'd faint with Sarah in her arms. She saw the whites of his knuckles closed around the phone, the grim determination on his face as he began to press the keypad and tap in her parents' number.

'No. Please don't,' she said again. 'Please don't. Mark, what is it?' Then without thinking, as a reflex action almost, to stop him from telling and upsetting her parents, she took the couple of steps to his side, and placed one hand on his arm.

In that instant as she touched him, time locked and she saw what was about to happen a split second before it did. She saw the phone thrown down and swinging on its cord, as his hand clenched into a fist and came towards her, its target pre set and inevitable. She heard the sickening thud as his fist hit the side of her head and felt the knot of pain explode in her cheek. She heard the cry that escaped from her lips as she began to fall. Down, down, the ground rising up, and Sarah snatched from her arms a second before she hit the floor. Then nothing.

Thirteen

Reds, greens and yellows, backed by a moving wall of darkness swam before her eyes. The colours came and went, grouping and reforming until they began to settle into a sickly orange hue. She was on her side with her right leg splayed awkwardly beneath her, and her right arm trapped under her body. She could hear Mark's voice in conversation, only his, with no reply. Close, but not immediate, not in the same room.

'Beautiful ... Yes ... Settling in fine. Yes, I will. Of course.' It was his best telephone voice, crisp and precise, the one he used when he wanted to impress.

Her eyes were still closed, her cheek was pressed hard against the cold, wet tile. The hardness seemed to amplify the throbbing in her head and the pain in her jaw. Aisha could taste blood, bitter and salty, and then felt it trickle from the corner of her mouth.

'Yes, feeding very well. Oh yes, most definitely,' he said. 'I will.'

For a moment, as she slowly regained consciousness, and her senses began to clear, Aisha wondered why she was lying so uncomfortably on the floor, while Mark was on the telephone in the lounge. Shouldn't he be in here with her, helping her to her feet if she'd fallen? Then she remembered what had happened and her eyes shot open in terror.

She saw the outline of the lower kitchen cabinets and the legs of the breakfast stools distorted in an orange haze. She blinked.

Her heart pounded and she took a deep breath, gulped in the air and tried to focus. In a while, she thought, when the jazzy patterns had quietened and she could do it without being sick, she would try and raise her head, then stand; and that was all she thought for some moments.

'Yes, thank you. We are.' Mark gave a little laugh. 'Absolutely!'

Aisha slowly raised her free hand and brought it up to her face. Uncoordinated and heavy as lead, she drew it across her mouth, then up to her eyes. Slithers of blood-stained saliva ran snake-like across her fingers. She swallowed and then ran her tongue around her mouth and swallowed again. Her bottom lip felt swollen and there was a cut to the inside of her cheek, but thankfully all her teeth still seemed to be in place. She slowly turned onto her back and winced. Placing a hand either side, she pressed down on the floor with her palms and heaved herself onto her elbows, then up into a sitting position. The room tilted and swayed, and she stayed very still, supporting her weight with her hands and trying to quieten her breathing. She mustn't faint and fall back now, she must concentrate on standing and finding Sarah.

Mark's voice floated in again, jovial and polite. 'Yes, I know. Very sweet. It fits perfectly. The pale lemon really suits her. You're so clever. I will.'

Pale lemon, Aisha thought, it must be her mother he was talking to. Her mother had knitted Sarah a lemon cardigan and Aisha had dressed Sarah in it before leaving the hospital. She reached up to the cooker and, clinging to the edge with both hands, hauled herself up. The nausea rose in her throat and she swallowed.

'Yes, tired, as you'd expect,' he said. 'I'll tell her when she wakes. Yes, of course I will. See you soon. Goodbye.' She heard the phone in the lounge clunk as it was set down.

Leaning on the cooker, Aisha stood very still and listened. It was quiet now. She ran her fingers over her cheekbone. It was hot and sore, but as she examined her fingers, she saw it wasn't bleeding. The only blood appeared to be coming from the inside of her lip. With another deep breath, moving hand over hand, Aisha slowly inched her way along the fitted units and to the sink. Taking out the bowl she turned on the cold tap, then spat. A globule of red saliva slithered round the sink before disappearing down the plughole. Aisha cupped her hands, filled them with cold water, then rinsed her mouth and spat again. Splashing cold water on the rest of her face, she turned off the tap and reached for the towel.

Leaning on the sink for support, she patted her face dry and listened. It was still quiet, not a sound. She expected to hear something – his footsteps, Sarah crying for her feed. Her eyes went to the wall clock, it was twenty past four. She must have been unconscious for nearly fifteen minutes, and her mind recoiled. Where was Sarah? She would be waking for her feed soon, she must go and find her. Heaving herself off the sink, Aisha began to make her way slowly across the kitchen and towards the lounge. She went past the wall telephone by the door, which was no longer dangling on its wire but had been returned to its cradle. Her head throbbed, her pulse beat wildly in her chest and the nausea rose in her throat. She concentrated on finding Sarah, to the exclusion of everything else. Moving slowly through the archway and into the lounge, Aisha suddenly stopped. Mark was at the far end of the room, on the sofa beneath the bay window, with Sarah cradled in his arms.

Aisha stayed where she was and stared the length of the room, uncertain and afraid. His broad shoulders were hunched forwards forming a canopy over the baby, the way some nursing mothers sat when feeding. Mark was smiling, smiling down at Sarah, who was awake but not crying. Aisha saw that he had the tip of his little finger in her mouth acting as a dummy.

Then he looked up, straight into her eyes. 'Your mother phoned,' he said. 'I told her you were resting and would call her back later.' His voice was normal, his expression was normal too, but Aisha found no relief in this. Fear and confusion gripped her. How could he sit there like nothing had happened? It was impossible, all of it, she didn't understand at all. Then he spoke again: 'Baby's hungry. Shall I make up a bottle? It must be well past her feed time.' Couldn't he see her swollen face or blood-matted hair? He must, so why didn't he say something? Didn't he know what had happened, what he had done?

Aisha stayed where she was and stared at him, not knowing what to say or where to begin. His denial placed it so far out of reach there was no starting point, no opening; she felt at his mercy.

'I'm feeding her,' she said at last, her voice far-off and unreal.

Mark smiled down again at Sarah. 'Yes, of course, I know. But I bought the formula in case you were too tired, or didn't have enough milk. It can happen to nursing mothers sometimes, particularly in the evening.'

She continued to stare at the two of them, together on the sofa, father and daughter, and searched in vain for the right words – a place to begin. Was he still expecting her to go and leave Sarah with him? Was that why he'd really bought the formula – so he could feed her after she'd left?

Aisha threw out her arms in despair. 'Mark!' she cried. 'What is it? What's happened? What are you doing?'

He looked up, his eyes widening in surprise, as though he hadn't the least idea what she was talking about. She could almost have believed him except for the pain in her head.

'Tell me!' she tried again, fighting back the tears. 'It must be bad to make you behave like that. Mark! You hit me, don't you remember?'

He flinched, recoiled, as though she had just spoken the unspeakable, but there was no sign of guilt or remorse. There was nothing beyond profound astonishment.

'What, Mark? What?' Her voice faded in defeat and his silence crackled in defiance.

He looked down again at Sarah, drew her closer, as though shielding her, protecting her and making her an ally – the two of them against her. Then slowly, without looking up, in a flat emotionless voice he said, 'You have destroyed me, Aisha. You have taken everything and left me with nothing. I'm finished.' His resignation and the inevitability added to her terror.

She fought to control her breathing as a rushing noise filled her ears. She mustn't pass out again, she had to stay in control. There was no telling what would happen if she collapsed now. She gulped in air. 'How, Mark? How have I destroyed you? Tell me. I've just come out of hospital with our baby. I haven't had time to do anything. How?'

He moved one hand to cup Sarah's head in his palm, and with the other, gently stroked her hair. 'I don't mean now,' he said evenly. 'Before. I realize it's not *all* your fault. I was blind, I wanted you so much. But to tell me while you were in hospital. That was cruel. Unforgivable. How could you treat your husband like that, Aisha? How?'

She stared around, trying to make sense of his words, to put reason where there was none. 'Tell you? Tell you what, Mark?'

She heard her voice high and panic-stricken. 'I haven't done anything. I don't understand.'

A tear escaped and ran down her cheek, stinging the grazed flesh on her cheekbone. Mark looked up, stared straight ahead, and for a moment she thought she saw the start of tears in his eyes too.

'That your use for me is over,' he said. 'That now you have what you wanted, I'm no longer needed. That you have thrown me away like a spent cartridge. Gone. History.'

Aisha heard the words and tried to make sense of what he'd said, but it made no sense at all. She searched the crevices of her mind, rummaged for a clue – something that would give her a lead. Had she made some chance remark that could have been misinterpreted and led to this? But no, there was nothing, she'd hardly said anything since arriving home. And at the hospital everything had been perfect.

'Mark,' she said in despair, 'I don't know. What have I said?'

'It's not what you said. It's what you *did*, as you damn well know.' His voice was rising again, losing its control. Aisha stayed very still, not daring to move or speak for fear of inviting another attack. 'Had you told me to my face,' he said, 'I might have been able to bear it. But leaving it out like that … I admit I lost it. Who wouldn't?' Suddenly his expression changed from anger to humiliation and defeat. 'It's still over there,' he said. 'I found it as you intended.'

Aisha slowly drew her eyes from him and followed his gaze across the lounge to the pine coffee table in the centre of the room. They had bought the table together before they were married and now treasured it as their first and, so far, only joint purchase. The unread newspapers were stacked at one end of the table, and next to them was an onyx elephant one of her relatives had sent from India. Beside that was the fruit bowl, two apples inside it, and lying next to the fruit bowl was her library book. She stared at the contents of the table, then up again at him, still unable to understand.

'The book,' he said. 'I read it last night. I assume that was your intention. But what a cruel way to do it, Aisha. Why not just tell me?'

She lowered her eyes again, and then, uncomprehending, walked across the room and to the coffee table. Sarah gave a little cry and Aisha looked over as Mark returned his finger to her mouth. She stooped to the table and slowly picked up the book. She stared at its plastic jacket, grimy from regular borrowing. It was a popular novel, an easy read. She thought she might have enjoyed it in hospital when she wouldn't have been able to concentrate on anything more serious, but in the rush of leaving she'd forgotten to take it with her. The picture on the front showed a woman holding a baby and it was entitled *Lisa's Baby*.

'You remember?' he was saying. 'You remember now, don't you? Read the blurb on the back if you need reminding, which I'm sure you don't.'

Mechanically, she turned over the book and scanned the half a dozen lines on the back. *Lisa, a thirty-something career woman, realizes her biological time clock is running out. Not wanting to miss her chance of motherhood, she joins a dating agency, where she works through a long list of men until she finds what she's looking for: James Case has the exact characteristics she desires in her child. She conceives, then leaves James, her use for him over.* 'A satirical look at our times,' one critic said. 'Very droll, with a neat twist at the end,' though what this twist was had been left unstated, and Aisha didn't know because she'd only read the first page.

She stared at the print, then up again at Mark. 'You surely don't believe …' she began, and stopped. 'You don't really think …' she tried again, but the words failed her, for clearly he did.

'I was beside myself,' he said. 'Coming home from the hospital last night and finding it there like that. I know I shouldn't have reacted as I did just now, but I'm gutted. I vested everything in our relationship, Aisha, now I'm left with nothing. I should have known, I suppose. I should have known it was too good to be true.'

He stopped and suddenly stood. Aisha started, and instinctively took a step back. Tucking the blanket around Sarah, Mark came towards her, arms outstretched, and placed Sarah in her arms.

'Despite what I said, I know she should stay with you. You're her mother. I must be the one to go. All I ask is that you let me see her sometimes. I won't make any fuss, I promise.' His eyes welled, his body hunched in defeat and then he turned and walked towards the hall.

Fear and relief gripped Aisha in equal parts and rendered her immobile. Relief, that there *was* a reason for what had happened and it was tangible and could therefore be explained; and fear, that Mark was going, going to leave her anyway. Suddenly she came to. 'Mark!' she cried, flying after him. 'Mark, stop!'

He continued up to the front door, then stopped, his back towards her, his shoulders slumped forwards. 'No, don't prolong it, Aisha,' he said without looking at her. 'Don't make it any more difficult than it already is. Please, Aisha.' His hand went to the doorknob and he began turning it, ready to leave. 'When I've found somewhere to stay, I'll contact you for access. Take care, and look after Sarah. I love you both. I always will.' He opened the door.

'No! No! Please don't go,' she cried. 'It's a mistake! A misunderstanding. I never intended you to read it. Believe me, please, Mark!'

He straightened, and letting go of the door, turned, his eyes again narrowed in accusation. 'No? What were you going to do then? Sneak off while I was at work?'

'No, I didn't mean ... I never intended ... I love you. I need you. I'll die if you go.' Her fear at being deserted overrode that of another physical assault, and she went right up to him and took hold of his arm. 'Please, Mark, please. Listen. Let me explain. I didn't mean any of it, honestly. I haven't even read the book. It's a dreadful, dreadful misunderstanding.'

He stared at her, a mixture of distrust and cynicism in his eyes. 'What are you trying to say? That your plan wasn't to leave me now you have the baby? Come off it. Give me some credit. I'm not that daft.'

'It's true, Mark,' she cried in desperation. 'How could I? I love you. It's just a story. Thousands of people have read it. It's not about us. You must believe me. Please, Mark, please.' Tears were streaming down her face and she was shaking uncontrollably. Her head throbbed and her legs trembled. 'Come inside and talk. You'll see it's a mistake. Really, I promise.'

He hesitated, and in that hesitation she saw the first sign of doubt, a small opening, a window in his previous unshakeable conviction of her guilt.

'Please,' she beseeched again, willing to beg if necessary. 'Please, don't go. I need you, Mark. So does Sarah. Please. I'm not the woman in the book. I wanted you first, then the baby followed. I want a proper family!'

His gaze went slowly from her to Sarah, then back again, as though he was struggling with what she was saying. His brow furrowed. 'Are you trying to tell me that you didn't leave that book for me to find? That you didn't marry me just to have a baby?'

'I wouldn't. I couldn't. Oh, Mark, no.' She buried her fingers in the material of his dressing gown, clinging to his arm and imploring him. 'Mark, you must believe me. I want us to be together. Always. Our baby is part of that. The product of our love, you said that Mark, please, it's true.'

His face began to crumple, slowly registering disbelief, and his arm slumped. 'Aisha, have I really got it wrong?' he slowly said. 'Have I made a dreadful mistake? Tell me, please tell me. I need to hear it.'

'Yes, yes, you have, Mark. Really. It's just a story. It's not us. How could it be? I wouldn't do that. I love you too much. Oh, Mark, please, come here.'

As he finally accepted what she was saying, he appeared for the first time to see the damage to her face. With an agonized moan, he clasped her to him, and burying his head in her hair, cried like a baby. 'Oh, my little love. What have I done? I've never hit anyone before. Now I've hurt the person who means more to me than life itself. I'm so sorry, Aisha, I'm so scared. Forgive me, I beg you. Don't make me go. I'll do anything if you let me stay, I promise.'

His body shook and his chest heaved as his sobs racked the air. It was an anguish so deep and harrowing that it made her almost as fearful as his previous anger. She held Sarah out to one side as she hugged and comforted him.

'It's all right,' she soothed. 'You're not leaving, neither of us is. We're going to be together always. We're one. All those months of planning and waiting for the baby have taken their toll. I understand. I know it's not you. Mark, please don't cry. Of course I forgive you. Please, Mark, I love you.'

Fourteen

*S*arah settled easily in her cot that night, surrounded by a mountain of soft toys and with the night light on low. The nursery and everything in it had suddenly found its purpose now Sarah had arrived, as though on the stroke of midnight a fairy had waved her magic wand and brought it all to life.

Mark and Aisha stood side by side gazing down at her, mesmerized and reluctant to draw themselves away. Sarah was so peaceful and serene in sleep that it was a humbling experience for them, and the indisputable evidence of their love, which they so badly needed.

'Come on,' Mark said at last, slipping his arm around Aisha's waist. 'You look exhausted. I'll do the night-time feed.'

She leant against him. 'I'll be all right after a few hours' sleep. She shouldn't wake again until two.'

'All right. But for goodness' sake wake me if you need help. Don't martyr on all alone.'

She looked up at him. 'Don't worry, I won't.'

Aisha adjusted Sarah's blanket one last time, then allowed herself to be led from the nursery and into their bedroom. She sighed when she saw her suitcase still unpacked on the bed; she'd forgotten all about it. 'I suppose I'd better unpack first,' she said and yawned.

'No, leave it. Take out what you need and I'll see to the rest first thing in the morning.'

Relieved that for once their usual orderliness could be overlooked, Aisha opened the case and took out her washbag and nightdress, then began dragging the case off the bed.

'No,' Mark said, springing to her side. 'No lifting, Aisha, you must take care. You're number one now.'

'You sound just like Tony,' she smiled. 'He was so kind and helpful, although he didn't stop talking. He told me all about his family and wife, and how you'd sent her flowers after her operation. Only, it was odd, he was convinced you had been with the company four years. I said it was more like eight. That's right, isn't it?'

Mark frowned. 'No. Where did you get that idea from?'

She shrugged. 'I thought that's what you said?' He shook his head. 'Well, it doesn't matter.'

She went into the bathroom and closed the door. At the sink she turned on the hot tap and waited for the water to run warm, while avoiding her reflection in the mirror. She'd already sponged the blood from her hair and cleaned up her face earlier, so there was no point in looking again and dwelling on it. After all, it was only a graze to her cheek and a small cut to her bottom lip, it would heal in a couple of days. 'We don't make mountains out of molehills,' her mother used to say to her as a child when she'd come in blubbering from a fall in the garden and had wanted lots of sympathy. It was Mark who needed the help now – to forgive himself and move on. He was beside himself with guilt and self-recrimination and had been apologizing all evening.

Aisha quickly showered, then dressed into a clean nightdress and tucked the breast pads into her bra. She was beginning to feel like a dairy cow with all the milk slopping around; no sooner were her breasts empty from one feed than they began to refill, then leak. Irene, the nurse at the hospital, had said it was perfectly normal, and that the problem arose when mothers didn't make enough milk. That wasn't going to be her worry for sure, she thought, and the formula Mark had bought would certainly go to waste.

'All right?' Mark asked attentively as she returned to the bedroom.

'Yes, I can't wait to get into my own bed.'

She sat on the edge of the bed and unwound her plait, while Mark took his turn in the bathroom. Aisha gave her hair a quick brush rather than the fifty strokes she usually gave it, and then eased back the covers and climbed in. She felt the soft down of the duvet mould luxuriously around her; a blissful contrast to the starched sheets of the hospital, which had crinkled like wrapping paper each time she'd turned over. She heard the rush of water as the tank in the loft refilled and Mark showered, then it stopped, and he returned to the bedroom, naked.

Aisha instinctively looked away. She doubted she would ever feel as comfortable about nakedness as he did, although she was getting better. She didn't immediately grab her clothes when he caught her dressing, or cover herself when he walked in on her in the bath or shower. When they'd been on their honeymoon, Aisha had explained that in her family they never walked around undressed as her parents considered it improper. Mark had laughed, but kindly, and had told her not to worry, then added he found her coyness quite endearing – a turn-on, he said.

Now Mark took a pair of clean boxer shorts from the drawer, pulled them on and slipped into bed beside her. He propped himself up on one elbow and gazed down at her; she saw the pain reappear in his eyes. She knew he was about to apologize again, as he had being doing all evening: tell her how ashamed he was, that he didn't know what had come over him, then ask if she could truly forgive him, for he was so dreadfully, dreadfully sorry.

Aisha didn't want to hear it anymore: she knew his reaction had been completely out of character, and had probably been brought on by all the anxiety surrounding the conception and birth of Sarah, and possibly also because of the way he had been treated by women in the past. Aisha knew that they had to put it behind them now, there was too much at stake and they had so much to be grateful for with Sarah. Mark opened his mouth to speak, but she laid a finger lightly across his lips. 'It's all right,' she said softly. 'I know. I forgive you, forget it now, please.'

With a silent nod of gratitude he kissed the tip of her finger, then reached over and switched off both their lamps. 'Spoons,' he said in the dark, snuggling up to her. She laughed and turned over. He nestled into the small of her back and draped his right arm over her hips. She closed her eyes, and to the familiar comfort of his warm breath falling lightly on her neck, very quickly drifted into sleep.

Aisha didn't know what time it was when she awoke. She came to with a start, her senses immediately alert. She thought she must have subconsciously heard Sarah wake for her feed – a sixth sense mothers seemed to acquire from very early on. Aisha lay in the dark, still half-asleep, and listened for Sarah's next cry, when she would leave the bed and go round to the nursery. Mark was still asleep, nestled behind her, his arm lying along her leg. His hips were pressed into the small of her back and through his cotton boxer shorts she could feel his erection. She knew now it was natural for this to happen sometimes when he was asleep, or first thing in the morning as he woke. Like his nakedness, it had

Cathy Glass

caused her some embarrassment at the start of their marriage, but now it was another shared joke: 'Sorry,' Mark would say when he woke. 'Henry has a mind of his own. Ignore him and he'll go away.' Unless, of course, they were going to make love, when she would turn over and into his arms.

Aisha shifted slightly towards the edge of the bed and listened for Sarah's cry. Maybe it wasn't time for her feed yet, although her engorged breasts told her it must be getting very close. She tried to see the clock on his bedside cabinet but it was facing away. Mark's breathing faltered, then she heard him swallow. Taking up the little space between them, his hand closed around her leg.

'Mark?' she whispered in the dark. 'Are you awake?'

'Yes, sorry. I wanted a cuddle. I've missed you so much, Aisha.'

'I've missed you too,' she said, and reached down and held his hand. 'I thought I heard Sarah. I'd better take a look.'

'No, I think I woke you. Sorry. I can't sleep. I need you, Aisha. I need to be close to you, to feel you.' She heard the longing in his voice, the heavy edge of urgency which normally preceded their lovemaking. But now, as in the last month of her pregnancy, he would have to be satisfied with a cuddle and their mutual promises of making up for it when they could. She went to turn over to face him but he stayed where he was, his body curled into hers, his erection pressing through his shorts against her back. He unwound his hand from hers and slowly slid it under her nightdress, so that his hand now rested on the bare skin of her stomach, between her pants and bra.

'You're so warm and inviting, Aisha,' he breathed. 'Just to touch you is wonderful after all this time. I love you so much.'

She felt his breath warm and moist on the nape of her neck as his lips gently rested against her skin. He began kissing her neck, soft little caresses, that despite the ravages of childbirth made her body tingle with desire.

'I need you,' he sighed again. 'I need something to ease the longing. I think part of my problem earlier was all that pent up emotion.'

'I need you too,' she murmured and squeezed his hand reassuringly.

'Can you give me something?' he whispered. 'I know we can't do it properly, but to have you close would be wonderful. And it would show me you have truly forgiven me.'

Aisha thought Mark meant masturbation, although he'd never asked her before and probably didn't like to ask direct out of respect for her. She had overheard two girls at the antenatal class laughing about a 'handjob' being the only way to get some peace when they were too big to make love. If this was what Mark needed to relieve the frustration and show him that she had really forgiven him, then she would do it for him. In the dark, below the covers. She was a married woman, she could masturbate her husband.

Aisha moved her hand round so that it rested on the outside of his shorts. She felt him stir, hard and warm, as he gave a little groan of pleasure. She would have to turn over to face him, but he was still pressed into the small of her back. Then his hand slid from her stomach to the top of her pants; looping in his fingers, he began to ease them down.

'Mark,' she said, slightly taken aback. 'We can't, not yet.'

'No, I know. It's OK, don't worry. I wasn't thinking of that.'

He continued to lower her pants to just under the cheeks of her bottom. She wasn't sure what he was thinking. Then he released himself from his shorts and she felt him stand hard and erect against her skin. The tip of his penis was resting lightly on her bottom, then suddenly it was between her cheeks.

'Mark,' she said again.

'Sshh,' he soothed. 'Trust me. I won't hurt you. Please.'

He began gently rubbing himself against her, a steady rocking motion up and down, using the crease of her bottom for stimulation. He moaned softly and she kept very still, her eyes unfocused in the dark. Was he going to masturbate himself this way, she thought, rather than her turning over and holding him? She was reminded again of her lack of experience, her ignorance of sexual matters; for all she knew this was something all married couples did, it was probably the norm. And although she would rather have been facing him, kissing and cuddling him, while she brought him satisfaction, if he wanted to enjoy her like this until they could make love properly then she would do her best to help him.

His breathing increased as his excitement grew until it was coming fast and shallow. As he moved up and down behind her, she pressed one hand on the front of her pants to keep the sanitary towel in place. Then he was holding the cheeks of her bottom and easing them apart. She felt the tip of his penis pressed hard against her back passage and she tensed.

'Mark!'

'Relax,' he breathed. 'I won't hurt you. Keep still. It won't hurt, I promise.'

He was pushing harder now, spreading her cheeks and pushing. It was difficult to relax, nearly impossible, for not only was it uncomfortable, but this was the place that ejected the body's waste, the very mention of which was considered dirty in her family. Harder still now, rubbing, pushing, trying to gain entry where he should not. Her muscles involuntarily contracted and fought to keep him out. It was more than uncomfortable now, it was starting to hurt. Should she tell him? He probably didn't realize he was hurting her. Then the pressure eased and one of his hands left her cheeks, and she momentarily relaxed. He was doing something behind her now, sucking, his fingers were in his mouth. Then his fingers returned to her bottom, now moistened with saliva, and he smeared it round the opening. He was hard up against her again, harder, and even more insistent now. He spread her cheeks wide apart then pushed, hard, harder still, and at last found entry. She cried out in pain.

'Relax!' he panted. 'For Christ's sake, relax!'

She tried. She tried to relax. She tried to think of something else as she had done in childbirth. But the dry grating pain drove into her and seemed to pierce her very being. Now, as when she was in labour, she tried to concentrate on her breathing and told herself it would soon be over and would be worth it in the end. But unlike before, she didn't have Mark to comfort and reassure her, for now he was working against, not with her. She thought of pulling away, telling him to stop; that it was hurting too much and was unnatural. But their peace was still tenuous, their emotion raw, and if she stopped him now he might see it as another rejection, and who knew where that would end? She grabbed the edge of the pillow and stuffed it in her mouth. She clenched the cotton between her teeth and ground down on it to stop herself from crying out. Then, just as she thought she couldn't take it anymore, that the pain was too much, and she would have to tell him to stop, he climaxed and his body froze. There was a second's pause and he withdrew. She felt the warm fluid trickle out and over her cheeks as he flopped onto his back with a sigh of satisfaction.

'God, I've missed you,' he groaned. 'I love you so much.' He reached for her hand and squeezed it but Aisha stayed very still, quiet, sore and humiliated.

She knew she had to say something, she knew she had to tell him that although she understood his needs she couldn't ever do that again. It wasn't a criticism of him, she was sure lots of couples did it, but it hurt too much and it wasn't right for her. She had to say something and she tried to formulate the words. But the opportunity to speak darts like a moonbeam and as quickly disappears. And once gone it cannot easily be retrieved without a confrontation or much, much worse.

At that moment they both heard Sarah cry.

'I'll have a wash while you feed her,' Mark said, getting out of bed. 'Give me a shout if you need anything. Love you.'

Aisha went to Sarah and fed and changed her; by the time she'd finished and returned to bed, Mark was curled on his side fast asleep. *Tomorrow,* she thought, *tomorrow I will approach him and explain how I feel. I will choose the right words and the right moment. Mark will understand because he loves me.* And she lay in the dark and convinced herself that in allowing him to do what he'd done, she'd proved that she'd truly forgiven him, and that their relationship would return to normal.

Fifteen

*A*isha tried to talk to Mark the following day as they sat on the sofa sipping their mid-morning coffee, which Mark had made. She rested her feet on the stool he had put beneath them and said, 'Mark, what happened last night … I …' But his quizzical look of non-comprehension meant that if she wanted to pursue it, she would have to explain and risk creating a scene, which was not only alien to her, but hardly the best way forwards. So she let it go and decided that if he ever approached her again in the same way then she would gently stop him, and say that although she appreciated such things were acceptable to some consenting adults, it wasn't right for her. But he didn't. Mark didn't ask for anything more than a cuddle until after her six-week postnatal check-up, when they made love properly, and then he was tenderness itself.

It had been five days since the inspector's visit, or was it six? Aisha was unsure, with no day or night on which to pin the time. Any sleep came in snatches, sitting in the chair, with the lamp on. It felt safer downstairs with the light on, she could see what was going on. Night after night, on guard, with the inspector's voice her only companion. Though sometimes Mark's voice butted in and corrected her when she'd got it wrong. 'Correctness is important,' Mark said. 'Be precise, and we won't have this problem. I won't have to get angry with you.'

Aisha tried, she tried to be precise, correct, tried to get it right, over the months, and then years that followed. She tried her best though she never succeeded.

'It's marriage,' Mark said, 'and parenthood. Learn to manage your expectations, Aisha, and we will be fine.' It's a phrase accountants use – management of expectations – and ironically her father used it too, though never in the context of marriage. Aisha tried desperately to 'manage her expectations'; she recalculated, reduced, and even cancelled some out. She analysed every action, word and phrase before she spoke; tried to eliminate double meanings and inconsequential remarks that could upset and provoke Mark. But it was like walking on eggshells – tread very lightly and you might make it to the end of the day – might, if you were very careful and lucky. Which apparently, she was not.

'So, when was the next time you saw the other side of Mark?' the inspector asked from the dark. 'When was the next unintentional act like the library book which provoked another out-of-character response?'

'Perhaps there wasn't one,' she said quietly into the empty room. 'Perhaps it really was a one off, and we put it behind us, and moved on, as I hoped. But you don't believe me, and of course, you would be right.'

One Sunday afternoon in early June, Aisha's parents were finally coming to tea. Sarah was eight weeks old and Aisha had wanted to invite her parents sooner, but what with one thing and another, she and Mark had never found the opportunity – there always seemed to be something that needed to be done. Her parents were due at three o'clock, and Aisha wanted everything to be just right to make a good impression, so did Mark. Together they had hoovered and dusted the house from top to bottom, made lunch, fed and changed Sarah, then settled her in the baby recliner in the lounge so that she could see what was going on. Aisha couldn't have been happier, for now they were making love again, it seemed they were even closer. It didn't matter that sometimes she had to pay particular attention to what she said and did, because quite clearly Mark was doing the same; they were both trying hard and having to readjust to life with a baby.

The new lace tablecloth Aisha had bought especially for her parents' visit was on the table, and she was in the kitchen washing salad and making a cucumber raita. She and Mark had agreed it would be a 'high tea' rather than dinner, with various cold dishes to suit all their tastes – a mixture of East meets West, Aisha quipped to Mark. He laughed and kissed her cheek appreciatively.

Mark began taking down the plates, cups and saucers from the kitchen cupboard ready to lay the table so they wouldn't have to do it when her parents arrived. Aisha noticed, as she seasoned the yoghurt for the raita, that Mark was using the normal china, the set he'd had before their marriage that was now dishwasher faded. OK for everyday, she thought, but not really suitable for her parents when they had an alternative.

'Mark, let's use the new Dalton,' she said lightly. 'You know, the wedding present from your office? We could christen it today.'

The radio was on and maybe he hadn't heard her, for he continued carrying the old china through to the lounge. Aisha left what she was doing in the kitchen and poked her head round the archway that led to the lounge. 'Mark, why don't we use the new China Blue? It's still in its box in the spare bedroom. Shall I fetch it?' It never crossed her mind that he might see it as a

131

criticism, a negative judgement of his choice, or she wouldn't have said it, obviously.

Mark stopped laying out the plates and then began collecting them together again, hurriedly, so that the china chinked together and made Sarah jump. Aisha wiped her hands on her apron and went over to the table with the intention of helping him, so that it would be less noisy. As she drew near, he spun round to face her, and she saw his expression, pinched and white, and realized her mistake. There was a moment's silence, a charged nanosecond before he shouted in her face.

'What? My things not good enough for you? I'll give you the fucking Dalton!' It might have been laughable, except of course there wasn't anything funny about his anger.

'Sorry,' she stammered, backing away, but not fast enough.

Large hands grabbed her shoulders and shook her like a rag doll. 'Mark, let's use the Dalton,' he mimicked, spitting in her face. Then he picked up the plates and pushed past her with such force that she lost her balance and fell backwards, cracking her head on the wall.

Sarah shrieked, but ignoring her and Aisha, Mark marched into the kitchen and slammed the plates on the work surface with such force that one cracked. Yanking open the integral door to the garage he went in and slammed it shut behind him. At that moment, the doorbell rang and Aisha realized in absolute panic that it was her parents, having arrived early. Through the shock, fear and horror of it all, and the sharp pain in her head, one thought dominated all others – her parents must not find out what had happened, and she prayed they hadn't heard.

She hauled herself up from the floor, touched the sore place on her head, then stood like a rabbit frozen in a car's head-lamps, not knowing what to do for the best. Go to Mark? Pacify

Sarah? Or answer the door? She knew she had to do all three, but in which order? Sarah was crying louder now so instinctively she picked her up. 'There, there,' she soothed, then looked anxiously between the rear of the house and the front door. The bell rang again. She felt her head and looked at her fingers; it was sore but not bleeding. She took a deep breath and began towards the front door. It crossed her mind, in the ridiculousness of the moment, that if Mark had wanted to hit her then he could have chosen a better day – one when her parents weren't expected.

Trying to remove the horror from her face, she went down the hall with Sarah in her arms and opened the front door. 'Mum, Dad, so lovely to see you,' she said, summoning a smile.

'Hello love, great to see you.' They both smiled at her naturally so that Aisha thought they couldn't have overheard and she breathed a sigh of relief.

'Come in,' she said, her thoughts racing. What was Mark doing in the garage? Her parents came into the hall and her mother kissed her, and then cooed over Sarah.

'Oh my,' she said. 'How she's grown!' Aisha felt a stab of guilt that her parents hadn't seen Sarah since they'd visited her in hospital.

Sarah was burbling happily now with all the attention.

'Look!' her mother exclaimed. 'She's smiling at her grandma. What a treasure. Hello Sarah. Can I hold her?'

Aisha placed Sarah in her mother's arms, then kissed her father and closed the front door. She led them into the lounge.

'How comfortable and homely you have made it,' her mother said, seeing the room for the first time. Her father hovered and looked like he was going to say something but thought better of it.

Aisha smiled at her mother. 'Thank you, do sit down,' she said with forced lightness. 'I'll just find Mark. I think he's still in the garage.'

Her father nodded – he could relate to a man tinkering in the garage. He sat on the sofa next to her mother and Aisha left them fussing over their granddaughter. She went through the kitchen and to the interconnecting door that led to the garage, then stopped, her heart pounding, her palms sweating. She'd no idea what state she'd find Mark in on the other side of the door or what he could possibly be doing, but she was desperate to smooth everything over as quickly as possible so that her parents wouldn't suspect anything was wrong.

She gave a little knock on the door, then slowly opened it. She could see Mark at the far end of the garage rummaging through his toolboxes, tidying them, she thought. Going right in, she closed the door behind her so that her parents couldn't hear. 'Mark, I'm sorry,' she said quickly. 'I didn't mean to upset you. My parents are here. Will you come and join us, please?'

There was no reply.

'Mark,' she said again, unable to hide her desperation. 'I'm sorry. Please come in. Mum and Dad are in the lounge, I want us all to be together and have a nice time.' Her words sounded pathetic, even to her ears.

Mark slowly turned, and she saw that his eyes were cold but not unyielding.

'I'm sorry I upset you,' she said again. 'It was completely unintentional. Will you come please so we can all be together like we planned?'

His gaze shifted from her to the car as though he wanted her to know he was considering his other option – of going out. At that moment, if she'd been in any doubt, she knew exactly where the power lay, and so too did Mark. They both knew it would have crucified her if she'd had to go back to her parents and admit something was wrong, that Mark wouldn't be joining them because they'd had an argument and he'd gone off in the car.

'Please, Mark,' she said again. 'It means a lot to me. I'm sorry.'

His gaze returned to her and he nodded. 'Apology accepted,' he said. 'Tell them I'll be there shortly.'

Relief flooded through her. 'Thank you, Mark. I do appreciate it. I'm so sorry,' she gushed. Then with a ridiculously light and forgiving heart, she returned to the lounge. 'Mark won't be long,' she announced gaily to her parents. 'He's just finishing off something in the garage. Oh, it's so good to see you both, so very good,' she chattered in nervous anticipation of Mark's arrival.

When he appeared ten minutes later, Aisha glanced at him anxiously, looking for any sign of his previous anger. But he appeared to be recovered and his usual charming self. He kissed her mother and complimented her on her sari – exactly the right thing to do because it was new, and the first time she'd worn it, which Aisha should have noticed if she'd been thinking straight. Mark then shook her father's hand and for the first time called him Dad; Aisha could see how touched her father was as he already looked upon Mark as a son. As Aisha sat nervously in the armchair and Mark talked politely and respectfully to her parents, always saying exactly the right thing, she dismissed the bump to her head as another silly misunderstanding: it was as Mark said – she needed to think before she spoke, which was something her father had pointed out many years ago.

Her mother unpacked the contents of her bag: baby toys and clothes for Sarah, flowers and chocolates for Aisha. Aisha's heart melted at her mother's thoughtfulness and the two of them went through to the kitchen to finish the last of the preparations for the meal. They worked side by side and chatted about Sarah's routine and how well she was doing, while the 'men folk', as her mother called them, sat in the lounge and talked business and cars. Aisha thought it was quickly turning into the afternoon she'd envisaged and her happiness was out of all proportion to what should have been a regular visit from her parents.

At five o'clock they sat around the dining table in the lounge and Aisha served the tea, using the old china. Her mother complimented her on the food: 'What a lovely spread, Aisha, you have been busy.'

'A great improvement!' her father joked. He'd never been impressed by Aisha's cooking at home, and used to tease her that she should keep to her banking and leave her mother to the cooking.

Mark agreed that Aisha had done them proud, and picked up his plate to help himself to the aubergine quiche. By pure misfortune he had the plate with the crack. He paused and looked pointedly across the table at Aisha. 'This plate is cracked,' he said, 'why didn't you use the new Dalton china for your parents visit? You know, the wedding present from my firm? Don't you like it?'

She met his gaze and felt the tingling sweat of fear creep up her spine; her heart began to race. *Not now, Mark, please*, she thought. *Dear God, not now.*

She looked around the table and saw her parents smiling at her, expecting a response. She forced down her fear and tried to keep her voice steady. 'Yes, of course I like it,' she said quietly. 'I must have forgotten, sorry. I'll make sure I use it next time. This will do for now, won't it?'

Mark nodded and continued serving himself, but she saw the smile that crossed his lips: the acknowledgement that he had won, was all-powerful and now fully in control. And when you've accepted it once, apologized, ignored, and allowed yourself to be humiliated, there's no going back. For once you cross that barrier, it's easier the next time – for the abuser and the victim.

Sixteen

*S*even years passed during which time Mark's occasional 'out of character' punches developed into a regular battering which left Aisha in fear of her life and Mark firmly in control. She lived as though balanced on a seesaw which was so finely tuned that she never knew when it was going to tip and send her crashing to the floor. Mark said that she should be more assertive and stand up to him. He said his mother had been the same, always kowtowing to his father, even though he battered her. Then one day she had sent him a solicitor's letter threatening legal action, and his father had changed immediately and had never hit her again; they were still together after nearly forty years of marriage.

But Aisha had forgotten how to be assertive, if she ever knew. Women in her family, her culture, didn't. It wasn't so very long ago that wives walked behind their husbands as a sign of respect and to emphasize their more lowly status. Aisha was no more likely to send a solicitor's letter to Mark than fly to the moon, and Mark knew that.

When Sarah was nearly two years old, Aisha discovered that she was pregnant again. She was being made to sleep downstairs by then, on the sofa, and Mark came to her once a week and took her roughly and out of necessity. It wasn't making love, for there was no love in it. It was more like marital rape, although Aisha never put up any resistance and would have never used that term. Mark always left straight after he'd climaxed to shower thoroughly. He said that because of her skin colour he couldn't tell if she was clean or not, and it was better to be safe than sorry; he didn't want to catch anything nasty.

So Aisha had another child, James, and the three of them lived isolated, in fear, and hidden from the outside world; and the beatings and mental torture continued. There were no visitors; they weren't allowed visitors, and Mark saw his friends away from the house. There was no money either. They had never opened a joint bank account, and when Aisha had first stopped work Mark had given her housekeeping money, which he'd handed to her in an envelope marked 'Aisha's Wages'. But by the time Sarah was six months old, that had been replaced by the odd £10 note left on the table after Aisha had asked for money to buy food. That too had quickly dwindled to a pile of loose change, which he threw in her face if she asked too often.

Once, out of desperation, she suggested that perhaps she should find a part-time job, in the evenings, to help out with the money. It was the wrong thing to say, but she was desperate and didn't know what else to do. 'No wife of mine is going to work,' Mark flared. The resulting battering left her right eye closed for three days, and a cut to her eyebrow which should really have been stitched, had he allowed her to go to the hospital.

When Sarah was three, she started nursery and Mark said Aisha could take her as long as she came straight home again. Aisha was never going to be one of the group of mothers chatting at the school gates, arranging coffee mornings and fundraising events. Head down, under a permanently knotted scarf to hide her cuts and bruises, and with James in the pram, she hurried straight there and back. She spoke to no one and no one spoke to her – like many victims she had become invisible and it was doubtful if anyone even noticed her. Another year passed, and then two, and time contracted for Aisha and it became meaningless. She took each day one at a time, concentrated on the little practical things like trying to feed and clothe the children on only a pound a day, and prayed that things would change.

There were no birthday parties for the children, no friends to tea. As Sarah and James grew and made friends at school, they seemed instinctively to know that it wasn't possible. Without any explanation, they knew that theirs wasn't a normal family and they would all suffer the consequences if anyone found out. The children never asked, not once, if they could invite a friend home to play, and the thought of what they were missing broke Aisha's heart more than anything.

'But how did it get to the point?' the inspector asked, with a scepticism Aisha had seen before. 'Why let it get so bad? And when it had, why stay? You could have left him, surely?'

Aisha shifted uncomfortably in her chair. How to make the inspector see? How could anyone understand other than another battered woman?

'It didn't just happen,' she said quietly into the dark. 'It stole up on me. Like a burglar in the night, it ransacked the house and took everything of value. I fully believed it was my fault and if I could only find the right way, the magic formula, then I could bring back what I'd lost. I was proud, Inspector, I couldn't admit what was happening even to myself. I was also frightened and completely isolated. By the time I realized, it was too late and I was impotent to act.'

'But your parents?' he persisted. 'Why didn't you tell them? They would have helped, surely? You were close once and you must have seen them?'

'To begin with we saw them occasionally, when Mark said it was convenient. But the times grew less and less frequent. Once, they dropped by unexpectedly, possibly even suspecting something, I don't know. Mark bundled us into our coats before opening the door. He was curt to the point of rudeness and said we were going out. We walked past them to the car and got in, then sat on the driveway until they had gone. I phoned them the next day while Mark was at work, and apologized. They were hurt, obviously – who could blame them? – and I couldn't tell them the truth. Mark stopped me using the phone after that, and if they phoned again I never got the message. But it would have crucified them to have known that the daughter they had invested everything in was a beaten, pathetic wreck. I wanted to protect them, and I really believed it was all my fault, and I had let them down. Survival bleeds you dry, Inspector, there's nothing left over for rational thought, let alone action.'

'But I still can't believe,' he said, 'I can't believe there was not one single person you could have turned to and confided in. The women's refuge? The Samaritans? There must have been somewhere you could have run to before it came to this?'

Aisha clasped her hands together. The room was very dark now and a familiar shadow was forming in the corner. 'There was one,' she said slowly. 'One person I went to in a final, desperate bid. Seeing him gave me the strength to do what I did, which was ironic when you consider what he was.' And she gave a little humourless laugh.

Seventeen

The two statues either side of the driveway were carved from grey stone and appeared to be a cross between a dragon and a dog. They were seated on their haunches and were nearly as tall as her; their huge eyes seemed to follow her with a fixed, unyielding scrutiny. Aisha should have known what they were, which part of the teaching they represented. To come here so badly informed, she thought, was disrespectful and presumptuous on the community's generosity.

She paused between the statues and looked up the drive to the rambling Edwardian house beyond. It stood in its own grounds on the edge of the green belt, surrounded by trees and open countryside, and wasn't as austere as she'd expected. There were no cars on the driveway, there wouldn't be. But there were net curtains at the windows, and the neatly cut lawn that ran out from the house was dotted with large terracotta pots much as you'd find in any North London suburb.

Aisha took another step and began falteringly up the driveway, forcing her legs onwards and forwards. To walk the length of the drive, ring the bell and wait to be admitted, then have to talk to someone she didn't know was more than she could bear. She doubted she was still capable of conversation; it had been so long since she'd spoken to anyone apart from the children, let alone a stranger. She could have turned and fled; run back down the drive and caught the next bus home, had she not gone to so much trouble. All those months of planning and saving the ten- and sometimes twenty-pence pieces, which she'd secreted in an old sock at the bottom of Sarah's drawer until she had enough for the bus fare. Then daring to stop at the bus stop on the way back from school and quickly memorizing the timetable in case he was watching her. Her heart had pounded uncontrollably as she'd arrived home and began calculating the time she would need: the length of the return journey, added to the walk either end, plus an hour spent there. Then having to choose a day, one from five, almost impossible with nothing to set them apart, and the risk spread evenly. She had finally decided on Friday because it was the last day she could possibly choose before beginning all over again the following week.

That morning, after Mark had gone to work, and before she took the children to school, she'd done the housework, set the potatoes and cabbage in salted water and cooked the brisket, ready for her return.

Yes, she could have turned and fled, had she not gone to so much trouble. And she knew that if she did, there would be no second opportunity.

Aisha stood in the tiled porch and looked at the old-style bell chime with its brass handle swinging on the end of a rod. The brass was so highly polished it glinted in the wintry sunlight; she was surprised that they bothered with such a secular chore as polishing when they must have more spiritual matters on their minds. She raised her hand and steeled herself, then gave the bell rod one short tug. She heard its single note echo down the hall and then peter out. She licked her dry lips and waited. No one came. She hadn't much time She tugged the bell rod again, and then the door began to open. Aisha instinctively took a step back.

She watched as by degrees he slowly came into view, then stood framed in the doorway and looked at her expectantly. She looked back at him and opened her mouth to speak, but all the months of preparation vanished; she stood helpless, and mute.

'Yes?' he said softly, after some moments. 'How can we help you?' His voice was low and almost choral in its serenity.

'I … I'm sorry,' she began. 'I'm sorry to disturb you. I need to talk to you.'

He studied her for a moment, as though gauging the level of her sincerity, his shaven head slightly bowed, his hands folded in the voluminous sleeves of his saffron robe. Then, releasing one hand slowly from its sleeve, he moved aside and gestured for her to come in.

Aisha stepped past him and into a long, bare, wood-panelled hall. The house was perfectly quiet, as though he was the sole occupant. The monk closed the door behind her and turned slowly to face her, his hands once more concealed within the sleeves of his robe.

'We have a visitors' room at the rear of the house,' he said softly. 'We can go there to talk if you wish. We won't be disturbed.' His voice was encouraging in its quiet confidence.

Aisha nodded. 'Yes, please.'

He glided round her as though on a cushion of air, only his feet were visible beneath the hem of his robe. She followed him down the hall, her footsteps echoing harshly on the wooden floor compared to the sandal silence of his own. He was short, only as tall as she, and his skin was more bronze than brown. Stopping at the far end of the hall, he raised his eyes briefly to hers. 'Would you like a hot drink? You must be very cold.'

'No, no thank you.' She smiled nervously, unsure of how she should address him.

He pushed open the door on their right and went in first. Aisha followed and looked anxiously around her. The room was bare except for an old upholstered chair and a marble altar dominating one wall. The altar was scattered with fresh petals and in the centre was a large wooden statue of Buddha, seated cross-legged. Slightly above the altar was a small leaded-light window, which looked out over the gardens at the rear. In the distance she could see the other brothers at work in the gardens, their robes little flicks of moving orange against a background of green and brown.

The monk bowed low before the altar then slowly backed away. Aisha was familiar enough with Buddhist teachings to know that you never turned your back on Buddha, and she waited a little behind the monk.

'Please, sit down,' he said, nodding to the one chair.

She went over and perched nervously on the edge while the monk lowered himself effortlessly to sit cross-legged on the floor in front of her.

He bowed his head and sat silently in prayer for a moment. With his shaven head and all-enveloping robe, his age was impossible to tell. After a moment, he slowly raised his head and studied her, quietly and at peace.

'Tell me your name, child,' he said, his manner echoing the gentleness of his voice.

'Aisha,' she said. 'Aisha Williams.'

'A Western surname?'

'Yes, I am married to an Englishman. My parents are from Gujarat.'

He nodded and the next question, which she had half-anticipated, held no hint of criticism. 'I don't think I have seen you or your family at the temple?'

'No, my father converted to Christianity many years ago. And my husband is an atheist. He doesn't believe.'

'And you, my child? What do you believe?'

Aisha hesitated, and felt again the imposition of her coming. 'I don't know. I was born a Buddhist. My parents' families still are. Was it wrong of me to come? I'm sorry if it was.'

His face flickered a smile and bore no trace of censure. 'No, it was not. All gods are compassionate, particularly in the face of pain and adversity.'

Aisha looked down at her hands wrung tightly in her lap, then up again at the monk. 'If it's so obvious,' she blurted, 'if my pain is there for all to see, why doesn't my husband see it? Why, if it's so obvious, does he continue? Why doesn't he stop if my wretchedness is so clear?'

The monk's eyes immediately dulled with sadness and she felt guilty for putting it there. He paused, and then asked gently, 'Your husband is responsible for all your pain?'

She nodded. 'I have tried, believe me. I have tried for so long, but nothing I do makes any difference. I still try. But he hates me more and more. I am now so unhappy and consumed by bitterness, I think things too dreadful to speak of.' She stopped. How could she expect him to understand? This holy man who lived segregated from the outside world. What would he know of marriage, her self-loathing and desperation? Did she even have the right to talk of such things in his presence?

He was still looking at her, compassion and concern on his face. 'The bruises on your face and neck, my child. Did your husband do this to you?'

Aisha pulled her coat closer around her neck and nodded. 'But it was my fault. Somehow I provoke him, though I don't know how. I try not to, God help me, I try. He says I have made him what he is. I must be evil, but I don't mean to be.'

The monk's eyes stayed with her, deep and unblinking, as though he was able to look into her very soul and see the pain within. 'You are too harsh on yourself. No single person can take all the blame. Not when two live as one.'

Aisha said nothing – her experience had told her otherwise.

'And you are alone in this?' he asked after a moment.

'Alone? I have two children.'

'But you yearn for no other man? I ask because of the Western acceptance of infidelity when all love has gone.'

Aisha looked at him and could have laughed at the ludicrous notion that she could in any way be attractive to another man. 'I am alone,' she said. 'I have never looked at anyone else. Never.'

'Then if you have tried to bring happiness to your union and failed, you must ask yourself if your suffering is great enough to leave. If you have looked within your heart and seen the truth, you have a duty to act, both for your own sake and that of your children.'

Aisha held his gaze, confused by his insight and candour. 'You speak as if you know of such matters?'

He gave a slow nod. 'We are not completely cut off from the outside world. We know what goes on. We simply choose to live away from it.'

She was silent for some time and the monk watched her serenely, waiting for her response.

'I can't leave,' she said at last. 'I am a prisoner. As surely as if I was locked in a cell with iron bars, I am a prisoner. I am nothing. I don't make decisions, I barely exist. The only way I can leave is to kill myself ... and, believe me, I have considered it.'

He was silent for some time, his head slightly bowed, and perfectly still. 'You made the decision to come here,' he said at last, looking up. 'That took a lot of courage.'

Aisha continued to look at him, this monk who with so few words seemed to see and know so much. 'Yes, but I will be going back.'

'You spoke of your father. Would he not offer you shelter in your time of crisis?'

She shook her head and tugged anxiously at her coat. 'My parents don't know, and I wouldn't ask. I couldn't harm them more than I have already. The shame it would bring on them would be untold. No woman has ever left her husband in my family. My parents wouldn't cope.'

'I understand,' he said nodding slowly, then his eyes flickered to the altar and back again as though drawing silent guidance and direction. 'What you need more than anything is time and peace to heal. You need respite from your daily cares to allow you the time to come to a decision. Without that, you will never be able to see anything, not with all your suffering.'

'I know, but how? How? Tell me. What can I do?' Her voice choked and she swallowed back the tears.

The monk paused before he spoke and when he did it was with the same calm reassurance and acceptance. 'Part of our house is a retreat, it is open to anyone who needs it. You can come here if you wish, with your children. You will have the peace and time you need. Your pain will not last forever, although it may seem so now.'

She stared at him sharply. 'But you don't understand. I can't. Mark would never allow it, never let me go. He would hunt me down and find me. He would stop at nothing to keep what he sees as his, what he says he has a right to. I would be placing you all in danger, not just me.'

The monk's eyes widened. 'What is this man? A giant? We have thirty brothers here. You will be safe. He is not Goliath.'

She lowered her gaze. 'He is to me,' she said quietly.

Yet sitting here enveloped in the monk's unassuming confidence and quiet inner strength, she could almost feel she could – she could collect Sarah and James from school, go home, quickly pack a bag and leave. Was it possible? Could she find the courage? Was there enough left in her? There would be time before Mark came home from work, if she was quick.

She wrung her hands in her lap and felt them cold and clammy. 'But even if I could come and stay here,' she said. 'I have no money. How would I pay for our keep?'

The monk smiled kindly. 'We do not ask for money. Only that you contribute in some small way to the community. Every skill is appreciated. Cooking, cleaning, or working on the farm. But only when you feel strong enough. Your immediate need is for rest and tranquillity.'

He waited again, exuding a peace and calm that seemed to empower the very air Aisha breathed. Could she? Was there still a small spark within her that could allow her to do this and see it through? An ember of self-preservation that hadn't been completely snuffed out in the last seven years, and with the monk's strength could be rekindled before it was too late?

'If I came,' she said suddenly, looking up, 'it would have to be tonight. If I made the decision to come it would have to be now.'

He nodded again, his calm and dispassionate features acknowledging this as he doubtless acknowledged all things. 'We can have a room ready. If that is your decision.'

A decision? Could she make one? After all these years could she make a decision to save herself and the children? Yes, she must. For the sake of Sarah and James, she had to, before it was too late. There wouldn't be another chance. 'I must,' she said. 'I must do it now. I'll come tonight. I have to go and collect my children from school, then I'll pack a bag and come. I will, I promise, but I need to go now.'

She stood. The monk nodded and then, raising himself effortlessly from the floor, went over to a small bureau behind the door. Sliding open the single drawer he took out a five-pound note and held it out to her. 'This is for your bus fare. I think it will be enough.'

She took the note and could have wept at his insight and generosity. 'Thank you so much. I only had enough to make this journey. I'll repay you as soon as I can.' She clasped his outstretched hand and pressed it to her lips. 'Thank you,' she said again. 'I must go now, I must go before I lose my courage. Pray for me, please. Maybe there is a way, there has to be.'

The monk slowly released her hand, then, bowing silently to the altar, backed towards the door. She followed him out, out of the room and down the quiet and empty hall, her heart racing, her thoughts soaring in a direction where they had never been before. She waited as the monk unbolted the front door and her eyes fell to a scroll hanging on the wall opposite. It was a quote from the Buddhist teachings. She hadn't seen it on the way in, but now the black lettering seemed to fly out at her.

'They do not dwell in remorse over the past,
nor do they brood over the future;
they abide in the present:
therefore they are radiant.'

'A favourite of mine,' the monk said, following her gaze. 'Samyutta Nikaya, 1,10. Carry it in your heart, child. We shall be waiting for you.'

Eighteen

*R*adiant. The word echoed in her mind as she ran down the path and to the bus stop. 'You look radiant tonight,' she thought Mark used to say in the early days when he'd told her how beautiful she was and that he'd love her forever. *Radiant*. It was a term she thought he'd used, but now she struggled to remember.

The bus came exactly on time and, handing over the last of her change, she took a window seat. She looked out of the window as her fingers curled around the five-pound note in her pocket and tried to steady her breathing. Her heart pounded and she felt hot and cold at once; she tried not to think about what she was doing but to concentrate on the journey and getting to the school.

An hour later she counted down the stops; the bus slowed and she stood. Making her way to the exit she waited on the platform until the doors swished open. She stepped off and began, head down, towards the school. It was drizzling now, the light but saturating rain of late November. She didn't have an umbrella, it had broken long ago and she'd never had the money to replace it. The wet quickly seeped through her headscarf, making her shiver with cold. She'd had nothing to eat all day and now wished she'd accepted the monk's offer of a hot drink. It would have helped a little.

She checked her watch again. It was nearly five to three, she was early because the bus had arrived on time. Her calculations had allowed for it being late – she knew how erratic the services could be. Turning the corner to the school she looked anxiously in all directions, half-expecting to see Mark, which was ridiculous because he never left work early, even on a Friday, and never collected the children from school. She was safe at least until six. There would be plenty of time.

There was only one mother already waiting on the pavement outside the school gates, but Aisha took up her usual place, well away from where the other mothers would eventually congregate. With her hands in her pockets, eyes lowered, she prayed the classes would come out on time at three fifteen. Sometimes they were five, even ten minutes late, if they had been noisy, or the classroom had to be cleaned up after art class.

It would have made sense to have gone in and asked if she could take Sarah and James early, on the pretence of a dental appointment or similar. But she'd never been into the school, not even for parents' evening; Mark had always insisted he went alone. Now if she went in on some pretext, they might suspect something, see her guilt and know, and she couldn't risk it, not with so much at stake. For guilt was what she felt, and was doubtless written all over her face – she was snatching the children while Mark was at work. It might even be illegal, she thought, though this was the least of her worries.

By three ten the entrance was a throng of chattering mothers, clustered under shared umbrellas, trying to keep bored toddlers in strollers under plastic rain covers. Aisha concentrated on the paving stone beneath her feet which was as familiar as her worn-out shoes. The stone glistened a deep grey from the rain, and she knew every inch of it, from the chipped corner on the left to the crack on the right, which sprouted a dandelion in summer. She shifted her feet and stared down at the concrete slab possibly for the last time. Where the children would go to school she'd no idea but she'd worry about that another day, for now she just needed to concentrate on getting away. At exactly three fifteen the bell rang from inside the school and her heart raced; the security gates buzzed and then opened automatically.

Aisha went into the playground, but instead of standing in her usual place, behind the other mothers and up against the railings, she walked further forwards, to the right, where she would be able to see the children as soon as they came out. She pulled her headscarf closer to her cheeks and watched as the main doors opened and the children began to pour out. A member of staff – she didn't know her name – stood on the steps, doing up coats and generally keeping an eye on the children as they left. Sarah and James were never in the first wave of loud, excited children, scrabbling to be out of school and home. They came more slowly, towards the end. Always together, and with Sarah's arm protectively around the shoulders of her younger brother. Aisha thought now, as she had before, that if anything positive had come out of the years of abuse and misery, it was the bond that had formed between brother and sister. She doubted it could be stronger, nor that it would ever change.

She spotted Sarah and James immediately, and stepping forwards, gave a little wave. A flicker of surprise crossed their faces when they saw she wasn't in her usual place. She watched them carefully as though seeing them for the first time as they picked their way around the other children. Sarah, with her jet-black hair and dark eyes, was still the image of her, while James had inherited some of his father's features; his hair and skin tone were lighter than Sarah's and he had hazel eyes. The two of them always appeared deep in thought and were far more self-composed than their more impulsive peers. *A very sensible child,* the teacher had written on one of Sarah's reports, *Sarah shows a maturity well beyond her years*. It had made Aisha cry when she'd read the report, for Sarah's maturity was at the expense of her childhood, which had been lost in the daily grind of surviving and having to support her mother.

Aisha bent to kiss her children as they came up to her, but instead of asking as she usually did, 'Have you had a good day?' and, 'Did you eat your lunch?' she said almost sternly, 'Put up your hoods. It's raining. Come on. Be quick.' Then, taking a hand in each of hers, she set off, faster than usual, towards the school gates. Only once they were outside the school grounds did she speak again, keeping up the pace and talking as she went. 'Now listen, both of you. I have something to tell you and it's very important. You are big children now and I need you to listen carefully. A lot depends on it.'

They looked up at her intrigued. There was an edge to their mother's voice which they hadn't heard before and which was both exciting and a little frightening.

'I haven't been home today,' she continued. 'After I left you this morning, I went on the bus, an hour away. I have been talking to a very kind man called a monk. Do you know what a monk is?'

They both nodded. She doubted James understood, he was too young, but she hadn't time to explain it all now.

'He is very kind,' she stressed. 'And he lives in a big house in the country with other monks, it's called a retreat. I went there because I have been so unhappy, we all have, and I needed to talk to someone and ask his advice. I have been telling him how things are at home and he wants to help us. He says we can go and stay there until I can think what to do for the best. I said we would.'

Cathy Glass

She paused and looked at them, trying to gauge their reaction, fearful they might object. It was, after all, their home and father she was leaving, and if they refused to go did she have the right to force them?

'Without Daddy?' James asked.

'Yes. It would just be the three of us.' She looked at his rain-spotted face, just visible under his hood and waited for his response, but none came. He just looked thoughtful.

'When?' Sarah asked.

'As soon as I've put a few things in a case. If we're going we must do it now. Otherwise ...' She stopped. 'I wouldn't be doing this if I didn't think it was right. You know how unhappy we are. I really can't take any more.' Her voice broke.

Sarah squeezed her hand reassuringly. 'I'll help you pack,' she said quietly.

'Thank you, darling.' She looked again at James. 'And what about you, James? What do you think?'

'Can I take my teddy?'

'Yes. You find it as soon as we get in.'

'Dad's going to be so angry when he finds out,' James added. 'He'll hurt you again.' Aisha's heart screamed, not for the first time, at what James had witnessed, and the gaping chasm in the relationship between father and son, and what should have been.

'No, darling, he won't,' she said. 'Once we're at the monks' house we'll be safe. They will look after us. And perhaps, in time, Daddy and I will be able to ...' but she let the sentence go unfinished. She knew to acknowledge any possibility of a reconciliation would undermine her present strength and resolve, and she needed it all, every bit, if she was going to see this through.

Aisha continued in silence, maintaining the pace with the children nearly running to keep up. Her feet squelched in her

156

leaking shoes as they moved quickly across the sodden pavements. She had to keep reining in her thoughts to the present and immediate, and banish all thoughts of the future. The five pound note was safely at the bottom of her pocket, her suitcase was on top of the wardrobe, the 103 bus which they would have to catch in the High Street ran every seventeen minutes. It would have helped to have had time to plan their escape, to have made a list of essential items, and pack. But then again, it was the very lack of premeditation that was allowing her to do it at all. Too much time and she would have lost her nerve, with no possibility of retrieving it or a second chance. 'You could never survive in the outside world,' she heard Mark say. 'You're useless without me.'

The rain was harder now, bouncing off the pavements and rushing along the gutters and down the drains. They were already soaked. The children would have to change when they got home if they weren't to catch cold – there would be enough time. She had a full hour to pack the basics, change, get on the bus and away from the area before Mark even left work. The next bit would be the worst – going into the house for the last time and taking what they needed. She would feel like a thief, taking things when Mark wasn't there, but they had to have the essentials, the rest didn't matter. She wondered if she should leave a note but the very thought of it, of writing *Dear Mark* ... made her falter. No, she would write to him later, she told herself, she could think about a letter when they were safe, and when she knew what to say.

She felt Sarah and James's hands in hers and gave them a reassuring squeeze. 'Nearly there,' she said. 'When we get in I want you to change out of your wet things while I pack. Put on your weekend clothes and leave your uniforms in the airing cupboard.

Sarah, will you make us a drink? And James, I want you to find your teddy. We've all got a job to do but we must be quick.'

The children kept close beside her like chicks around a mother hen as they approached the corner and the turning to their road. The daylight was quickly fading and the drab, wet skies of a dismal winter afternoon were closing in. Still holding hands, they rounded the corner as one. Then stopped dead. They stared in disbelief and horror. Halfway down the street, parked at the kerb outside their house, was Mark's car.

'He's home!' Sarah cried. 'He must know!'

Aisha stared, unable to believe what she was seeing. 'He can't know,' she gasped. 'I didn't know myself until this afternoon. It's impossible.' Yet something told her that it wasn't, and he did.

'What are we going to do?' Sarah asked, letting go of her hand to go round and comfort her brother.

'I don't know,' Aisha began. 'I ...' But the words fell away.

But how? When? Why? He hadn't followed her that morning on the bus, she would have noticed, she was sure. Yet he never came home this early, never. He often got back after nine on a Friday, and some nights he didn't come home at all. Perhaps he was ill? Perhaps he'd left work early because he was unwell? But if he was, why was the car out of the garage? He hadn't taken it to work that morning, he'd used the tube as he did most days. The car had been in the garage that morning when she'd left, she was sure. But why wasn't it now?

'Aren't we going to the monks' house?' James asked between sobs.

Aisha fought to regain control. 'No. Now, listen. You have to forget everything I've told you. Everything. Do you understand? We will go in as normal. I've just collected you from school. James, you can read your book to Sarah while I make us a drink.

Act perfectly normal. Forget everything. I know it's difficult, but you must.'

Sarah nodded as James sniffed. Aisha took a tissue from her pocket and wiped his face, then waited while he blew his nose.

'Good boy. Now, no more crying. Don't cry and we'll be all right.' But her heart and mind cried out and told her otherwise, for not only were they not going to escape, but Mark would be furious if he knew she'd been out of the house for longer than the twenty minutes it took to collect the children from school.

James pushed the tissue into his pocket and tried to smile, but found it impossible. Sarah took his hand.

'OK, now come on.' Aisha said, and went in front while the children followed a little behind. They continued up the street, the house drawing closer with each step.

Perhaps Mark had only been in for a short while, she thought, which was why his car was outside. Perhaps he'd just got in, for whatever reason, and had taken the car out of the garage ready to use later. Aisha couldn't remember him doing that before, but it wasn't impossible. In which case, her absence was accountable. She'd been to the school to collect the children and now she was coming home. But if he had been in for longer and was aware of her absence, she needed an excuse. But what? What excuse could she possibly give for being gone for longer than the school run? She had no shopping with her and anyway Mark knew she didn't have money to buy anything. Likewise, he knew she didn't have friends to visit, and no family to speak of. A doctor's appointment? But the surgery wasn't open in the afternoon, only mornings and evenings, and that could easily be checked. A walk? It was the only possibility. Yes, she would have to say she had gone for a breath of fresh air. He would be angry, but hopefully no more than any other time when he'd phoned to check on her and she'd been asleep and hadn't answered immediately.

The children drew further back as they approached the house. The lights were going on in the neighbouring houses as the last of the daylight disappeared. Aisha saw their hall and lounge lights were on too, but had no idea what that meant, other than that Mark was in. The up-and-over door to the garage was down as normal. She stopped at the front gate and pressed the latch, pushed the gate open and waited for the children to catch up. They went up the short path, Sarah and James together, slightly behind her and still hand in hand. At the front door Aisha stopped and bent down to whisper to the children.

'Act perfectly normal, all right?' They nodded, and her hand trembled as she took the key from her pocket and turned it in the lock.

As she opened the inner door, she said loud and cheerily, in case Mark could hear. 'Come on, quickly. I think Daddy might be home.'

She smiled, trying to lighten their load, but their large eyes stared back silent, unblinking and afraid. She closed both doors, then busied herself in the hall, helping James out of his sopping wet shoes and coat. Sarah tried to unbutton her coat, but her cold, wet, shaking fingers refused to cooperate. 'Here, let me,' Aisha said, and started to undo the bottom buttons on her coat as Sarah continued fumbling with the top.

They heard the interconnecting door to the garage slam shut in the kitchen and Sarah jumped. James froze and looked as though he might cry again. 'Sshhh, shhhh,' Aisha soothed quietly and placed a finger to her lips. She draped their coats over the radiator in the hall to dry as Mark's footsteps left the tiled floor of the kitchen and disappeared into the carpet of the lounge.

Then another sound, the rustle of his nylon overalls, growing closer as he approached the hall. Aisha knew then for certain that he hadn't just come in, but had had time to change out of his suit and had been tinkering in the garage. Sarah knew it too and gave a little cry.

A few seconds later, Mark appeared through the lounge door and stood in the hall, surveying them.

'You're back,' he said flatly. 'Where have you been?'

'To school,' Aisha said, making her voice light and even. 'To fetch the children.'

'No. Before that.'

She looked at him, trying to gauge his mood, but as often happened it was impossible; his controlled expression said nothing beyond he wanted a reply, and offered no clue as to what he was thinking or what lay in store.

'Before that?' she said lightly. 'I went for a walk.'

'In the rain?'

'It was nice earlier. I had a headache and wanted some air. I'm sorry. If I'd known you were coming home early I wouldn't have gone.'

He looked at Sarah and James and then again at her. Any minute now, she thought, any second and he would come towards her and strike. Sometimes he made her wait, as though savouring the delay, like a cat toying with a mouse. She never knew the exact moment when the blow would come, only that it would.

'Go upstairs and get dried off,' Aisha said to Sarah and James, wanting them out of the way. Usually she had them in their rooms before Mark came home in the evenings, and at weekends they played upstairs if he was in the house.

The children took a step towards the stairs, then stopped as their father's arm shot out and blocked their way.

'Hey. Not so fast,' he said. 'What's the hurry? Don't you want to see your daddy?'

Aisha instinctively put herself between the children and him and placed an protective arm around each of their shoulders. 'They're wet, Mark,' she said evenly. 'They need to change.'

'In a minute. They won't melt. First they can tell me if they've had a good day. That's what children are supposed to do when they first come in from school.'

Sarah and James said nothing, they just stood looking up at him, large eyes rounded in fear. Aisha gave their shoulders a little squeeze of encouragement.

'Yes,' they replied together.

'My God! You're like a couple of robots.' Mark laughed. 'Put some life into it, for goodness' sake!'

'Yes thank you, Daddy,' Sarah said with more conviction, aware of what was at stake.

'That's better,' Mark said. 'And what about you, James? Did you enjoy school?'

He nodded and managed a bleated, 'Yes.'

Mark laughed again and dropped his arm from the stairwell. 'OK, off you go; go and amuse yourselves. I need to speak to your mother.'

Sarah remained where she was while James ran upstairs. She looked at her mother, waiting for her permission and reassurance. She would never abandon her mother unless she told her to.

'Go on,' Aisha nodded. 'Do as your father says.'

Sarah hesitated again and then went upstairs.

'Well?' Mark said, drawing himself up squarely. 'Aren't you going to ask me?'

She searched his face, trying to think of what she should be asking. What she had forgotten. The floorboard squeaked overhead as Sarah crossed the landing and went into James's room.

'Ask you what?' she said quietly.

'Why I have come home early. I mean, I don't normally. I'm a creature of habit. So what makes me suddenly take a half-day's leave on a Friday and come home early?'

She heard the 'half-day' and felt sick. Half-day. Three, possibly four hours. Not even she could have been walking for that length of time, especially in the rain.

'What brings you home early?' she said, her voice slight and unsteady. 'You don't normally.'

'No. Quite so. I don't. So it must be something pretty big. Very special to bring me home at lunchtime.'

'Lunchtime,' she repeated and she felt her knees tremble.

'Yes.' He smiled. It was a wide, broad grin, that seemed to hold none of his usual derision, but was doubtless just a different ploy. She never knew exactly how he was going to play it, and this was different again from anything she could remember. 'I've been in the garage all afternoon,' he confirmed with another grin.

Aisha hadn't heard James's bedroom door close and she knew the children were probably both listening. 'Shall we go into the lounge?' she said, not wanting them to hear. She walked past him and expected the first blow.

She heard his nylon overalls rustle behind her, but the blow didn't come. He followed her into the lounge and she turned to face him, putting what distance there was between them.

'I've bought something,' he said, his voice light and almost jovial. 'I've bought myself a present, a treat, for doing well at work. I collected it at lunchtime and came straight home. It's in the garage and I want you to be the first to see it.'

She looked at him from across the lounge, studied his face, his body language, for some clue. But there was nothing beyond self-satisfaction and something almost indefinable, which could have been joy.

'A present?' she asked lamely. 'For doing well at work?'

'Yes. That's what I said. Come on. You've kept me waiting long enough. It's in the garage and I want you to be the first to see. I've been waiting all afternoon.'

He turned, ready to go, while she stayed where she was. The garage. No, she didn't want to go in there. He kept it locked and she and the children were never normally allowed in. If she went into the garage it would be more difficult to get away. The up-and-over door was down at the front so the only exit was through the kitchen. If he locked or barred that door, she would be trapped with no means of escape.

'Come on then,' he said again, an edge of impatience creeping into his voice. 'I want to get cracking, before it gets dark. Best foot forwards.'

There was no alternative so she followed him. To run now would incite his anger even more, and where would she run to? Not upstairs. She didn't want the children to witness another assault. And not out of the house because she had already learnt that if she fled the house he locked the doors, and wouldn't let her in again until the morning.

'I always wanted another one,' he called over his shoulder as she followed a few paces behind him. 'It's the one thing I prom-ised myself when I could afford it. And now I can!'

He reached the interconnecting door to the garage, but instead of opening it, he turned and stood with his back against it and looked at her. There were still none of the telltale signs which over the years she'd come to recognize – the slight tensing of his brow, the brief narrowing of his eyes, the colour imperceptibly ebbing from his lips, all of which gave her the precious few seconds' warning to cover herself for protection or to run. But there were none of these.

'Close your eyes,' he said. 'I want it to be a complete surprise. I'll tell you when to look.'

She followed his instructions and did as he said. She brought up her hands and placed them palms down over her eyelids. Sometimes compliance persuaded him out of it; sometimes, but not always.

'No peeping,' he called, his nylon overalls rustling.

She stood a yard or so in front of him, eyes closed and hands blocking out the light. She was even more vulnerable now, unable to see, with no idea where he was and no chance to interpret and cower. She heard the handle on the door lower and then the door creak open. She felt the front of cold air rush in from the garage. And she thought objectively, without emotion, that the saving grace of him attacking her in the garage was that the children wouldn't have to see or hear.

Nineteen

With her hands covering her face, Aisha heard Mark's footsteps and sensed his approach. She closed her body down, ready for the attack. Eyes screwed shut and face shielded by her hands, she hunched her shoulders forwards, and brought her elbows inward to protect her stomach. But instead of the expected blow, the first vicious thump that would spearhead the rest, Mark continued past and round her. Stopping just behind her, she felt his hands on her shoulders. 'You mustn't look until I tell you,' he said. 'I'll be annoyed if you do.' His voice was light and his fingers rested gently on her shoulders, his touch just like it used to be a lifetime ago.

She went with him as he eased her forwards, steered her towards the open door. 'Mind the step,' he said briefly. 'We don't want you tripping over.'

Aisha raised one foot, then the other, and stepped over the small concrete plinth and into the garage. She felt the cold air encase her and smelt stale engine oil combine with more recent exhaust fumes. It crossed her mind that he might be planning to gas her, asphyxiate her with carbon monoxide from the car, but she dismissed it; if and when he did eventually kill her, he'd make it look like an accident – a fall from the top of the stairs or drowning in the bath. Apart from which, the car was outside, and if he raised the garage door, she would make a run for it.

'Keep your eyes closed until I tell you,' Mark said again in the same conciliatory tone.

They stopped just inside the garage and his hands left her shoulders as he came round to stand in front of her. She felt him take hold of her arms, just above her wrists, it was still a light touch with no pressure, not his usual painful grip when he was about to hit her. He began edging her sideways to the right, a little down the side of the garage, then stopped. Positioning her with her back against the wall it was as though he was lining her up for something and every muscle in her body tensed. His hands left her arms and he moved away. She heard the door to the kitchen close, then his footsteps recede across the concrete floor, towards the centre of the garage. Her hands were still covering her face and she felt the moisture from her breath condense warm onto her palms. Her heart thudded violently as she strained for any sound that would give her a clue, a hint of what he was about to do, and that crucial second's warning with its chance of escape.

His footsteps stopped in the middle of the garage and there was a small silence before she heard a sound of crinkling and scraping, as though heavy-duty polythene was being dragged over the concrete garage floor.

'Nearly ready,' Mark called, his voice animated with excitement. 'The great unveiling!'

Aisha's mind circled and darted as she stood behind her self-imposed blindfold and waited. Her thoughts fled to corners that she hardly dared consider, and where she hadn't ventured in years. Was it possible that after all this time Mark really did want to show her something? Share a purchase? But he never shared anything with her, not even a thought, unless of course it was another cruel joke, like the Christmas present he had gift-wrapped which had turned out to contain his dirty washing.

'OK,' he called. 'On the count of three you can open your eyes.' Then: 'One. Two. Three. You can look now!'

With every muscle taut and ready for flight, Aisha slowly lowered her hands and blinked into the fluorescent light. She blinked again and it took a moment for her to realize, to comprehend what she was seeing. In the middle of the garage, beside a heap of dark blue polythene, Mark stood facing her, feet apart, arms folded across his chest, posing proudly beside a huge, red, gleaming, brand-new motorbike. Aisha blinked again and allowed herself to breathe, then let her arms fall to her sides.

'Well? What do you think?' he said grinning. 'Isn't she magnificent? Top speed of a hundred and eighty. She'll do the ton easily.'

Aisha looked at the bike with its immaculate paintwork, glinting chrome and spotless black tyres and didn't know what to think. She could see the garage reflected in one of the wing mirrors, which stuck out like antlers on either side of the handlebars. She looked between the bike and Mark, and for the briefest of seconds wondered what it had cost.

'Well?' he said again, waiting for her reply. 'Isn't she absolutely beautiful?'

'Yes,' she said at last.

Mark laughed indulgently, and unfolding his arms, relaxed his pose. 'Come on over here,' he said, waving for Aisha to join him, 'and I'll tell you all about her. You won't understand the jargon, but believe me, she's the best. Bikes have come a long way since I was a teenager. I can't believe I've actually got one. It's been my lifelong ambition to own another, and now I do!'

Aisha could see that he was beside himself with excitement, like a child with a new toy. She moved slowly forwards, towards the centre of the garage, relief and confusion mingling in equal parts. Clearly Mark had treated himself and he wanted to show her. She looked at the shiny toy and thought sadly of everything the children had been denied, and could have wept.

'Look! Just here!' he said, squatting down on his haunches and pointing. 'This model has just been released.' Aisha bent slightly forwards and saw the name *FIREBLADE* emblazoned in glinting chrome on the side of the bike. 'It's the latest,' Mark exclaimed. 'I had to put my name on the reserve list nearly a year ago. This will be one of the very first on the road. You won't see another bike like this, believe me, Aisha. Not for ages.' He paused, waiting for her response.

She nodded, amazed, not so much by the bike, but that he had actually used her name.

'Right,' Mark continued, 'I'll explain about the engine first.' He tapped just below the chrome nameplate. 'It's got a 918 cc liquid-cooled, four-stroke engine with new dual concentric valve springs. That means there's optimum performance through precise valve operation from anywhere in the powerband. When you throttle back it goes like hell. I drove carefully bringing it here, but later I'm going to open it up properly on the motorway.' He waited again for her reply.

'I see,' she said.

'The manufacturers have used the very latest magnesium ACG for all the casings. Not only on the engine cover but here on the oil pan trim, and here too.' He tapped various parts of the casing, which to Aisha looked more like thick black plastic or thin metal. 'It's reduced the bike's weight by over 100 grammes. And together with the modified cowls, which are sleeker and more aerodynamic, it has lessened wind resistance, which in turn has made it even faster.'

'Faster than what?' Aisha asked, trying to think of a question as Mark paused and looked at her again.

'The previous models.'

'I see.' She nodded again.

'Now, down here,' he said, shuffling sideways on his haunches towards the rear of the bike and signalling for her to follow, 'is the latest pro-link suspension system. It's mounted in the swing arm, here.' Another tap. 'Its effect is to isolate suspension stress, which in a nutshell means sharper handling, particularly on corners.'

Aisha looked at the metal contraption which ran from the bike to the centre of the rear wheel. 'I understand,' she said nodding.

'And of course, there's the latest anti-locking device on the breaking system. I mean, you couldn't have this much power without it.'

'No,' she agreed. 'You couldn't.'

Mark stood and straightened. Aisha followed suit. 'Now to the front and the headlamps,' he said.

He ran his hand up from the rear, over the leather seat and towards the front, caressing the bike like the outline of a curvaceous woman. Aisha followed him round so that they were both at the front, facing the bike head on. She was standing so close to him now she could smell his aftershave, the same brand he had used since they'd first met, a poignant, bittersweet reminder of what used to be. For years she'd only smelt it in the bathroom after he'd been in there in the morning, and at other times when he was this close to her it was her fear she smelt.

'The headlights are slim, low-profile, dual-line beam, multi-reflector,' he said, touching her arm. 'They combine to project a more brilliant, aggressive forward image. You'll appreciate, Aisha, that on a bike they serve a double purpose. Not only do they allow the rider to see, but more importantly to be seen. Most accidents involving bikes aren't the rider's fault, but happen when a car or lorry doesn't see them and suddenly pulls out. This system increases the bike's visibility considerably.'

'Yes.' She looked sideways at him as he continued with the advantages of the 43 mm HMAS front fork, which she understood was something to do with the steering. Mark was talking to her, using her name, making eye contact and touching her arm, wanting to draw her into his excitement. He pointed out the 'state-of-the-art immobilizer' so that the bike couldn't be stolen, and she began to wonder. Was it possible that in fulfilling his lifetime ambition, reaching the fruition of his dreams, Mark had resolved an inner conflict, one born of frustrated desires, and had turned a corner? Was it possible that this was his way of reaching out to her, an olive branch of shared attainment, his way of bridging the gap? She allowed herself to be drawn further into his enthusiasm and wondered some more.

'This is the automatic ignition,' Mark said. 'I'll give you a blast.'

'So you don't have to kick-start them anymore?' she asked, remembering the lads who had owned old motorbikes at university and could never get them started.

Mark laughed, but not unkindly. 'No, that was years ago. Have a listen to this.' He took a key from his overall pocket, and inserting it in the lock, fired the engine. She started as the bike burst into life, a deep and very powerful throb that reverberated around the garage walls.

'Mark, the children will wonder what's going on,' she shouted over the engine noise.

Mark laughed, and giving the engine a couple more revs, turned it off. He moved down the side of the bike again, caressing the leather seat as he went. 'Well, that's the tour over,' he said, glancing up. 'What do you think, Aisha? Impressed eh?'

'Oh, absolutely,' she enthused. 'I can see why you're so excited.'

He looked very pleased, and as she watched him, standing in awe of his bike he suddenly seemed disarmingly childlike. She caught another glimpse of the old Mark, the one she used to know, who was vulnerable in his masculinity, and kind to her. And her heart softened and began to yearn for everything that had been and could possibly be again. It didn't matter that he had spent a fortune on the bike, for doubtless he would make it up to them in his way, another time – if this was truly the turning point as she now desperately wanted to believe.

'I'm glad you approve,' he said. 'I can't wait to take her out and see what she can do.'

'Yes, but be careful – it's raining out there, you know,' she said, which she recognized as something her mother would have said – the limiting note of caution.

He laughed again. 'Don't you worry. I've bought all the gear. Stay there and I'll show you. You can tell me what you think.'

Aisha watched as Mark strolled proudly to the rear of the garage and retrieved a large parcel from the beneath the shelves of tools. The brown paper had been loosely rewrapped and Aisha remembered the parcel arriving by express delivery at the beginning of the week. She'd had to answer the door, and when she'd given it to Mark that evening, he had actually thanked her. The paper rustled as he shook out the contents, and then held it up against him. It was an all-in-one zip-up leather suit. Red, exactly the same shade as the bike, but with luminous white flashes running the length of each side. He winked at her, and kicking off his shoes, stepped out of his overalls and into the suit, zipping it up to the neck. He posed again before her, arms folded and legs apart, proudly wanting her to see and appreciate. If Aisha thought a balding, middle-aged man, clad from head to foot in tight red leather looked faintly ludicrous, she certainly didn't say.

'Amazing,' she said and smiled approvingly and prayed this really was the turning point.

'Boots,' Mark said, returning to the shelves and picking up a large cardboard box. 'Knee-length, to give added protection. The lower leg is the most vulnerable part of a rider, although this bike's cowls offer better coverage than most.'

Aisha watched intently as he lifted the lid off the oblong box and took out a pair of long black leather boots. Placing them at his feet, he stepped in, one at a time and drew up the inside zips.

'Now the helmet,' he said. 'Obviously the most important accessory of all. It has three-density energy absorption and is made from the latest high-grade polycarbonate, which means it's virtually impenetrable.'

He took another box from beneath the bench – this one had a photo of the helmet on the side – and carefully took out the helmet. Not red this time, but metallic silver, with an almost-black visor. It was very large and looked an odd shape, she thought, elongated to the front.

'To protect the whole of this area,' he explained, rubbing his chin and neck. The helmet's silver casing glinted in the fluorescent light, but Mark didn't put it on, instead he tucked it under his left arm, and assumed the pose of a triumphant Grand Prix winner.

'Well? What do you think?' he asked, his eyes sparkling in the light as he waited for her approval.

'Very smart indeed,' she said, and clasped her hands together in admiration. 'Not only do you look the part, but it will obviously give you excellent protection. And keep you warm?'

'Yes, that's right. I haven't bought the gauntlets yet, you know – the gloves bikers wear. I've had to order them, they didn't have my size in red. I'll use ordinary leather gloves for now.'

'Very sensible and so smart,' she said again. Aisha knew that appearance had always mattered to Mark as much as practicality.

He smiled. 'I'm so glad you approve. I thought you would.'

Standing there in the strange intimacy of the garage, feeling included and appreciated, she was sure now. In realizing his dream, it was the answer to hers, and they could reset the clock and begin again. They hadn't been this emotionally close for a long time, not since their troubles had begun, and it was impossible it could be anything else – his sincerity and openness were so obvious and intense. This was his way of reaching out to her, of saying he was sorry and he hoped they could repair the damage and be a couple again. Aisha's thoughts went fleetingly to the monk who at this very moment was preparing a room for her and the children. She would have to write later and apologize, explain what had happened – that she and Mark had finally found a way forwards – and she would return the monk's five-pound note. She knew the monk would understand, and she might even take the children one day to meet him – a day's outing in the school holidays. She was sure they would like to see the monk, and he them.

'So, you approve?' Mark said again, carefully returning the helmet to its box. 'You can see why I was so excited?'

'Oh, yes. I'm so pleased for you. It's important to have something you really want. To achieve an ambition.'

She took a few steps towards him. *Now what?* she thought. How should they progress from here? It would take time, obviously, to rebuild what they had and start again. Hours of talking, possibly with a counsellor. She'd always thought that if they ever reached this point they should seek the help of a professional. Someone who could guide them through the pitfalls of their relationship and steer them to a better understanding. She wondered if she should be the one to suggest it, for men didn't immediately think of counselling, did they? A Radio 4 programme she'd once listened to about Relate, the marriage guidance service, had said as much. In over ninety per cent of referrals it said, it was the woman who made that first call. Their partners and husbands happily attended the counselling sessions, but hardly ever initiated the first appointment.

Mark turned to face her, suit and boots still on. 'I'm glad you like it,' he said. 'I knew you would want to share it with me as soon as possible.'

'Oh, yes, I do like it. I'm so pleased for you. The children will be too, particularly James, he loves motorbikes. Shall I fetch them?'

'In a minute.' He paused. 'So, you really do approve?'

'Oh, yes, I do, Mark, really.'

'And you can see why I wanted to share it with you?'

'Yes. I'm so pleased you did. We ...' She wrung her hands together and searched for the right words, the ones that would acknowledge what they had been through, and lead them forwards to a counsellor. She would suggest it now, while there was just the two of them, before the evening took over and she was busy with the children, and Mark with his new bike. 'Mark? I've been thinking—' she began.

'So, you can imagine ...' he said interrupting her, his voice slightly dropping, 'you can imagine how disappointed I was when I came home and found you weren't here.'

'Yes, I'm sorry,' she said. 'I wouldn't have gone if I had known. But it was pleasant earlier. I thought a walk would do me good.'

'And did it?' he said, his eyes widening. 'Did it do you good?'

'No, I got wet.' She hesitated. 'I'm sorry. It was silly of me to go.'

She looked at him and he looked back. There was a silence that seemed to stretch the length of the garage, broken only by the odd cracking of the polythene as it yawned and stretched. And in that silence, she felt the first few grains of sand shift, as the previously firm ground lost some of its stability and the tide began to turn. Yet the surface appeared to remain calm like a millpond, with no ripples.

'I'd better make sure the children have changed out of their wet things,' Aisha said. 'Then I'll make us dinner and you can tell me more about the bike.' She smiled and began walking towards the door, instinctively putting as much distance as possible between them. One step. Two steps. Then the first wave crashed as the sand was sucked from beneath her feet, and his voice echoed around the ceiling and bounced off the walls.

'So, where the fuck were you all afternoon?'

He was behind her, moving in closer, taking up the ground. Only a couple of steps to the door, not that far, not that far at all. But she didn't make it. He sprang like a lion felling its prey, landed on her back and brought her down. Knees first, then her elbows and face, bouncing off the rough concrete floor. Aisha heard a cry escape from her throat and strangulate as the air was cut off. Flat down on the floor, head pressed sideways, her cheek grating on the dry concrete. Her mouth began to fill with blood as his fists pummelled her back, her head, shoulders, neck, anywhere he could find.

'You bitch! Whore! Lie to me, would you! I'll teach you!'

She tried to cry out, but she was cut short by the blows raining down on her neck and head. He was going to kill her this time for sure. She knew she couldn't survive this. The force of the blows, their ferocity ... he was going to smash her to pulp on the hard concrete floor.

And perhaps it was this realization, or some residue of courage that had stayed with her from her conversation with the monk, or her anger at the way she'd allowed herself to believe, or maybe it was Sarah's hysterical cry of 'Mum!' from outside the door, but strength rose within her as it never had before and Aisha began to struggle and fight back. She thrashed her arms, kicked her legs, twisted and turned for all she was worth, trying to dislodge him from her back.

'Bitch! Whore! I'll teach you to lie to me, you fucking cow!'

Sitting astride her legs, he tried to grab her flaying arms and pin them to her sides. But the more he tried to restrain her, the more her anger and strength grew. She struggled and fought back, fighting for her life. A life that she finally realized was a life worth fighting for. Not only for her sake, but for that of the children.

'Mum!' Sarah shrieked again, and opening the door to the kitchen, screamed.

She heard James sobbing. 'Dad, stop! Stop! Dad!' he begged.

With a sudden burst of strength, she arched her spine, threw herself backwards, and managed to force him off. He was beside her now, shouting in her face, still trying to grab her arms. With a second burst of strength, she brought up one knee, sharp and hard, straight into his groin. He let out a cry like she'd never heard before, and his grip momentarily relaxed. She seized the moment, and summoning all her strength, hurled herself towards the kitchen door.

'Out now!' she yelled to the children.

'Run, Mummy, run!' Sarah screamed.

Aisha raced through the interconnecting door and then slammed it shut. She turned the key. 'Quick! Out the front, go now! Run!'

Sarah grabbed James as Mark landed with a thud on the other side of the door. 'You bitch. Wait till I get hold of you.' His fists pounded the wood.

She cupped her nose to stem the blood and raced after the children – out of the kitchen and through the lounge. They only had a few seconds before he would go to the front of the garage and release the up-and-over door. Then he would kill her without a doubt. She saw Mark's keys on the hall table and grabbed them. She threw open the front door. The children hesitated.

'Get in his car. Now!' she screamed, pushing Sarah and James out through the porch. Blood dripped from her nose and she tried to pinch it as they ran down the short path and onto the pavement. She pressed the fob to the car and mercifully the locks flew up. She tore round to the driver's door as Sarah bundled James into the back, and slammed the door. Left hand over her nose to stem the blood, she jabbed the key into the ignition with her right hand.

'Please, dear God, let it start,' she breathed.

The key turned and the engine fired, just as the garage door began to rise.

'He's coming! He's coming! the children shrieked hysterically.

Into first gear, she released the handbrake, at the same time pushing the accelerator down hard. The tyres screeched and they shot forwards, leaving Mark on the drive shouting her name.

Twenty

*D*own to the end of the road, Aisha stopped the car at the T-junction and peered at the dashboard. She found the light switch, clicked it on, and the road ahead lit up. Grappling with the steering column, she found the wiper arm and pushed it to the top. The wipers flicked furiously and the windscreen cleared.

'Fasten your seat belts,' she shouted to the children as she extended her own.

She inched the car forwards, up to the white line, and paused. She checked in the rear-view mirror and saw the road behind was clear. Her foot hovered above the accelerator pedal as she waited for a gap in the traffic to turn right. The cars were relentless, non-stop in both directions. She wanted to turn right and then go up the High Street, and out towards the M25. She knew where to join the motorway, and it would be easier than trying to find her way through the country roads in the dark: easier and safer.

She drew the back of her hand across her nose and sniffed; she could feel the congealing blood settle in the back of her throat. She checked the rear-view mirror again; a white van drew up behind obscuring her view. Then she checked the wing mirrors and the road. More traffic, it was endless. Finally a gap seemed to be appearing in the headlamps further up, in both directions. Was it big enough? She wasn't sure. She waited, hands clenching the wheel, pulse soaring, scanning the road both ways. It was

179

difficult to judge the approaching space in the dark and rain, and with so many cars, and so long since she'd driven. Touching the accelerator, she took up the slack on the clutch, then, pressing her right foot down, seized the gap in the traffic. The car lurched, but thankfully didn't stall. She changed up into second, then third, another jolt, but she was driving; incredible after all these years. And more incredible – they'd got away!

Aisha steadied her breathing and concentrated on the tail lights in front, then without looking down, delved into her cardigan pocket for a tissue and wiped her nose.

'Are you all right?' she asked the children in the back. They were so low in their seats she could only see the top of their heads in the rear-view mirror.

'Yes, are you?' Sarah's little voice faltered.

Aisha nodded, then she braked lightly as the traffic slowed to join the High Street. Gradually her pulse settled. It was still very busy with late-night Friday opening and she continued up and down the gears, and past the shops. She was getting the hang of the gear changes now; it was astonishing what you could remember when you had to. The wipers were still going full tilt and she felt for the wiper arm and turned it down a notch so that they settled into a slower, more steady rhythm.

'We're going on the motorway to the monks' house,' she said. She hardly dared believe the words herself.

'I'm cold,' James murmured.

Aisha glanced down at the dashboard, saw what she thought was the heating dial and turned it on. Warm air began to circulate round their feet.

The High Street ran out and the first sign for the M25 appeared. The interchange was about a mile away and Aisha knew she wanted to head west. The road widened and the traffic began to gain speed and she changed up into fourth gear. She wasn't sure where fifth gear was, but she didn't need it now, she would worry about that later.

'I'm hungry,' James said.

'Sshh, quiet,' Sarah pacified.

Aisha stared through the windscreen and concentrated on the road ahead, while her thoughts coursed between anger, astonishment and exhilaration at having got away. How dare he? How could he? How dare he lure her into the garage like that, make her believe in him and then attack her! What a fool she'd been, what an idiot, and not just now, but in all the years gone by. But somehow, miraculously, with the monk's encouragement, she had got away not only that but she was driving his car! His bloody precious car which she'd never been allowed to touch, let alone drive; a family car which had only ever left the garage with him in it. She bet he was angry, furious, pacing the garage and probably trashing the house. Just as well she wasn't there to see it, she knew what he would do to her. But that was past now, history, and would never happen again. That she'd had to leave all their possessions behind, and the children and she only had the clothes they stood up in, didn't matter. At the retreat she could telephone her parents, and once she'd explained what had been going on she was sure they'd help her. Now she'd escaped and was away from Mark she was already finding her thoughts were beginning to clear: thoughts, plans, and actions. Who knew what the future could hold, for now she'd made the decision to get away, all things were possible. Mark could have his car back later, when he was calmer and less likely to kill her.

A large illuminated signboard appeared and the traffic began to slow. Aisha changed down into third gear, then second, and it didn't jolt this time. She saw the roundabout ahead and remembered it from years ago when she used to drive – left to Heathrow and right to the Dartford Tunnel; she flicked the indicator to left. She had to concentrate hard now, to get onto the roundabout and then the motorway. She watched the red brake lights of the car in front, and the traffic coming from the right. The queue of cars gradually moved forwards, filtering onto the roundabout, and then it was her turn. She pulled onto the roundabout and then immediately turned down the first exit and onto the slip road to the motorway.

They were gaining speed, the cars in front and behind, going down the slip road to join the fast-moving traffic on the motorway. With the indicator flashing and in third gear, Aisha glanced through her side window at the cars coming along the motorway to her right. They were going fast, very fast, and she couldn't see a space on the motorway. One set of headlights seemed to follow another, but she kept the speed going – she knew she couldn't slow or stop, but had to filter in. She felt a moment's panic as the end of the slip road approached and there was still no sign of a space, then a van flashed and held back, letting her in. 'Thank you,' she said out loud, and gave herself a mental pat on the back – *I'm doing well,* she thought.

The windows were misting up, but she'd no idea how to direct the air onto the windscreen, and she was going too fast to search for the dial now. Leaning forwards, she rubbed the glass with the sleeve of her cardigan and then glanced at the speedometer. The needle hovered on sixty, but it seemed much faster with all the cars and lorries, and the three lanes moving in parallel. She checked the mirrors, then somehow managed to find fifth gear. It was where it had been on her old car – the one she'd had before her marriage, a lifetime ago. Aisha touched her nose; she could still taste blood, but it had finally stopped bleeding. The front of her cardigan must be covered in blood and she probably looked a right state. But who cared? They had escaped, and she was driving, and when they arrived at the monks' she would be able to wash it; everything was going to be all right.

'OK?' she asked the children, her voice nervously light. 'You didn't know Mummy could drive, did you?'

'No,' they chorused together.

'Is there a radio?' James asked, recovering slightly and hoisting himself up in his seat.

Aisha felt for the radio dial and pressed the knob. It was preset to Magic, a popular London radio station, and the DJ was announcing the next song. An unexpected chart success, he said, which had gone straight to number one. An upbeat religious reggae tune settled beneath the rain and wind as Aisha concentrated on the car in front and those to the right of her in the middle lane. She remembered to check her mirrors every so often to see what the vehicles behind were doing. The conscious thought she was giving to this was like taking a driving test before driving became second nature.

'I'm sorry,' she said to the children after a moment. 'I'm sorry for everything. You shouldn't have suffered as you have. I promise I'll make it up to you as soon as I can.'

'It's not your fault,' Sarah said quietly. 'You didn't do anything.'

'I should have acted sooner. All these years. What's it done to you two?'

For sitting here in the car and driving, a sense of normality had begun to return: an objectivity which was allowing her to view the past and see it for what it was. All that time, she thought, how could she have let them suffer? Yet it had taken a monk, and another brutal attack, to finally spur her into action. She had become petrified into acceptance and compliance. If someone

had said to her a day ago, 'Get in the car and drive,' she would
have said, 'No, I can't possibly; I'm useless, I've forgotten how.'
Yet here she was after all this time, driving as competently as
everyone else. And if she'd got this far, and re-mastered this skill,
who could say what else she was capable of? It was amazing what
you could do when you had to; she had amazed herself, the
children and probably Mark too.

'I'm hungry,' James said again.

'It's not too far,' she said. 'Only about twenty minutes. Once
we're at the retreat the monks will look after us. I'll ask them for
something to eat.'

Aisha was almost certain which turn off the motorway she
wanted and Radwood, the nearest town to the retreat, was sure
to be signposted. But she couldn't visualize the country lane the
house was in. The bus would have approached it from a different
direction, and in the dark and rain it would look very different
anyway. There was no rush, she told herself, she could take her
time and drive around if necessary, and if she still couldn't find
it, then she would stop and ask for directions – that would be the
sensible thing to do. There couldn't be many Buddhist retreats in
the area, she thought. In fact when she'd looked in the phone
directory, there'd only been two listed. She relaxed a little, and
took comfort in her newfound ability to make rational, objective
decisions and act on them, and her new ability to keep the children safe.

The radio was playing S Club 7 now and their old hit 'Reach
for the Stars'. It rang out, up-tempo in beat and uplifting in
lyrics, and the words were inspiring and ironic. Sarah was absent-
mindedly mouthing the chorus and Aisha was reminded that
here was another thing they'd been deprived of: music. Theirs
had been a house without cassettes, CDs, radio, MP3s, DVDs; the

list was endless. And, she thought sadly, without laughter too. She and the children had been trapped in a barren dessert, not only cut off from other people, but happiness. *You bastard*, she thought. *I really hate you for what you've done – not just to me but the children.*

Aisha rubbed the windscreen again and remembered to check the mirrors. She returned her gaze to the front and then checked the mirrors again. Further back, four or five cars behind, a bright headlight was visible on the outer edge of the inside lane. The driver was trying to pull out and overtake. *Idiot*, she thought, *he'll have an accident or, worse, cause one, trying to overtake in this weather.*

'Reach for the Stars' had been replaced by a more downbeat Jennifer Lopez song – this was more her type of music. Aisha had forgotten how much she used to like music, in the days when she'd had likes and dislikes. She remembered she'd always had music playing in her car and in her bedroom at home – while working at the desk her father had made. Mozart and Tchaikovsky had been two of her favourites, they'd been *Mark's favourites too*, she thought bitterly, remembering their first conversation all those years ago.

She glanced at the speedometer, the needle was still hovering above 60 mph which was fine. The middle and outside lanes weren't travelling any faster, the whole of the M25 was moving as one in the Friday evening exodus from London. She glanced at the children: James was snuggled into Sarah and she was watching the cars through her window. They both appeared more relaxed now.

Aisha looked to the front again and thought of the monk who was waiting for them with a room prepared, and the life from which she had so incredibly managed to escape. A roar of an engine sounded from behind and she glanced in her wing mirror. She saw the bright headlamp – the one that had been trying to overtake before – move out again, still trying to overtake. An uncomfortable tightness settled in her chest as she realized it was the single headlamp of a motorbike and not one of a pair from a car. *Don't be silly,* she told herself, *there will be any number of motorbikes on the motorway, of course it's not him.*

She kept glancing in the mirror, watching the bike as it forced a gap between the inside and middle lane. Then it accelerated out and round the car in front, until it was behind her, hovering at her rear offside wing. She looked in her wing mirror but the driver was hidden behind the bright light of the headlamp. Then the bike began to move out again, ready to overtake her. Her heart clenched and her mouth went dry. Could it be? Was it possible? Another roar of engine and the bike was beside them outside her window, hovering between the lanes at 65 mph. She looked, saw it, and knew – the white luminous flash running down the side of the biker's red suit. 'My God! It's him!' she cried, and she had to fight her panic to keep the car straight.

The children screamed and clung to each other. Aisha looked frantically between her side window and the road ahead. He was directly next to her, riding parallel, the white luminous flash glowing against the dark red of his leather suit. His elongated helmeted head turned slightly towards her like some giant insect, looming in the night. Aisha clutched the wheel to keep the car on course and, feeling for her door, pressed the central locking.

A car horn blared angrily at him from behind for blocking the lanes. The bike engine revved; then it moved forwards, alongside her bonnet and out into the middle lane. Another roar and it had disappeared between the cars, into the rain and dark ahead.

'He's gone!' Aisha cried to the children. 'Calm down, please. He's gone!' Her heart thumped wildly and her hands sweated as she clenched the wheel and stared straight ahead. 'Please! Calm down!' she cried again. 'I can't drive.'

Dear God! Now what? she thought. He was on the motorway! But how? Had he followed them from the house, so far behind she hadn't seen? She remembered the white van drawing up behind them as she'd waited to turn out of their road. Had he been behind the van and followed them all this way? It was possible; she'd been so busy concentrating on driving and on the road ahead she wouldn't have necessarily noticed. Had he followed them or did he know where they were going? Did he know about the monk? Was it possible he'd found out somehow? It would explain why he'd chosen today to collect the bike and come home early.

'Sarah,' she pleaded, 'please stop James from crying; I can't think.'

Aisha swallowed hard, peered ahead – up the lanes of traffic – and tried to think. There was no sign of a motorbike's single red tail light in among the pairs of car lights. If he did know where they were heading he could be going ahead to lie in wait at the retreat for when they arrived. She shivered, every muscle in her body tensing in fear as it had done in the garage. There was no way she could park the car on the driveway at the retreat and make it to the front door if Mark was already there and lying in wait. Even if she and the children ran across the driveway, they wouldn't be able to make it. She thought of the secluded drive with its hedges and trees, and the bell she would have to ring, and then be answered before they were safe. No, it wasn't possible, Mark would grab them as soon as they stepped from the car. Her stomach contracted and she felt sick with fear. She swallowed the bile rising in her throat.

'Mum, what are we going to do?' Sarah asked, her small voice breaking.

'I don't know. Please, just look after James, will you. I'm trying to think.'

James was still sobbing uncontrollably and it was making driving very difficult. What with the dark, the rain, her terror, looking at the tail lights in front, and all these cars and lorries, her head was spinning. If only she had a mobile, she could have phoned the monk or even called the police. She could have pulled off, stayed locked in the car and phoned 999. But there'd been no credit on her mobile for years and she didn't even know where her phone was now. No money for a mobile, clothes, or even food, only a brand new motorbike.

Without a phone, and with no way of contacting anyone for help, something told Aisha it was better to keep going. It felt safer to be moving; he couldn't get in while they were in the car. But what was she going to do? Spend all night circling the M25 like a motorway equivalent of the Circle Line? And what about petrol? She hadn't thought of that. She looked down at the dashboard, scanned the array of illuminated green symbols and dials, and found the petrol needle. Dear God, it was already approaching red. Fear gripped her, and she felt as useless as Mark had always said she was.

'Sarah, you must stop James crying, please,' she repeated, though she could have wept herself.

You thought you were getting clever, she heard Mark say. *Not so clever now, are you? Trapped in the dark and rain and about to run out of petrol. What are you going to do? Panic? I told you you'd never make it without me.* And she thought of what would happen if she went back now and knew she couldn't, for one way or the other – by his hand or her own she would surely die.

How much petrol had she got left? She glanced again at the dial. Probably no more than half a gallon, which in this big car meant nothing. Probably not enough to get to the retreat, even if she found it first time.

'I'm scared,' James said, his sobs at last subsiding.

'It's all right,' Sarah soothed, sounding older than her years. 'Don't worry, he's gone. We're safe now.'

But for how long? Aisha thought. How long could they keep going? She checked all around, but there was no sign of the single headlamp, just endless pairs of lights shimmering through the surface spray and rain. Did she have enough petrol to get them to a service station where she could run in and ask for help? But where was the next service station? None had been signposted and she wasn't even sure they had them on the M25; she couldn't ever remember seeing one on this stretch of the motorway. Should she turn off? Take the next exit and stop at the first house she came to and run in and ask for help? *Could you call the police, please. My husband is trying to kill me.* Would they believe her? With all the dried blood down her front, and the state she and the children were in, they might. But supposing she turned off and he was following her, and there wasn't a house or they didn't answer the door? What then? Perhaps she should pull onto the hard shoulder and wait for a police car to pass. Hadn't she read somewhere that the police regularly patrolled the motorways? But how often? Ten minutes, twenty, every hour? She'd no idea and it felt safer to keep moving, with the doors locked.

Then she saw him. He was waiting on the hard shoulder. Terror gripped her. There was no mistaking his large frame, the white stripe of his leather suit glowing luminous in the passing headlights. He was standing astride the bike, one leg raised,

189

ready for the off. His helmeted head flicking back and forth as he scanned the passing cars, looking for them in his car. There wasn't enough time to pull into the middle lane so cars could shield them, there was too much traffic, moving too fast. Aisha clenched the wheel and looking straight ahead continued steadily past him.

'He's there!' Sarah shouted. James shrieked.

Then they heard the roar of engine as the bike accelerated off the hard shoulder and onto the inside lane. Aisha looked in the mirror and saw it tuck itself in half a dozen cars back. The children sunk low in their seats and covered their heads with their hands again. Aisha looked in the mirror as the single headlamp pulled in only a few cars behind them. *He was right about one thing,* she thought, the bike's multi-reflector beam he'd spoken of in the garage certainly projected a strong forward image; its light was dazzling and unmistakable.

Her eyes darted nervously as she monitored the bright light's progress. There was another roar of engine as the bike throttled and began to overtake. Her heart pounded and she was sweating, despite the cold. A car horn blared from behind and the single headlamp closed in. It came up between the inside and middle lane, then forced in behind her, almost riding on her bumper. Close, far too close. There was no stopping distance – if she had to suddenly brake he would go straight into her. And the confession she'd made to the monk earlier that morning briefly touched her mind: *I am now so wretched and consumed by bitterness, I think things far too dreadful to speak.*

The throb of the bike's engine drowned out the radio and the headlight began to move outwards again as he accelerated up beside them. He paused outside the window, his giant helmeted head with its black visor leering in at her like a creature of the night. Then another blast of engine and he'd disappeared, the power of the bike projecting him into the night.

'Has he gone?' Sarah whispered, daring to peep out.

'Yes, for now,' Aisha said.

Yet Aisha's voice was low and oddly dispassionate as her mind suddenly became calm and focused. She thought of the garage where she'd squatted down beside him, wanting to share and see everything. How she had allowed herself to believe and forgive – the hope, the optimism, her plans for counselling and their future, before he had killed it dead

The traffic picked up speed slightly, 67 mph, 68 mph, and a signboard appeared. Radwood was listed, it was the next exit, the one which should have taken them to the retreat. She peered through the mist and rain, then down at the speedometer – nearly 70 mph. The road cambered slowly to the left and then she saw him again on the hard shoulder. Waiting, watching, looking over his shoulder, looking for his car with them in it.

'Keep down,' she said to the children. She drew herself up in her seat, then continued steadily along the inside lane and past him.

He accelerated out and forced a gap in the traffic a short way back. Cars hooted loudly. It was a dangerous game he played – this cat and mouse, driving aggressively. It could escalate into road rage in drivers who weren't as compliant as she – or how she used to be. Aisha remembered her naïve acceptance in the garage, his attack, and all the years of punishment and degradation, and knew it would all continue if he got to them and forced her to go back. She looked at the red tail lights of the car in front, and then at the bike's single white beam in her wing mirror. Two cars blocked the bike's path, keeping him back for a few seconds.

Aisha's thoughts remained quiet and composed. She glanced in the rear-view mirror at Sarah and James, both slunk low in their seats and secured under their belts. The radio was still on, the DJ was playing a request, and inviting listeners to phone in with theirs. Aisha thought she might one day, she might phone in, for she had plenty of requests, though not all for music.

The bike's light flashed to full beam and its horn blared, ordering the cars to part and let it through. The drivers let him in; they had little choice if they weren't about to cause an accident and knock him off his bike. He was riding two cars behind her now, in a few seconds he would be up to her bumper, then level and overtaking. She saw the final signboard for her exit and looked again at the speedometer. The needle was hovering over 65 mph and Aisha began to do some calculations: the speed and distance equalling the stopping time if she were to suddenly brake. She used to be a good judge of speed and distance, in the days when she was good at things, and drove. 'You drive like a man,' her father had once said, by way of a compliment. Aisha remembered how good she used to be, and all that she and the children had suffered, and knew she couldn't go back now or ever.

The single light was directly behind her now, hovering on her offside wing. The bike's engine was revving, getting ready to come up beside them once again. She glanced between the front and wing mirror, and gripped the wheel very tightly, every muscle in her body tensed.

'Keep under your seat belts,' she said to Sarah and James.

The bike's engine roared and pulled out. Aisha ticked off the seconds, judging which would be the correct one. The bike was level with Sarah's door now, moving alongside them at 68 mph. Soon, in another second, he would be level with her door, then he would accelerate again, disappearing and re-appearing until they had run out of petrol, when he would finally catch them. He began to draw level with her door, now exactly level, and in that split second she swung her left arm up and over and brought the wheel round, hard right. Hard down, taking their car straight into the middle lane, as hard and fast as she could. She heard a horrendous crunch of metal as the car jolted and spun and the white stripe on the suit disappeared. Then she was braking, braking for all she was worth, spinning, and trying to avoid the other cars.

Tyres screeched, her wheels locked, and they pirouetted out of control. Round and round on the slippery road surface in a dance being mimicked by other cars outside. Steer into a skid, she remembered from the Highway Code, all right in theory, but impossible in practice. There was no time to turn in one direction before you were heading off in another. She clung to the wheel as the car travelled sideways and began to rock; she prayed it wouldn't turn over. Then as fast as it had started it stopped, bang, straight into the front of another car and they were finally still. Nose to nose, facing the wrong way down the fast lane but miraculously, unbelievably, still upright.

Twenty-One

It was quiet, so very quiet in the aftermath of the accident, with only the hiss of steam escaping from the engine. It was as though time had taken a breath and was deciding what to do next before exhaling. A freeze-frame of events between the past and future, a brief and silent window in the present, before action needed to be taken.

The first thing Aisha did was to check the children were unhurt. They were dazed and shocked, but otherwise all right. They'd been huddled low in their seats so she was sure they hadn't seen exactly what had happened, which was a huge relief. The next thing she did was to switch off the radio. It seemed irreverent to leave the music playing given that people were probably hurt. She wondered where Mark was and if he was trapped under her car, but decided even if he was he couldn't get to them – not with her door crushed and a car rammed against the other side. So she folded her hands loosely in her lap, rested her head back, and waited. She couldn't do much else as they were trapped in the car but also she felt quite happy waiting. After everything that had happened that day, she found it quite relaxing to simply sit and wait. They weren't in any danger, and doubtless someone would get them out eventually.

The children seemed content to sit and wait too, now that she had reassured them they were safe and it was only a matter of time before help arrived. They had calmed down, and Sarah had rubbed a patch clear of mist on her window and the pair of them were now watching the activity unfolding outside. And there was plenty of it, Aisha thought. What five minutes before had been a reasonably free-flowing motorway now looked like the chaotic end of a dodgem ride at the fair. Vehicles had come to a halt at every angle across the three lanes: nose to nose, bumper to bumper, at right angles, and parallel. Some still had their head-lights on, while others had been plunged into darkness by the impact. As she surveyed the carnage, she saw car doors and windows begin to open, and the occupants clamber out. The calm in the wake of the accident quickly gave way to a chaos of movement with people darting around like a disturbed colony of ants. Shouts, exclamations, calls for help and reassurance filled the air as drivers and passengers checked on each other, and then their vehicles. *What a mess,* Aisha thought, *what an unholy mess.* But that was as far as her interest went for quite a while – a vague and passing assessment on what was happening outside which seemed separate from her and the children.

The wipers were still chuntering back and forth and she lowered the lever on the steering column so the wipers would clear the windscreen every fifteen seconds. The engine had cut out on impact but she left the keys in the ignition so the wipers and heater worked. Through the windscreen, she could see steam rising from the bonnet of the car in front – a misty spectre spiral-ling into the cold night air. As Aisha looked, the driver's door slowly opened and a woman in her late sixties got out. She stared at the bonnet of her car which was coupled with Aisha's in a weird act of intimacy, then made her way, dazed, towards the grass verge where others were starting to gather. Two cars behind hers was a lorry, its cab towering fortress-like over the surround-ing mayhem. The driver had switched on his interior light and

Aisha could clearly see him talking on his mobile, while looking around, presumably reporting on what he saw. Aisha watched as he leant across, and, opening his door, continue his report hanging half out of the cab. *He must have a good view up there*, she thought. *Panoramic.* And her other thought was that his consignment of Heinz food was going to be rather battered and very late.

Further over to her right, Aisha saw a man in shirtsleeves, sopping wet but apparently unhurt, picking his way between the cars. He stopped and looked in each vehicle as he went, and seemed to be checking on any occupants, though many of the cars were now empty, their doors left raggedly open in the unscheduled exodus. Aisha charted his meandering path towards them as he came closer and closer, and finally up to her door. He tried opening her door with the handle, but it wouldn't budge, then he squeezed in behind their car and tried the rear door, but that wouldn't shift either. He returned to her side of the car and motioned for her to wind down the window. She pressed the button set in the armrest; and the window grated and managed to lower itself a couple of inches before stopping.

'I'm a nurse,' he said, his mouth to the gap, and looking at the children in the rear. 'Does anyone in here need emergency first aid?'

Aisha shook her head and wondered how he would get in if they did. She noticed there was an ugly scratch on his forearm which he seemed to be unaware of.

'No, thank you, we're fine,' she said. 'But it's very kind of you to ask. I appreciate that.'

He looked at her oddly; perhaps politeness wasn't the correct response at a time like this, she thought. He hesitated and a large raindrop ran down the centre of his nose and dripped onto his already sodden shirt.

'I'm sure others need you more than us,' she added. 'Was anyone badly hurt?'

'It seems we've all been pretty lucky from what I've seen so far. Mainly cuts and bruises, one fracture, apart from the poor guy on the bike. Hopefully he'll make it but ...' He shook his head. 'The emergency services are on their way.'

Aisha nodded and thanked him again. Seven years of fear evaporated and her one thought was that she and the children were safe at last. She pressed the button to raise the window and, turning to the children, she said quietly, 'I think there is a chance your father is badly hurt. If so, I hope in time you will find it in your hearts to forgive me.'

They looked at her and said nothing and she recoiled from what they could be thinking, for in making them all safe she had taken away their father – possibly for ever. She was silent for some time and the children were quiet too.

Presently two police cars and three ambulances arrived, their blue lights flashing and sirens wailing, closely followed by two fire engines. Sarah and James moved to the window to watch the activity. Ten minutes or so later the male nurse reappeared, this time with a police officer whom he showed to their car. Aisha lowered her window the two inches again and looked at him questioningly. The PC was young and bore a very earnest expression. 'How are you and the kids doing?' he asked, shining his torch into the back seat.

'We're doing all right, thank you,' Aisha said.

'We'll have you out as soon as we've cleared a space for the cutting gear. Shouldn't be too long.'

Aisha thanked him and raised the window again. She and the children watched and waited as more ambulances arrived and left, in a relay of advancing and retreating lights and sirens. After a while James became restless and remembered he was hungry; with the promise of a meal with the monks gone, he wanted to know when they were going to have dinner.

'I really don't know, love,' Aisha said. 'And I'm not really in a position to find out, am I?' He moaned a bit longer and then returned his attention to the window.

Every so often, one of the police or fire crew knocked on her window to reassure them it wouldn't be much longer. Each time she wound down the window the two inches, smiled and thanked them, then shut it again to stop the rain coming in. One police officer asked if there was anyone she would like to contact to reassure them they were safe, as the accident was now being reported on the news.

'No, thank you,' she said. 'We're not expected by anyone.' She paused. 'Is it possible to have a drink of water please? We're all rather thirsty.'

'Sure, I'll see what I can do,' the police officer said, then added with a wink at the children, 'it won't be Coke though.' But his joke was wasted on Sarah and James because they'd never had Coke, not at £1.35 a bottle; it was tap water or nothing.

The police officer returned shortly with three plastic cups of water, which he carefully eased through the gap at the top of the window. Aisha thanked him, and before he left he said again they would be out very soon. She switched on the radio and heard that the M25 was at a standstill anticlockwise, between junctions twenty and twenty-five. A multi-vehicle pile-up, it said, that wouldn't be cleared for at least four hours. She switched the radio off again – she already knew most of that, and more. She knew who was responsible; for once she was the maker of news.

* * *

Nearly half an hour passed and then it was their turn to be released. She and the children sat up and took notice as a hive of activity began outside their car. Four burly firemen in dark protective suits, two with clear visors attached to their helmets, congregated down her side of the car. She lowered the window the two inches again as they asked so she could hear their instructions.

'We're going to have a go at prising this off first,' one of the firefighters said, tapping her door. 'If that doesn't work we'll bring over the cutting gear.' Another firefighter told her and the children to move to the far side of the car and turn away. Aisha leant over the back of her seat and positioned the children against the far door, huddled into each other, and then she slid into the passenger seat.

'Turn away,' the fireman repeated as he inserted a massive crowbar into the hinge and began levering.

There was a hideous metallic rip that sounded like a ring pull coming off a giant can, only magnified a million times.

'OK,' the firefighter called, and Aisha turned back to look. The door was in his hand, torn off like a sheet of paper, and he was leaning it against the bonnet.

'Dear me,' she said, 'that wasn't very strong.'

'No,' he joked. 'It's like opening a can of beans with these modern cars.' Aisha thought how angry Mark would be if he could see his car now and hear it referred to as a can of beans.

She stayed in the passenger seat and helped first James, then Sarah clamber over the handbrake and into the driver's seat, where another fireman reached in and lifted them out. Aisha then slid across and felt his big strong hands under her elbows, helping her out and keeping her away from the jagged metal of the hinges. As she straightened and stood next to Sarah and

James, a paramedic draped blankets around their shoulders. Aisha appreciated this small kindness – it was still raining and they hadn't had time to grab their coats on the way out.

'Where are we going?' she asked the paramedic as he guided her and the children round the damaged cars.

'To the ambulance, to check you over,' he said.

'I don't want to go to hospital,' Aisha said, holding back.

'No, you needn't if you're OK. But we'll check you all in the ambulance as a precaution, we're doing it with everyone.'

'All right,' she agreed. 'But how will I get home?'

'Someone will take you. Don't worry.'

So she didn't. She'd worried enough for one day and was now feeling strangely light-hearted.

As they approached the ambulances parked on the hard shoulder, the paramedic reassured the children that there was nothing to worry about, and asked them if they had ever been inside an ambulance before. James, suddenly finding himself the centre of attention, began agitating about food again. An elderly couple who'd just been given the all-clear and were coming down the steps of the ambulance heard him.

'You have these, dear,' the woman said, delving into her bag and producing a packet of crisps, and a small bag of sweets. 'They were for my granddaughter, but I don't suppose we will be going there now. Not after all this.'

Aisha thanked her, feeling a pang of guilt for being responsible for stopping her visit, and told James to say thank you too; then she and the children continued up the steps and into the startling brightness of the ambulance. There was something faintly disturbing about the fluorescent light and the clinical neatness – the meticulously labelled stowaway cupboards on the walls. With a shudder, Aisha realized it reminded her of the garage and the last time she'd been under a glaring overhead light, surrounded by precise, almost fastidious attention to order. She pulled the blanket closer around her and sat on one of the long seats, while Sarah and James sat together on the other. The two paramedics introduced themselves as Joe and Chris and started checking the children, testing their reflexes, then their sight and hearing. They talked to them as they worked and gently asked them questions: Did it hurt anywhere? Had they banged themselves in the accident? Sarah and James looked at her and shook their heads; the smell of cheese and onion crisps filled the ambulance and James clung protectively to his bag.

'Offer one to Sarah, that's a good boy,' Aisha said. Joe and Chris laughed as James reluctantly stuck the bag under his sister's nose and then withdrew it again before she had time to take one.

'Don't want one anyway,' Sarah said, and Aisha frowned at them both.

Satisfied the children were not injured, Joe looked at Aisha. He assumed the cuts and bruises to her face and the dried blood down the front of her cardigan were a result of the accident. This suited Aisha as it meant her injuries didn't require any further explanation which might have been awkward. Joe talked to her as he shone his pencil light in her eyes; and asked her name, date of birth, what day of the week it was, and if she had any dizziness or double vision; she answered no to all. Then he ran his hands over her cheekbones and pressed lightly and asked her if it hurt.

'No,' she said again, 'not really.' She could have added that this hurt was nothing compared to how she had got the injury, and all the hurt that had gone before. Aisha found Joe's concern, and his touch, quite pleasant after all the years of neglect and abuse, and would have liked to have told him what really hurt and possibly confessed, but of course she didn't, for what would have been the point in that?

Joe finished examining her and then said that while there was no obvious trauma to her head she should go to the hospital for an X-ray, 'to rule out a hairline fracture of the skull'. Without thinking, her guard momentarily lowered by his kindness, she replied, 'No. It was only my nose he caught,' then immediately realized her mistake. 'I hit my nose on the steering wheel,' she said quickly. 'But I'm all right now, it stopped bleeding a while ago. Really, I'm fine, thank you.'

'I'm sure you are,' Joe said patiently. 'But an X-ray is a sensible precaution after any severe blow to the head.' Aisha thought of the many severe blows she'd had to her head, none of which had resulted in her going to the hospital for an X-ray, whether it was sensible or not.

'No,' she said again, firmly but politely. 'I'll see my doctor in the morning if there's a problem.' Joe had to accept this and told her that if she felt unduly tired, or suffered any visual disturbance she must go straight to casualty.

'Yes, I will. Thank you.'

As she and the children left the ambulance, two police officers appeared from the shadows, and Aisha was momentarily startled. They had their notepads already open and the WPC addressed her. 'We're taking everyone's contact details,' she said. 'Do you feel up to answering a few questions?'

Aisha nodded. She wasn't sure how much of a choice she had, and she knew she'd have to be careful, but then surely she'd had enough practice at thinking before she spoke? She also knew the police would have spoken to enough witnesses by now to have gleaned some of her role in the accident, the motorway had been packed, someone must have seen something.

'We are conducting the interviews in the police cars as it's so wet,' the WPC said. 'I'll look after the children in one car, if you'd like to go with my colleague in the other.'

Aisha looked over to the hard shoulder and to the two police cars, their lights still slowly flashing. Sarah stayed where she was and looked to her mother for confirmation.

'Go on. I'm fine, darling, really. You take good care of James.' She held Sarah's gaze and Sarah gave a slight nod. Aisha hoped neither of them would say anything untoward, for children can be so honest.

Sarah walked beside the WPC while James, eager to explore the police car, went on ahead. Aisha glanced at the officer at her side as they began towards the second car. What was it they said? It was a sign of your age when the policemen started to look younger? He couldn't have been more than twenty, she thought. The orange light flashed on her face as the PC opened the passenger door and waited for her to get in. Closing it, he went round to the driver's side. It was warm inside and surprisingly comfortable, and quite different from a conventional car. Aisha's eyes travelled over the dashboard with its maze of coloured dials and switches, and something that looked liked a small computer mounted in place of the glove compartment. The PC shut his door against the seeping rain and then turned to a clean page in his notebook. She looked ahead at the police car parked a few yards in front where the children were. She could see the outlines of their heads: James's was just visible in the driver's seat, with the WPC in the front passenger seat, and Sarah was in the back. The lights on the roofs of the two cars continued to revolve slowly like synchronized beams from a lighthouse.

'Can I start with your name, please,' the PC said. She told him, spelling out 'Aisha', which always caused a problem.

'Thank you. What can you tell me about the accident?'

Aisha could see his reflection in his side window, highlighted every so often by the flashing light, his pen poised above his notepad ready to take down her answer.

'I think it might have been my fault,' she blurted. 'You see, it was dark and wet, and he came up so fast … I just didn't see him until it was too late. If it was my fault I'll never forgive myself.' She sniffed and blinked back the tears, genuinely regretting she was causing so much upset to so many people; it wasn't in her nature to hurt others.

'Please, don't upset yourself,' the PC said. 'I probably shouldn't say this, but from what I've heard it was the fault of the bike rider. By all accounts, he was driving like an idiot. An accident waiting to happen, if you ask me.'

So young and innocent, Aisha thought, he obviously felt sorry for her. Laying his pen on his pad he reached into the door pocket and took out a wad of tissues. He passed them to her and waited while she wiped her eyes and blew her nose.

'When you're ready,' he said gently. 'I've only a few questions, it won't take long.'

'Thank you,' she said, moved by his kindness.

'Your car is the silver BMW, registration MAR K12?'

'Yes, it was my husband's.'

'And when, and from where did you start your journey?' he said, writing as he spoke.

'From home. At roughly 5 o'clock.'

'And where is home?' he asked, and she gave him her address. 'Where were you going to? Is there someone expecting you? Someone you should contact?'

'No. We were going for a short drive and then home again. There's no one expecting us.'

'A rough night for joyriding,' he said, trying to lighten her mood.

'I know. But my husband insisted on it, to make sure we were safe. You see, I hadn't driven for some time, and he wanted me to get used to the car, so I could use it for shopping and collecting the children from school. That was why he was travelling so close on his bike – to help me if I got into difficulty. Do you know anything more about him? How he is?'

She looked at the PC and waited.

His pen froze in mid-sentence and his face visibly paled. He couldn't have been in the job very long, and she wished she hadn't had to do this to him.

'It was your husband on the bike?' he said at last.

She nodded. 'It couldn't have been anyone else.'

'Wait there and I'll get someone to talk to you. I'm so sorry. I didn't realize. No one did.' He scrambled out of the car, leaving her alone.

Aisha looked to the front – at the outlines of her children in the police car and kept her mind steady. The PC returned almost immediately with a more senior officer who said they were telephoning the hospital now to see if there was any news. He too asked if there was someone he could contact for her, and Aisha said there wasn't. The senior officer hovered outside the car with the PC, both waiting, she assumed, for news from the hospital. When he answered his phone Aisha knew straight away from his expression what he was going to tell her. But he broke the news so gently and professionally that she hardly felt a thing – her husband, as he was now referred to rather than *the idiot on the bike*, was, he was sorry to say, pronounced dead on arrival at the hospital. He reassured her that everything that could have been done to save him was done, and that he had been unconscious

and therefore hadn't suffered. Aisha wasn't surprised that Mark
was dead, for she doubted anyone could be knocked off a bike at
70 mph and survive. Not even Mark, with all his power and
omnipotence, could do that. Her thoughts went to the crash
helmet, the cost of which would have kept them in food for
months, and was supposed to have saved him in an accident but
clearly hadn't.

The police put her composure down to shock – the reason
why she hadn't said anything earlier about it being her husband
on the bike, and why she wasn't hysterical now. The senior officer
then explained that they would need to take a statement from
her, but offered to leave it until the following morning. Aisha said
that she'd rather get it over and done with now, so Sarah and
James were fetched from the other car and the three of them
were driven to the police station.

Once inside the station, the children were taken to the office
to be looked after while she went to an interview room with the
PC to make her statement. When it was finished the PC fetched a
detective inspector who introduced himself as Stan Calder, and
said how sorry he was. He brought her tea in polystyrene cup,
which Aisha thought was very kind, but when she took the first
sip she retched – it had sugar in it. It wasn't his fault, the inspector wasn't to know that Mark had banned all sweet things from
the house. It wasn't so much the cloying sweetness after so long
without which had made her sick, but the recollection of the
punishment that she knew would follow if she drank tea with
sugar in and got found out. Like many things, it produced a
reflex action.

The inspector read her statement back to her – it was short,
there wasn't much to say really. It was dark and wet, and Aisha
hadn't driven for a long time, and it was the first outing for Mark

on his bike. She said he had been following very close and must have suddenly decided to overtake. Aisha cried openly as the inspector read the statement, and the words fell between them into a void of regrets and what might have been. He waited patiently until she composed herself and then took a gold pen from his inside jacket pocket, and passing it to her, pointed to where she had to sign. Aisha hesitated before she signed, not because of the contents of the statement, but because it had been so long since she'd had to sign anything that she'd forgotten her signature, and had nearly written Hussein instead of Williams.

As Aisha signed her statement, and then handed back the gold pen to the inspector, she wondered if Mark had known. Had he seen it coming? Did he know? Had he suffered the expectation of pain and torture as she had done all those years? She sincerely hoped not, for no one should suffer like that, not even Mark.

Twenty-Two

It was after eleven o'clock by the time Aisha and the children were finally heading for home, driven by Steve, with Lisa in the passenger seat, the same two police officers who had looked after Sarah and James at the police station, and with whom they had built up a rapport. And while Steve and Lisa's conversation in the car was subdued, tempered by the knowledge that the children's father was dead, and they had yet to be told, James in particular had become quite lively, and rather a chatterbox. Now in his second police car of the evening, he considered himself something of an expert, and was explaining to Aisha and Sarah the workings of the various instruments on the dashboard, and when and how they should be used. Lisa had indulged him while on the station forecourt by giving the police car's siren a whirr, but now explained it was illegal to use it on the road, unless they were going to an emergency.

'Couldn't we pretend it's an emergency? Please?' James begged. 'No one will ever know.'

'No, love, not even the police can break the law.' Lisa turned to look at James in the back with compassion in her eyes; very soon this little boy's excitement was going to be quashed by the worst news any child could ever hear – the death of his father.

'I'm going to be a policeman when I grow up,' James said, his voice rising with passion. 'I'm going to put naughty men in prison and lock them up, then they won't hit women!'

'That's enough.' Aisha said gently, worried that James might say more than he should. 'Steve needs to concentrate on driving, and it's difficult if someone is talking all the time.'

'Well, if you're good, James, and work hard at school,' Lisa said, 'I'm sure you will be a policeman one day.'

James grinned, satisfied.

When they drew up outside the house and Steve cut the engine, a heavy silence fell in the car as all five of them looked out towards the house. It was exactly as Aisha and the children had left it when they had fled in terror only six hours before. The downstairs lights were still on, and the garage door was open. Mark, presumably hadn't shut it before he'd given chase in fury. He had closed the front door though – or had they? Aisha couldn't remember. The house seemed to stare out at her as evidence of what had happened, and why.

'Did you leave the garage door up?' Steve asked, glancing at her.

'My husband must have,' Aisha said quietly. 'He came out last.'

'I'll close it,' Steve said. 'It's easy pickings for the opportunist.'

Then suddenly she realized that she wouldn't be able to get into the house – her front door keys were in her coat pocket in the hall, and Mark's were still in the ignition of the car.

'Oh,' she said. 'I'm locked out. My house keys are in the car.'

'Is there a back door?' Steve asked.

'Yes, but that's always kept locked. There's a door at the rear of the garage which goes to the kitchen, but I think that will be locked too. I'm sorry. I should have realized. I didn't think. I'm sorry to be so much trouble.' Apologizing for her failings came easily to Aisha; she was a liability, Mark had been right.

'Don't worry,' Lisa said, turning and smiling at the children. 'We'll get you in somehow.'

They climbed out of the car and stood on the pavement; Aisha held back and waited for Lisa and Steve to go up the path first before following with the children. She felt a moment's panic as she went up the path, as though in returning to the house they were returning to their old lives. She could almost believe that Mark was inside waiting for her, furious at what she'd done and ready to punish her.

Steve checked the front door and then went into the garage. Aisha followed, with Sarah and James either side of her, and stopped just inside the up-and-over door. The garage was still brilliantly lit by the overhead florescent strip light which seemed to highlight what had happened and her guilt. The heavy-duty polythene cover from the bike lay in the centre of the garage, the open boxes that had contained his boots and helmet were on the shelf. Mark's discarded nylon overalls, which he'd taken off to try on his leather biker's suit, were beneath the workbench. Further over to the right, she saw the exact spot where she had fallen, where he'd pounced on her and brought her down. Aisha looked at the grey concrete for any telltale sign of blood, but couldn't see any. The children nestled into her side, and she draped an arm round each of their shoulders and held them close.

'I don't suppose there's a window open?' Steve asked.

'No, my husband was very security conscious.'

Apart from the garage, Steve's expression said. He went to the door that led to the kitchen and tried the handle.

'The key is in the lock on the other side,' Aisha said, and gave the children a reassuring squeeze.

Steve bent down and peered through the keyhole, then straightened. 'Wait there,' he said. 'It shouldn't be too difficult to pick the lock.' He winked at James as he went out of the garage and to the police car.

'We're not allowed in here,' James said quietly to Aisha, his face serious.

'It's all right,' she reassured him. 'You're not touching his tools.'

'My son isn't allowed in his father's garage either,' Lisa said, and threw Aisha a muted smile.

Aisha nodded. She looked around at the shelves of neatly labelled jars of nails and screws, the tools hanging in a fastidious line over the cupboards which lined the walls. The garage had always been Mark's domain, his presence now was almost tangible. Once they were in the house, she thought, she would lock the door from the kitchen to the garage, and never set foot in here again. They had no reason to come in here, there was nothing they would need, and the house would feel safer with the interconnecting door secured against what had been Mark's room.

Steve returned holding what looked like a small screwdriver. Lisa joined him at the internal door. He knelt down and Lisa watched as he began prodding and poking the keyhole. A minute later, there was a small click; Steve lowered the handle and the door opened. He stepped into the kitchen, picked up the fallen key and reinserted it in the lock on the inside.

'That's cool,' James said, impressed. Steve smiled.

'Thank you so much,' Aisha said.

'Would you like us to come in and stay for a while?' Lisa asked.

'No, we'll be all right now. Thank you both so much.'

'Have you got someone coming to help you?' Lisa persisted.

'Yes,' Aisha lied.

'Well, if you're sure then. Take care, all of you.' She smiled at the children.

'You'll make it in the force one day,' Steve said to James, ruffling his hair as he passed. James grinned, and the three of them stood together while Steve and Lisa went out through the garage. 'I'll close it,' Steve said, reaching for the up-and-over door.

'Thank you.'

Aisha and the children watched as the garage door slowly lowered, gradually cutting off the dark outside before shuddering the last few inches into position. In silence, the three of them then turned as one and entered the kitchen. Sarah and James stood very close to Aisha as she switched off the light in the garage and then locked the door. She took the key from the lock and, opening a kitchen drawer, slid the key under a pile of tea towels, then closed the drawer.

'Is that for us?' James asked, spying the pans of prepared vegetables and cooked brisket Aisha had left ready on the hob that morning.

Aisha looked at the pans and could hardly believe it was her who had put them there that morning. It was as though a different person had prepared the meal and cleaned the house before going to see the monk, and in a way, it was.

'Yes, but I need to talk to you both first, then I'll make you something to eat.'

Taking a hand in each of hers, she led Sarah and James through to the lounge and sat them down either side of her on the sofa, an arm around each of them. She felt their little bodies warm and yielding, trusting, leaning against her.

'You are big children now,' she began, the words poignantly familiar – the ones she'd used when she'd met them from school and had told them about the monk, 'so I need to tell you something, and I know it will hurt. It will cause you lots of strange feelings, conflicts. We will need to talk a lot.'

'Mum?' Sarah said, her little mouth trembling. 'He's dead, isn't he?'

Aisha looked down into her daughter's eyes, which held a mixture of childhood innocence and adult maturity. 'Yes, darling, he is,' she said softly, and braced herself for the blame that she knew could destroy her relationship with the children forever. For whatever Mark had done, he was their father, and he was dead.

'I'm sorry,' Sarah said slowly. 'But not as sorry as I should be. He won't be able to hurt you anymore will he, Mummy? And I'm not sorry for that. Is that wrong?'

Aisha squeezed her daughter's hand and felt her eyes fill. 'No, love. I'm sure we all feel the same. It's very difficult – very confusing.' She looked down at James, and he rubbed his eyes.

'I'm the same,' he said simply. 'And I'm tired and hungry. Can I have something to eat and go to bed?'

She kissed the top of his head and swallowed hard. 'Shall we talk more in the morning?'

The children nodded solemnly, and James rubbed his eyes again.

Aisha hugged them hard, and as she did, her gaze fell across the room. Everything seemed so alien and distant now Mark was gone. It was as though she was sitting on someone else's sofa, in someone else's lounge: the three of them in a stranger's house, which in many ways, she supposed, they'd always been. She gave the children another hug and then released them.

'Now, if you go and get changed and ready for bed, I'll make you something to eat and bring it up to you,' she said.

'What, in bed?' James asked, astonished.

'Yes, would you like that?'

'But we aren't ...' he began and stopped. Aisha knew he was about to say, 'We aren't allowed to eat upstairs.' It had been one of Mark's many rules – no eating away from the table, not even an apple – and, like most of Mark's rules, Aisha had enforced it, believing it was for everyone's good.

'It's OK,' she said. 'You can have supper in bed tonight, nothing will happen to you. I'm in charge now and I say it's all right.'

Sarah and James looked at her, and she could see that they almost believed it – that their mother was in charge. So much had happened since she'd met them from school that she appeared a different person now.

Sarah and James didn't want to go upstairs alone, and if Aisha was honest she wasn't too keen on the first trip up either. The whole house was like a mausoleum, a monument to Mark; reminders of him and his regime were everywhere. It made her realize just how little about the house had changed since she'd moved in nearly eight years before. He hadn't made any compromises, no alterations to accommodate her – the house and everything in it was, and always had been, his. Such poignant and overwhelming reminders of a husband, so soon after his death, would have reduced another woman to hysterical tears, but the only emotion Aisha felt was utter relief mingled with a residue of fear. For while she was at last safe from another beating, she couldn't throw off the unsettling feeling that Mark wasn't so very far away, and given the right circumstances could appear at any moment and continue where he'd left off.

She went with the children to the foot of the stairs and switched on the landing light from the hall. Then, putting on a brave face for the sake of the children, she led the way up the stairs. First she went into Sarah's bedroom and switched on the light, then James's room, and finally the bathroom. She didn't go into the main bedroom – it was Mark's bedroom and she hadn't slept in it for years and certainly couldn't face it now – she firmly closed the door. In the morning, after she'd slept and felt stronger, she might venture in, but she doubted she could sleep there ever again.

With the upstairs lit, Sarah and James were happy to be left to wash and change, while Aisha returned downstairs to the kitchen. She lifted the lids on the pans of vegetables; she wouldn't cook them now, it was too late, and she doubted any of them could eat a full meal, they were past it. Instead, she strained the brisket, sliced it and laid thick slices between the last of the bread. There was no butter or margarine because Mark never ate sandwiches or toast. But the thick slices of meat would make this feel like a feast for the children. She opened the fridge and found a carton of juice, which was still half-full. Mark liked his freshly squeezed orange juice; it always had first call on her meagre budget. She poured the juice equally between the two glasses for the children, then filled the kettle and set it to boil for a mug of tea for her. There was no milk, but it didn't matter because she was used to drinking black tea – Mark had never taken milk in his tea or coffee so there was never any in the house. Arranging the plates of sandwiches on a tray with the glasses of juice, she carried it upstairs.

Sarah and James were washed and changed and both propped on the pillows in Sarah's bed, waiting for their supper.

'Here we are,' Aisha said, proud that at least she could give them something decent to eat. She placed the tray between them on the bed. 'Try not to spill it on the duvet.'

Their eyes lit up. 'Are you having some?' Sarah asked.

Aisha nodded. 'Later. When you've eaten,' she said from habit; she always made sure the children were fed before she ate.

She kissed the tops of their heads and then sat on the end of the bed as they ravenously ate the sandwiches. The last

Cathy Glass

twenty-four hours were now catching up and Aisha suddenly felt absolutely exhausted. She waited until the children had finished eating and had emptied their glasses of juice, then she lifted the tray off the bed.

'Can I sleep here?' James said snuggling down.

She didn't see why not. 'If Sarah doesn't mind.'

Sarah shook her head, and yawning put her arm around her brother. Tucking them in Aisha kissed them both goodnight. 'Sleep tight,' she said. 'Call me if you need me.' She kissed them again and, leaving the bedroom door open so she would hear them if they called for her, she came out and went downstairs.

In the lounge she suddenly realized how cold the house was and felt the radiator – it was stone cold. Of course the heating would be off, she thought, Mark had it set for an hour in the morning, while he washed and dressed, and two hours in the late evening for when he returned home. The rest of the time the house was freezing; in winter she and the children had often worn their coats to keep warm. *Not anymore*, she thought, *here's something I can change now, and without any fear of a beating!*

She went into the kitchen and to the boiler mounted on the wall at the far end, and peered at the programmer. It was a digital display, with the time showing on a small Perspex screen, and three buttons on the right. It wasn't immediately obvious how to alter the settings, she'd never been allowed to touch it and she had no idea where the instruction sheet was. Then she spotted an additional little button on the left of the box, marked 'Constant'. *That's it,* she thought, *constant.* Constant heat, constant hot water, and even constant peace might all be possible now. She pressed it, the boiler fired, and she heard the radiators creak as the pump sprung into action and the hot water began to circulate. At the same time a familiar angry voice came from behind

216

and made her jump: 'What the hell do you think you're doing? Switch it off. Now!'

She nearly did. Aisha found her finger poised, ready to push the button to switch the boiler off again, before she realized. 'No,' she said out loud, spinning round and confronting the empty space. 'I won't and you can't make me.'

Leaving the programmer on constant and ignoring the boiled kettle and last slice of brisket, Aisha hurried out of the kitchen and into the lounge. What she needed now was sleep more than anything else; she was physically and mentally exhausted. In the lounge she dragged the armchair away from the centre of the room and to one side, where she backed it flat against the wall so that nothing could get behind it. She flopped down. She would sleep now and then tomorrow after she'd slept she'd be able to think what to do. All the lights were on, the children's bedroom door was open so she'd hear them if they woke, and the house was warming up. *Tomorrow*, she thought, *tomorrow ... when I've slept.* She rested her head back and stared at the ceiling as it swam in and out of focus before her eyes closed and she drifted into a fitful sleep.

Twenty-Three

'*Y*ou haven't got his will?' Aisha asked shocked. 'But you're his bank.'

'Yes, but it hasn't been deposited here, I can assure you, Mrs Williams. I have looked personally.'

'Well, can you at least tell me what's in his account, so I've got some idea? I'm desperate.'

'I'm sorry,' the girl on the other end of the phone said. 'Until we've had sight of Probate or Letters of Administration, I can't release any details. Our hands are tied.'

'What am I supposed to do? I've got two children and no money!' Aisha pleaded.

'I'm sorry,' the girl said again. 'If you had an account with us then we could perhaps have arranged a loan. All I can suggest is that you contact the Citizen's Advice or the DHSS. There really is nothing we can do at present.'

'All right,' Aisha said defeated and put down the phone. Of course Mark's bank would want Probate or Letters of Administration before discussing his account with her. She would have known that from all her years in banking had she stopped to think about it. So where on earth was his will then? If he'd even bothered to make one, that is. It was typical of Mark to leave his wife so ill-provided for, she thought. Her mother knew exactly where her father's will was, together with all the paperwork, and £100 emergency money, should he meet an untimely end. Now

218

here she was with no money, and no hope of getting any in the foreseeable future. What was she supposed to do?

Aisha looked at the phone on the hall table as if it was to blame and then turned to her coat on the hall stand. Rummaging first in one pocket and then the other, she pulled out the monk's crumpled five-pound note, plus two twenty-pence pieces which was the change from her bus fare. 'Five pounds and forty pence,' she said out loud.

She knew it took months to process a will, even longer if there wasn't one, and Letters of Administration had to be applied for. How were she and the children supposed to live in the meantime? There was nothing in the house apart from half a packet of cornflakes and the uncooked vegetables on the stove. Worried sick and with a pounding headache Aisha stuffed the money back into her coat pocket and went through to the lounge. Sarah and James were spread on the floor in front of the television where they'd been all morning. Much to the children's amazement – for their father had forbade it – Aisha had switched on the television for them when they'd got up, and here they were still watching two hours later, mesmerized by the colourful cartoons. 'Could you please turn the volume down a little,' she said, 'I'm not feeling so good.'

'Sorry Mum,' Sarah said and took the remote from James.

'Thank you. Keep it low, please. I haven't finished on the phone yet.'

Aisha returned to the hall and slowly picked up the handset. There was nothing else for it, she was going to have to phone her parents and ask them for a loan. She daren't waste her last £5.40 on bus fares to and from the DHSS, apart from which she wasn't feeling at all well. Her head throbbed and she ached all over, probably from the restless night spent in the chair.

Despite the heating being on constant, she'd been so very cold. Perhaps she was sickening for something, she thought, that's all I need!

With the phone in her hand, she went to key in her parents' number and then realized with a stab of guilt that she'd forgotten the area code; it was so long since she'd phoned them – so long since they'd spoken. Heaving out the telephone directory from under the phone she flicked through the pages to the list of area codes. She ran her finger down until she found her parents' code and then stopped. What on earth was she going to say to them, suddenly phoning after all this time? What would they say? What would they think? She knew she needed to apologize, but after that, what?

Taking a deep breath she braced herself and carefully keyed in the code followed by her parents' telephone number. She could hear the children's cartoon on the television coming from the lounge. Her heart raced and her stomach churned as the phone rang and rang but no one answered. *Perhaps they're out?* she thought. *Or perhaps they've even moved house? Would they have told her?* She thought they would.

Cutting the line she tried again, pressing in the numbers slowly to make sure there was no mistake. This time it was answered immediately. 'Hello, 5644.' It was her mother's voice, hesitant and out of breath. Her mother's voice. Tears sprung to Aisha's eyes. She had almost forgotten she had a mother, let alone one she could phone. She tried to speak but nothing came out. 'Hello?' her mother said again.

'Mum,' Aisha finally said. 'It's me, Aisha.'

'Aisha?' her mother repeated, unsure.

'Yes Mum. It's me. I'm sorry it's been so long but I need your help. Mark's dead and I haven't any money. Do you think you and

Dad could lend me some?' She knew it was coming out all wrong but she hadn't the presence of mind to put it differently – more politely. It went quiet on the other end of the phone. 'Mum? Are you still there?'

There was another silence and then her mother's small, uncertain voice again. 'Aisha? Is that really you?'

'Yes, it's me. I'm sorry it's been so long, but Mark was killed in an accident yesterday and I haven't any money. I'm desperate. Can you help?'

'Killed? In an accident?' she repeated in the same faltering voice. 'Yesterday? Are the children safe?'

'Yes. They are. They're all right.'

'And Mark is dead, you say?'

'Yes.'

It went quiet again. Aisha heard the phone clunk as it was set down and then again as it was picked up. There was a short silence followed by her father's voice, authoritative and demanding. 'Aisha, is that you? What's going on? Your mother is in tears. You say Mark is dead?'

'Yes, Father, he was killed in an road accident yesterday. The children and I are unhurt, but I haven't any money to buy food, can I borrow some? Please.' She could have simply thrown herself on her parents and asked for help, but having spent so many years obsessed and worrying about money to feed and clothe the children, this single thought still dominated.

There was a long pause during which Aisha could hear her mother crying quietly, then their muffled voices, before her father came on the line again, formal and direct. 'Aisha, if as you say, you have been widowed, we have a duty to help. We will give you what you ask for. But our grandchildren, Aisha? Why did you reject us and not let us see them for all these years?'

Her heart clenched. 'I don't know,' she said lamely. 'I really don't know now. I think it had something to do with Mark. I can't think straight at present.' She stared into space and searched for the answers, but now Mark had gone so too had his threats, intimidation, and the reason she'd behaved as she had.

She heard her father's sharp intake of breath as he used to do when she had displeased him as a child. 'We will help you. How much do you need?'

'I'd be grateful for anything. You don't have to see me if you don't want to. You could put the money in the post.'

'Aisha,' he said firmly, 'we will come to your house. I will give you some money and we will see our grandchildren at the same time. I appreciate you have been bereaved and are not yourself, but I expect you to show us the same civility as you would any visitor. Is that clear?'

Visitor? she was about to say, *we're not allowed visitors, didn't you know?* But she realized that was no longer true. 'Yes, Father, thank you so much. When?'

'We'll be there in an hour. Goodbye Aisha.'

'Goodbye,' she said, and put the phone down.

She stood still for a moment, trying to take in the conversation she'd just had with her parents after all this time, and then went into the lounge where the children were as she'd left them, on the floor in front of the television. 'Sarah, James,' she said, 'your grandparents are coming to see us; they are on their way. You'd better get dressed quickly.'

The children looked up at her from the floor with a mixture of surprise and delight. 'Grandma and Granddad?' they said together. 'Coming here?'

'Yes, you know – my parents,' she clarified, unsure if they remembered who they were.

'Have I met them?' James asked.

'Yes, but it was so long ago, you probably don't remember. You were only little.'

'I can remember them, just,' Sarah said. 'I liked them, they were kind.'

'Yes, they are very kind people.' She swallowed the lump rising in her throat. 'Now go and get dressed, please, and make sure you have a wash.'

Sarah and James jumped up and scampered off upstairs, chattering excitedly about the forthcoming visit of their grandma and granddad. Aisha looked at the mess they'd left on the floor: cereal bowls with crumbs from the cornflakes they'd eaten dry; half-drunk glasses of water, the cushions from the sofa dotted on the floor where they'd sat watching television. She sighed; they were only children but at present everything was such an effort. She stooped and picked up the cushions and returned them to the sofa, then collected the bowls, spoons and glasses, and switching off the television, carried them through to the kitchen. She dumped them in the sink together with her mug of half-drunk black tea, and returned to the lounge and sat on the sofa.

Sarah and James reappeared, washed and dressed, and looking as presentable as was possible in their worn-out weekend clothes. The children went to the bay window and stood side by side behind the net curtains watching passing cars and looking out for their grandparents. Every so often James called out, 'Is it a black Mondeo? A green BMW? A red Astra?' wanting to be the first to spot his grandparents and showing off his knowledge of cars.

'I don't know, love,' Aisha said over and over again, exhausted. 'Wait until a car stops outside the house and then call me. I'm

going to close my eyes for a bit. Wake me, if I fall asleep.' She
rested her head back and massaged her temples to try and ease
the throbbing. If she could just sleep for a while, perhaps her
head would clear and then everything wouldn't seem such a
burden. She heard the children's hushed tones continue their
commentary and then fade as her eyes closed. A little while later,
she came to with a start as James squealed with excitement.

'Mum! It's a blue Ford! They're here!'

'He's right, Mum,' Sarah added. 'They've parked outside.'

Aisha hauled herself to her feet and running her hands over
her hair, joined the children behind the net curtains at the
window. She should probably have brushed her hair and had a
shower but the energy required for all that was beyond her at
present. At least she'd changed out of the bloodstained cardigan
she'd been wearing the day before. She couldn't remember doing
it but she must have taken it off when they had got back late last
night — it was still lying on the bathroom floor.

The three of them watched as the doors to the car slowly
opened and her parents climbed out. Aisha's heart lurched at the
sight of their once familiar outlines now distanced by the passing
of time. How they'd aged, she thought, how different they
seemed now, she would barely have recognized them if she'd
passed them in the street. Her father was dressed in a suit and tie;
he never wore casual clothes when he left the house. Her mother
was wearing a dark green sari under a three-quarter-length coat.
As Aisha watched she saw her pick up the hem and shake it free
in a quaint little gesture that she now remembered from her
childhood. Once they were out of the car her father went round
testing all the doors, a habit Aisha had once found irritating but
now seemed strangely comforting. She watched him offer his
arm to her mother and they began slowly towards the garden

gate. Her father was much thinner, and his usual upright shoulders were now slightly stooped, making him appear even shorter. Her mother had gained weight, but walked slowly and seemed to be using her father's arm for support. And her black hair, which always used to be plaited, was now grey and knotted in a tight bun on her neck. She was carrying a shopping bag, and if Aisha wasn't mistaken, it was the same bag she'd brought with her to the hospital when Sarah had been born. How long was it since she'd seen them? She really had no idea. They'd seen James as a baby, but not at hospital as she'd only been in one night. Did they come here? She thought maybe once, perhaps when James had been a toddler. Then there was their unexpected visit when Mark had sent them away, and they'd never been again. Aisha couldn't remember exactly when that was, for like most of the last seven years, it had blurred into a fog of beatings and survival.

Aisha waited until they rang the bell before going to answer the door. Her mother was standing just behind her father in the porch; they both looked sombre, lined and small. 'Hello,' Aisha said as lightly as she could, trying to raise a smile. 'Good to see you, please come in.' She stood aside to let them pass. She wasn't sure if she should kiss them, but they made no attempt to kiss her so she didn't.

Her father nodded stiffly as he walked by her into the hall. 'Aisha,' he said formally and that was all.

Her mother followed him in and glanced in Aisha's direction, her face pained and lined; then she looked at Sarah and James standing awkwardly further down the hall.

'Say hello to your grandparents,' Aisha encouraged as she closed the front door.

'Hello,' the children said and smiled shyly.

Her father went up to them and leant forwards so the children could kiss his cheek. Her mother joined him and kissed Sarah and James unselfconsciously. 'Hello loves,' she said in the same small voice Aisha had heard on the phone. She sniffed and Aisha wondered if she was crying, but she had her back to her so she couldn't see.

'Shall we go into the lounge?' Aisha said, and nodded to Sarah to lead the way.

Once in the lounge, they all stood about awkwardly, avoiding each other's gaze. Aisha thought how strange it was seeing her parents in the house after all this time. 'Would you like a drink?' she offered. 'I'm afraid it can only be water or black tea. We haven't anything else.'

'No, thank you,' her father said tightly. 'We don't need a drink.'

Aisha shrugged. 'Well, sit down then, won't you?' She waved to the sofa. 'Shall I take your coat, Mother?'

Aisha waited while her mother slipped off her coat and then handed it to her without meeting her eyes. Her parents perched side by side on the sofa while Aisha hung her mother's coat on the hall stand and then returned to sit opposite them in the armchair. James and Sarah hovered, uncertain, and then came and sat on the floor beside her feet. There was another uncomfortable silence as Aisha looked at her mother and she in turn looked at the children. Her father sat very still, his gaze concentrated on the floor.

'Thank you for coming,' Aisha said at last. 'I'm sorry it's been so long.' She paused. Her father shifted position, crossing one leg over the other, while her mother looked at the children.

'So, how are you both?' she tried again. 'Keeping well, I hope?' She knew it sounded ridiculous after all this time but what else could she say?

Her father looked up sharply. 'How are we? Aisha, how do you think we are? You shut us out of your lives for years and then suddenly phone with all this.' He waved his arm as though encompassing all the problems she'd ever had.

'I should think you're pretty angry,' she said. 'I would be. But if it's any consolation, things haven't exactly been good here either.'

Her father shot her a warning glance, reminding her he was her father and expected respect. 'I'm not talking about now,' he said. 'I realize you've suffered a dreadful bereavement, and I'm truly sorry. But all this time, Aisha. Don't you think you owe us an explanation, if not an apology? After all we've done for you. How could you treat us so cruelly?'

She looked at him carefully. *Cruelly*, now there was a word she understood and knew a lot about. More than either of her parents could ever begin to imagine. She knew she should open up and explain, but not now. She hadn't the strength now and wouldn't know where to begin.

'I really don't know how I treated you so badly,' she said quietly. 'I'm sorry.' And she was sorry. Sorry she'd hurt them, sorry she'd phoned and got them involved, sorry she'd met Mark, and sorry she'd ever been born. 'Sorry!' she said again with more force than she should.

Her mother began to cry and her father looked at her accusingly. 'Now see what you've done.' He put an arm around his wife and comforted her while Sarah and James watched them, intrigued. They'd never seen a man comforting his wife before; hitting, shouting, yes, but not actually trying to make her feel better. Aisha saw the look on their faces and could have wept.

'I'm sorry, Mum,' she said more gently. 'I didn't mean to upset you.' She wanted to go over and hug her parents but she didn't think she had the right to, not after all these years and the way she'd behaved.

After a few moments her mother took a lace handkerchief from the waistband of her sari, and drying her eyes, looked at Aisha. 'We've come here to help, love,' she said gently. 'Not to be angry with you. I've brought you and the children something to eat. It's not much, but it's all I had ready.'

'Thank you, Mum,' Aisha said quietly. 'That was kind of you.'

She and the children watched as her mother reached down into the shopping bag at her feet, and unzipping it, took out two polythene containers and a glass bottle with a screw top. 'It's the *dhal* you used to like, but it's not so spicy. Your father doesn't like it too hot now. And a *chappati* – I made them last night – and some mango squash. It's all I had ready. Would the children like some?'

Aisha looked at her mother as she meekly offered up the food she used to lovingly prepare for her as a child. Like many mothers, food and love were inextricably linked. The years fell away and Aisha remembered her parents' visit to the hospital when Sarah had been born, and the food she'd brought with her then in that same shopping bag. She remembered how proud and excited they'd been and how much they were looking forward to being grandparents and idolizing their grandchildren. But that had never happened and it was her fault.

'Thank you, Mum,' Aisha said, and touched Sarah's shoulder, who stood and went over to her grandmother.

'Thank you, Gran,' Sarah said smiling and took the boxes. James joined her and they went through to the kitchen.

'Will she be able to reach the bowls and glasses?' her mother asked.

Aisha nodded. They heard Sarah open a kitchen cupboard and take out the crockery, followed by Sarah saying how nice the food was and James agreeing. Aisha looked at her mother and could see how pleased she was. Her father seemed to have softened a little too, she thought. The three of them were quiet; it was so difficult to know what to say. Then her mother broke the silence, and turning to her husband she said quietly, 'Please give her the money, Ranjith.'

Aisha watched as her father reached into his inside jacket pocket and took out his wallet; it was black leather with his initials in gold. Aisha remembered her mother giving it to him for his sixtieth birthday years ago. Opening the wallet, he stood and came towards her. 'Here is a hundred pounds, Aisha, to see you through.' He held out the twenty-pound notes.

Aisha stared. She'd never seen so much money, not for a long while. 'I don't need all that,' she said. 'Ten or twenty pounds will be plenty.'

'Nonsense,' her mother said kindly. 'That goes nowhere nowadays. Take it, Aisha and let us know if you need any more.'

Her father nodded and pushed the money towards her. 'It will be months before things are sorted out. You can't live on nothing.' Aisha stared at him still shocked, for that was exactly what they had been doing – living on nothing.

He placed the notes in her hand. 'Thank you,' she said quietly. 'I'll pay you back as soon as I can.'

'Don't worry about that now,' he said and returned to sit beside her mother.

Aisha looked at the two of them sitting side by side on the sofa, loving, supportive and respectful of each other, even after a lifetime of being married. *That's how it should have been for me,* she thought bitterly and her bottom lip trembled and her head throbbed.

'Do you want to talk about it?' her mother suddenly asked, almost as if she suspected some of what had been going on.

Aisha shook her head and felt her eyes mist. 'No, Mum, not yet.'

'Well, when you do, you know where we are,' she said tenderly. 'Is there anything else you need? How will you manage – organizing the funeral and everything? There's so much to do.'

Aisha shrugged, she hadn't really thought that far ahead. She'd been too worried about trying to find some money so they could eat to think about the funeral. Sarah's voice called from the kitchen, 'Mum! Can we have seconds?'

'Yes, of course. Have as much as you want,' Aisha said.

Her mother smiled, pleased that they were enjoying her cooking as Aisha had done. Then glancing at her husband she sat forward earnestly. 'Aisha, we won't stay long now but I was wondering … would it help if Sarah and James came back with us and stayed for a few days? It would be easier for you and we would like it so much, wouldn't we?' She looked at her husband for confirmation.

Her father nodded. 'I'd be pleased to have them,' he said. Then, looking straight at Aisha: 'But can you not tell me why you haven't let us see them before? And why you never returned our calls? And the accident? You've said nothing about that. What happened and where?'

'It was on the motorway,' she began and stopped. She met his gaze and the years rolled back. Suddenly she was a little girl again, vulnerable but with her father to protect her. It took all her self-control not to tell him but she feared the outcome. For seated here with her parents and with the children's chatter coming from the kitchen, a normality had returned as it had done briefly in the car. It was impossible to imagine, let alone explain how she had got into the position she had, and then done what she had done. 'One day,' she said softly. 'But I can't tell you now.'

He nodded slowly. 'You are a grown woman, Aisha. I must accept that, although I won't pretend we haven't been hurt.'

'I know, Dad, believe me I know. We've all been hurt in this.'

She stood and wiping the back of her hand over her eyes went over and kissed them both, then went through to the kitchen where the children had just finished eating. 'Gran has asked if you would like to go and stay with her and Grandpa for a few days?' she said.

Sarah and James looked at her wide-eyed and amazed – the invitation which was the norm for many children was a first for them.

'What? Sleep there with my teddy bear?' James asked.

'Yes, if you'd like to? Just for a few days.'

'Will you be all right alone?' Sarah asked, as always concerned for her mother.

'Yes, things are different now. I'll be fine, and we can phone each other every day.'

They scrambled down from the breakfast stools and went through to the lounge. 'I'm coming to stay with you, Grandpa.' James said squeezing himself between his grandparents on the sofa.

Sarah, more reserved, hung back. 'Are you sure you'll be all right alone?' she whispered to her mother.

'Yes, I'm sure. Now you go and talk to your grandma while I go upstairs and pack a bag for you and James.' Finally reassured, Sarah sat on the sofa, and as Aisha left the lounge she heard her mother asking Sarah if she enjoyed school and Sarah saying she did.

Upstairs, Aisha went to the cupboard on the landing where she knew there was an old holdall that had once been Mark's. Taking it out she unzipped it and going through to Sarah's room lay it on her bed. She opened the door to the built-in wardrobe and began searching through. James's clothes were in here too as there wasn't any furniture in his room except for the bed. But as she looked she realized just how few clothes the children owned. Apart from their school uniforms, which had had first call on any money, and the clothes they were wearing now, there wasn't much else. She found a dress for Sarah that still fitted, a pair of joggers with a top for James, and a few pairs of pants and socks for each of them. Folding these into the holdall she picked up the children's nightwear from Sarah's bed and put that in too. Then James's teddy and Sarah's rag doll which were in the bed. Aisha went through to the bathroom, and taking their toothbrushes and face flannels returned and tucked them into the side compartment of the bag so they wouldn't dampen the clothes. Zipping up the holdall she carried it downstairs, embarrassed that her parents would shortly be unpacking it and seeing the contents. Leaving the bag in the hall she went through to the lounge where Sarah and James were now chatting easily with her parents. If her parents wondered why their grandchildren weren't more upset at having just lost their father they didn't say, and it crossed Aisha's mind again that possibly they had some idea of what had been going on in their short lives.

'I've packed what they have,' Aisha said to her mother, 'but I'm afraid there isn't much. The rest is in the wash,' she lied. 'If I give you some of this money Dad gave me, could you buy them another outfit each, please?'

She put her hand into her cardigan pocket ready to draw out the notes but her mother said, 'Keep that, we'll take care of some new clothes. It'll be a nice treat to take them shopping, won't it Ranjith?' Her father nodded.

'What about school on Monday?' her mother now asked. 'Shall I phone the school and tell them what's happened and that the children won't be going for a while?'

'Yes,' Aisha said, again having not thought that far ahead. 'That's probably what we should do.' She felt relief that finally someone else was in control and knew what to do. 'Thanks, Mum. That would be very helpful.'

'We won't have another accident, will we?' James suddenly asked, concerned.

'No,' her father said, patting his shoulder reassuringly. 'I'm a very careful driver. I've been driving since I was seventeen and I've never had an accident.'

'Cor, that's a long time,' James said and his grandfather smiled.

Her parents stood and the children did likewise; they all went into the hall. Aisha hugged the children, and Sarah asked again: 'You will be OK without us, Mummy?'

'Yes, I will, don't worry. I've lots to do, and I'll phone you every day. It'll be like a little holiday for you.' But as soon as she'd said it she knew the comparison was futile, for the children had never been on holiday – something else they'd been denied.

Aisha gave the children a final kiss and hug each and then hugged and kissed her parents. They didn't resist. Sarah took hold of her grandma's hand, while James stood proudly beside his grandfather. They went out the front door and Aisha went with them and then waited on the pavement as her mother settled the children under their seat belts in the rear of the car, and her father put their bag in the boot. Her heart ached at the sight of her parents finally allowed to be grandparents – something they should have been doing for years. As her mother straightened, Aisha threw her arms around her. 'I love you,' she said. 'I've always loved you.'

'We love you too, darling, take care and look after yourself. We'll speak soon.'

Aisha stayed on the pavement and waved until the car was out of sight. Then she returned up the path and into the house where she shut and bolted the front door. How quiet and lonely the house now seemed without Sarah and James. She wandered around the downstairs unsure of what she should be doing, or feeling, and then sat in the armchair and rested her head back. Thoughts came and went as she stared into space and the wintry light of afternoon slowly faded into dark. Just twenty-four hours before she'd fled this room in fear of her life. And although she'd run in terror, aware of what Mark would do if he caught her, her conscience had been clear. Now she carried a weight so heavy that if she didn't tell someone soon it would very likely destroy her and drive her mad with guilt.

Twenty-Four

*A*isha woke to the sound of knocking followed by the ring of a bell. It was growing louder, more insistent. *Bang. Bang. Ring. Ring.* What a noise, she thought as she surfaced, it was enough to wake the dead. Her eyes opened. The room was now lit by the morning sun and she realized that someone was at the door, calling through the letterbox. 'Mrs Williams? Hello? Are you in there? It's Inspector Calder, Stan Calder. Police.'

Aisha jolted forwards out of the chair, across the lounge and down the hall. Sliding the bolts, she flung open the front door and stared at the two of them. Dishevelled and disorientated from sleep, panic gripped her. 'What's the matter? The children? They're not hurt?'

'No,' the inspector said. 'That's not why we're here. I'm sure they're fine.' Relief flooded through her. 'I'm sorry we frightened you,' he said, 'but we have a few questions about the accident. This is my colleague, WPC Lewis. May we come in?'

'Oh yes, yes of course, come in,' Aisha flustered. 'The children are staying with my parents, I thought something had happened to them.'

Leaving the inspector and his WPC to close the door, Aisha stumbled back down the hall and into the lounge, dizzy from waking so suddenly and then standing too quickly. She returned to the chair. 'I'm sorry. I must have dropped off. I haven't been sleeping. Do you have the time?'

WPC Lewis looked at her watch. 'It's ten thirty. Are you all right, Mrs Williams?' she asked, concerned. 'Is there anything I can get you? You shouldn't really be alone at a time like this.'

'No, I'm fine, really,' she said. 'What was it you wanted?'

'Just a few points to clarify. It's nothing to worry about.'

As they sat on the sofa Aisha saw them glance around the room, taking it all in. She felt rough – all night sitting in the armchair, drifting in and out of consciousness, you could hardly call it sleep. And the nightmares that had plagued her while she slept and had continued each time she awoke: the shadow, the familiar outline of Mark, accompanied by his voice. She could almost have believed he was there, accusing her, like a revenging ghost.

'It won't take long,' the inspector said. 'It's more a formality.'

Aisha thought there was now a certain formality in his manner, compared to the last time she'd seen him – at the police station when she'd made a statement after the accident and he'd been so kind and thoughtful. When had that been? she wondered. Yesterday or the day before? She really didn't know; she was losing track of time, with no sleep and all the worry.

The inspector cleared his throat and leant slightly forwards on the sofa. Aisha looked at him, and tried to focus and understand what he was saying. 'Mrs Williams, there are a few points in your statement I need to clarify, if you don't mind. You said it was the first time in years you had driven. Could you tell me how long exactly?'

Why did he want to know that? She thought, immediately going on guard. And what was the right answer? She'd had plenty of practice in the past trying to find the right answer, but still hadn't perfected it. 'Five or six years, I think,' she said. 'We sold my car when the children were little. Mark said we didn't need it.' *Be careful,* she warned herself, and tried to clear her head. 'We didn't need a second car,' she said evenly. 'Living so close to the shops and tube, there was no point. Why? Is there a problem?'

'No, just clarification.' He nodded and the WPC wrote on the pad she had opened on the arm of the chair. 'And your husband wanted to go with you on your first outing to make sure you were safe?'

'Yes, that's correct. Mark thought it would give me confidence if I knew he was following. He also wanted to try out his new bike.'

'Not the best choice of evenings,' the inspector said dryly. 'The road conditions were atrocious. We had three separate RTAs on the M25 that night.'

She wasn't sure if it was a statement or a question but the inspector appeared to be waiting for her reply. 'I know,' she agreed and shifted in the chair. 'I was worried before we left. I said we should wait. The weather might have been better over the weekend.'

She stopped and glanced at the WPC, who had her eyes down and was still writing. Then she looked again at the inspector who was looking at her as though expecting her to say something else, but what? More detail? She didn't know. She wasn't very good at lying, she'd never perfected the art; unlike Mark.

'I should have insisted we waited,' she added. 'I knew I would remember how to drive. You don't forget that skill in five years, but Mark hadn't been on a motorbike in over twenty years. I should have stopped him and refused to go.' She tried to read the inspector's expression but it was impossible.

'I know how painful this is,' he said, lowering his voice respectfully. 'Try to remember it *was* an accident. We won't keep you much longer.' He paused again but clearly hadn't finished yet. She shifted again in the chair and tried to concentrate. 'Mrs Williams, could you explain exactly what happened in the moments leading up to the accident? I know you covered it in your statement, but I'm trying to get a more detailed picture.'

Aisha felt a little nerve start to twitch in her neck. 'I'll try,' she said, 'but it's all a blur ... it was dark and it all happened so quickly. I remember seeing Mark in the wing mirror, he was travelling a few cars behind me, three, I think. The car in front of me slowed to about fifty and I saw a space in the middle lane so I indicated and pulled out. Mark must have been trying to over-take at the same time and ...' She stopped and in the silence she heard the horrendous crunch of metal and splintering glass and felt the jolt as the car wheels went over the bike, just as it had done that night.

'I'm sorry, Inspector, that's all I can remember,' she said.

The inspector nodded sympathetically. 'Thank you. That's more or less what the other witnesses said. And the car was owned and maintained by your husband?'

'Yes, as far as I know.'

'We're having the car and the bike checked by forensics for any sign of faulty brakes and steering. Another formality, I'm not expecting to find anything.'

No, you won't find anything wrong with the car or bike, Aisha thought, *although wouldn't it be wonderful if you did – proof that it wasn't my fault after all!* The inspector had stopped talking now and was looking at her. She wondered if she was supposed to add anything, but couldn't think what, so she just nodded.

'Well, that's it then, Mrs Williams,' he said. 'Thank you. I'm sorry to have had to call on you at this time. I can file my report now.'

Aisha didn't think she'd added much beyond what she'd said in her original statement but he was standing now ready to go. 'We've notified your husband's parents,' he said, 'as you asked us. 'Is there anyone else who should be informed?'

Aisha thought. 'His work, I suppose.'

'We'll see to it first thing on Monday. Anyone else?'

'I don't think so.' In truth she'd no idea who Mark knew or anything about his life outside the house. His life had always been separate from hers and the children's so she didn't know who should be informed he was dead. But she could hardly admit that to the inspector.

'We'll leave you to it then.' The WPC also stood, closing her notepad. 'Thank you for your time, Mrs Williams.'

The inspector nodded and the two of them began towards the hall. But as they passed the bureau on the way out of the lounge the inspector paused and looked at the photograph. 'Is this Mark?' he said, picking it up.

'Yes. It was taken soon after we met.' Aisha looked at the photograph he now held: her and Mark seated side by side on the bench beneath the oak tree. 'Mark stopped a passer-by and asked if he'd mind taking our photograph,' she said quietly. 'We were so much in love then, Inspector, I thought it would last forever.'

The inspector looked at her, his grey eyes reflecting empathy. 'I lost my own dear wife last year, after nearly thirty years of marriage. The hurt fades, but it never completely disappears. At least your children are safe.'

'Yes, thank God they are. I'd die if anything happened to them.'

'One last thing,' the inspector said, returning the photograph to the bureau. 'I know it sounds trivial, but I will need to see your driving licence and the car's insurance at some point. If you have them to hand, I can take them with me now if that's easiest.'

Aisha stared at him. 'I've no idea where they are, Inspector. My husband looked after all the paperwork.'

'Don't worry. You can put them in the post, save you a trip to the station.' He nodded a goodbye and continued into the hall where the WPC was waiting. Aisha followed them to the front door. 'Thank you for your time,' he said again. 'Look after yourself. I'll be in touch.'

She smiled weakly and watched them go; then closed the door and drew the bolts. She stood in the hall, her mind racing. Her driving licence? The car's insurance? Where were they? She didn't have a clue. She hadn't seen her driving licence since she'd moved in, and she'd never seen Mark's car insurance – there'd been no need as she never drove the car. And a familiar and threatening voice returned – the one that had told her not to turn on the heating and had haunted her during the night: *Now you've done it. You weren't insured to drive my car. They'll know you took it without permission and that'll be the end of you and your story!*

She spun round to confront him but the space behind was empty. There was only one thing to do, she thought, find the insurance and prove him wrong.

Twenty-Five

*S*hirts. She had never seen so many shirts and most of them were brand new! Half a dozen were still in their cellophane wrappers, with matching ties laid diagonally across the chest. There was every shade of blue, grey and beige, to match his suits and casual jackets. The ones Mark had worn had been washed, pressed and folded, and looked as new as those in the packets. 'I wonder what silly sod spent hours ironing these,' Aisha said out loud. And a now familiar voice came back: *You did. You stupid fool. Repeatedly. Because, as usual, you could never get it right.*

Aisha yanked out the drawer as far as it would and, scooping up the shirts, dumped them in the bin liner. It was already half-full and was going to the charity shop, together with the two bin liners she'd already filled. She hadn't intended clearing his things out now, it had happened as a result of looking for his car insurance, her licence, and hopefully his will. But far from giving her some relief as she hoped it might, being in his bedroom and going through his belongings had made her grow increasingly agitated and angry, as though in disturbing Mark's clothes she was disturbing him.

Closing this drawer she opened the one below. She gazed at the meticulously neat piles of underpants, which had been bought by his mother from Marks and Spencer and sent in the post each Christmas. Although Mark hardly saw his parents, his mother still sent him pants and socks every year. Aisha received a headscarf and the children a ten-pound note each, which had been a lifesaver and went on food.

'As if you weren't old enough to buy your own sodding pants!' Aisha cried out loud, tearing off another bin liner. 'Allowing your mother to buy you pants at your age! That's weird.' She grabbed the pants in handfuls and stuffed them in the bin liner.

In the same drawer, to the right, lay piles of his white cotton handkerchiefs. Dozens and dozens, starched and ironed to perfection. Three piles were perfect triangles with points so sharp you could cut yourself. The other two piles were squares, with their edges exactly aligned. Mark always had three clean handkerchiefs each and every day, triangles in the jacket pockets – breast and inside pocket, and a square one in his trouser pocket ready to shake out if he sneezed. Three a day, every day, rarely used, but crumpled and left for her to wash and iron, just the same. Careful not to disturb their shape, for she hadn't wasted hours to have them creased now, she took them out and laid them in the rubbish sack, on top of his underwear. And as she did she remembered the handkerchief he'd used to mop the droplets of rainwater from his face on their first date. It cut through her like a knife, for to think of the Mark she had met and loved was more than she could bear.

Closing this drawer, Aisha slowly stood, and then went to the double wardrobe, which was solely Mark's. It was crammed full of his suits, hanging lifeless in their polythene jackets like Bluebeard's women. Mark liked his suits, he thought he cut a dash in his suits; a ladies' man, a man about town: a cad, Aisha thought. He wore his suits in strict rotation, a new one every weekday. He took them to the dry-cleaner on a Saturday morning and he collected the five from the previous week at the same time. A wardrobe full of suits. Twenty-five? Thirty? She'd no idea.

Unhooking them from the rail a couple at a time, Aisha folded them in half and laid them in bags for the charity shop. Soon, another three bags were full.

With the rail in the wardrobe clear, she could now see the full extent of his footwear: a four-tiered rack of shiny leather shoes, sitting obediently in pairs as though under starter's orders. 'Four racks, each containing six pairs of shoes,' she counted out loud. 'That makes twenty-four. And not your mass-produced, high-street rubbish either. Oh no, yours had to be handmade by a cobbler in the City.' Aisha had no idea how much they'd cost, and it was probably better she didn't know. She reached in and took out the first pair and ran her hands over the smooth soft leather. You could tell they were good quality by their rich, deep shine, and their suppleness. She bent the toe up and watched it spring back, unmarked, without a crease.

'How many pairs did the children and I have?' she said, stuffing the shoes into another bag. 'One each. That's all. And even those, we couldn't afford to have repaired. Fuck you! You bastard. Well, you won't be needing your precious shoes now. Not in the state you're in!'

With the shoe rack clear, she tied the tops of the bags, sat back on her haunches and surveyed them. Some lucky bargain hunter was going to find a real prize in the charity shop. Then it occurred to her that Mark owned a newer, more expensive piece of footwear – the boots he'd been wearing at the time of the accident. She wondered if they were still on his feet. Did they put corpses in the morgue with boots on? She didn't know. But even if they didn't, no one was going to be interested in bloodstained boots, even if they were expensive and had only been worn for a few hours. Stacking the bags along the landing, she returned to the bedroom and looked around. She was doing well, progressing quickly, though she admitted it helped not having the children home. It was surprising, she thought, how little time it took to remove someone from a room when you put your mind to it and got down to the job in hand. A good deal less time than it took to remove them from your life, she thought.

Ignoring the small cabinet which contained her own meagre assortment of clothes, she opened the door to the large built-in cupboard. Like all the other drawers and cupboards in the bedroom it had been Mark's and he had told her to keep out. Aisha remembered how she'd obeyed Mark's order as though the doors might have been booby-trapped. *Don't you dare go in there! No dear, I won't.* And she hadn't, ever, even when he was out of the house, so great was his power. Inside the cupboard a matching set of empty suitcases was stacked at the bottom, and Aisha thought they may as well stay there for now. Beside the cases was a brand new set of golf clubs and two similarly pristine squash rackets. She remembered they had 'taken Mark's fancy' years ago so he had treated himself, but they'd never been used. Aisha thought she might be able to sell them later, and raise some much-needed cash. She moved them to one side and revealed a box of Christmas decorations – bought for their first Christmas together and untouched ever since. *Christmas,* she thought bitterly, *some joke Christmas was. There wasn't much peace on earth in their house.* On the top shelf was another cardboard box and it looked vaguely familiar. Aisha reached up and carefully slid it down.

Squatting on the floor, she peeled off the browned Sellotape and lifted the lid. With a flash of recognition, almost déjà vu in its intensity, she realized it was her box, one of the ones she'd packed when she'd left home and had moved in with Mark after their marriage. She took the top item and unwrapped it from the old newspaper, and discovered Tina, her favourite doll. The next parcel contained half a dozen little china elephants she had collected as a child, and the next a babushka doll her father had given her. Aisha delved deeper and found some old paperwork: greeting cards – twenty-first birthday and graduation – bank statements from years ago, her birth certificate, and postcards from India tied with a ribbon. And yes! Eureka! Here was her driving licence! It was the old-style paper type, and she unfolded it and read the print. She had passed her test when she was eighteen and of course it was still valid, it ran until she was seventy! *Terrific,* she thought, *that should keep the inspector partially happy at least. Thank goodness.*

Closing the flaps on the box (she hadn't time for a trip down memory lane now), she tucked the licence into her pocket, and leaving this box to one side, returned to the built-in wardrobe. There was a new digital radio still in its box on the shelf – another 'it took my fancy' purchase of Mark's, and a Nike bag with new sports towels in it, but no file, box or folder that could conceivably contain his paperwork. Closing the door to the wardrobe, and buoyed up by the discovery of one essential item, Aisha tore off another bin liner and went through to the bathroom. She didn't expect to find the car's insurance in the bathroom, obviously, but she wanted to clear it of his things while she was still in the mood. There was too much of him in the bathroom, too many personal items; Mark had been clean if nothing else. And the smell of his damn aftershave and deodorant still pervaded the house as though he was there and using it. *Well, not anymore,* she thought.

The mirrored wall cabinet was too high for her to see in properly – it had also been banned from her use too – but it was where most of his toiletries were. Aisha stood on tiptoe, slid open the doors and peered in. It was stacked to overflowing with deodorants, aftershaves, colognes, and a very expensive male French perfume which Mark had bought from Harrods when he'd felt like treating himself. No wonder the house reeked of his aftershave with this lot in the cupboard, she thought. Holding the rubbish sack open with one hand, Aisha ran her other hand behind the neat lines of bottles, aerosol cans and jars, and flipped them forwards. Metal collided with glass as they landed in the bag, making a merry tune, and one she found quite satisfying.

On top of the cabinet, Aisha could see two electric shavers, still in their boxes and hardly used. Why Mark had needed two electric shavers when he mostly wet-shaved, she had never understood, but like everything he bought for himself, it had to be the latest and the best. Jumping up she flipped them down and caught them in mid-air. They were impersonal enough to be given away, or even sold if she knew someone who would buy them. She placed them on the floor beside the bin bag and then turned to the towel rail. It contained his towels, bath and hand, folded precisely in half and half again, deep blue and luxuriously soft. She and the children had never been allowed to use his towels and had had to make do with an old one – one shared between three – which was so old that it would have been relegated to the dog's basket, if they'd been allowed a dog. Aisha tugged his towels off the rail and stuffed them into the rubbish bag. A waste, but she could never have brought herself to use them, even if they were thoroughly laundered. Last but not least was his electric toothbrush, mounted on the wall to the side of the washbasin. She lifted it from its stand and dropped it into the bag, knotting it securely. She would have to find a screwdriver and remove the wall bracket later.

Straightening, she caught sight of her reflection in the mirror over the hand basin. God, she looked a mess, no wonder her parents and the inspector had done a double take when they'd first seen her. Her hair, which she hadn't brushed since the accident, was now straggled half in and half out of the plait. And her eyes, sunken from lack of sleep, were circled by dark rings and seemed to stare, almost deranged. The skin on her cheeks was taut and dry, and lighter than it should be – she looked ill. And her clothes, which she'd been wearing for days, were now so crumpled that they looked as if she had been sleeping in them, which come to think of, she had. As Aisha stood mesmerized and slightly unnerved by what stared back, she felt again the uncomfortable sensation that she was not alone. The shadow that seemed to form at the corner of her vision, the brief movement behind her in the mirror, and still the smell of his aftershave, so that it seemed Mark was still there and watching her.

She spun round, threw the bin bag out of the bathroom and onto the landing, then hurried downstairs. In a frenzy, she tore around the lounge, seizing everything of Mark's that came to sight. Once she had removed all his possessions from the house it would empty itself of him, she thought. The gold carriage clock, the crystal glass vase, his umbrella, and a collection of Reader's Digest short stories. She darted round and dumped them in a pile in the middle of the lounge floor; then racing through to the kitchen, she flung open the drawers and cupboards. She stopped. Everything in the kitchen was his, as was the furniture, linen and electrical appliances. For despite Mark's initial promises of the two of them choosing some replacements together, they never had, and she couldn't throw out all the crockery, pans and cooking utensils, never mind the sofa and dinning table – she and the children would have nothing left. Seething with her anger and resentment, she kicked shut the lower cupboard doors, then went back into the lounge. She paused. Tucked down beside the sofa she saw his briefcase, sitting where he must have left it on Friday. Grabbing it with both hands, she pressed the lock: no combination, that was lucky, and it sprung open. Wrenching the two sides of the briefcase apart, she turned it upside down and shook it hard. The contents cascaded down onto the carpet in a waterfall of pens, papers, envelopes, and sweet wrappers.

'Sweet wrappers!' She dropped the briefcase and stared in disbelief. Toffees, bon-bons, chocolate éclairs, aniseed twists, handfuls of wrappers from a mixed assortment which Mark must have bought and eaten in secret. Aisha stared, incredulous, then dropped to her knees and began picking the wrappers over, examining them closely as if they were a rare species of insect which, at any moment, might develop legs and scuttle off.

'How could you?' she said. 'How could you? When you forbade the children sweets even on their birthdays and at Christmas? You said you never ate sweets, which was why your teeth were so good. You bastard! You fucking hypocrite! I hope you rot in hell.'

And the voice, with its confident assurance, answered back as she thought it might: *You're wrong again. What I said was I didn't eat sweets as a child, which is why my teeth were perfect.*

'No you didn't!' she cried. 'I heard you, I know what you said, so did the children. You're a liar! Liar! Liar!'

Anyone chancing to peep in through the window would have seen a woman on her knees laughing and crying hysterically, and shouting into an empty room. But no one did. And the retired couple next door simply raised their eyes knowingly, and talked of something else, as they had done every other time they'd heard a disturbance from their neighbours' house.

But wait, what was this? Aisha's attention focused again on the contents of the briefcase. Here were some official-looking brown envelopes. She began opening them, taking out the contents, and setting them on the floor beside her. A pension report, that was hopeful; one part of the new-style driving licence, the other section was probably in his wallet, wherever that was; a contract for work – apparently he had changed his job two years previously with a starting salary of £85,000! *Thanks for telling me!* she thought angrily. And here was the bike's registration document, filled in ready to send off, and also the bike's insurance. *Getting warmer,* she thought. She opened the next envelope, which contained a copy of his birth certificate, then the next, which was the car's blue registration document with correspondence from an insurance company. She flipped over the pages stapled at one corner and read the titles: 'Renewal Notice', 'Schedule', 'Certificate of Motor Insurance'. This was it. Her heart beat loudly in her chest as she ran her finger down the boxes of small print – *Certificate number, Car Registration number, Effective date of commencement, Person or classes of persons entitled to drive.* This was the section she wanted, her mouth went dry as she read: *The following are insured to drive this car: The policyholder. Any person with the permission of the owner, provided that the person holds a licence to drive the vehicle or has held and is not disqualified from holding or obtaining such a licence.*

She stopped and reread it. Yes, it applied to her – she was a driver with a full licence, never mind that she hadn't had his permission, they weren't to know. Thank goodness. She breathed a sigh of relief. She *was* insured to drive his car. Hallelujah! She put the insurance certificate to one side and with tears of gratitude and relief streaming down her face, continued through the remaining papers. There was no sign of his will and the rest of the papers were work documents, together with an address book.

Aisha sat back and stretched out her legs which were stiff from kneeling, and wiped her wet cheeks on the back of her hand. She began turning the pages of his slim, gold-edged, sleek address book, which she thought might hold clues to his life outside the house. There were names she didn't recognize, there was no reason why she should; she had been excluded from his life when she had given up work and was at home with baby Sarah. Yet it was eerie seeing Mark's neat distinctive handwriting, in fountain pen, not biro. Some names were obviously work contacts; others, male and female, had been entered under their first name only. There were email addresses, mobile numbers, and website addresses. Aisha returned to the front of the book and went down the first page again, methodically going through: *Alan, Abbott Holdings, Astute Accountancy, Ann* – whoever she was she had her own website. She turned the page. *B. Brian*, with an email address, website and mobile. How sophisticated these people were. *Bikers Galore, Bikers Ahead, Beemax, Bertram Hold-ings* – that was his pension company, she had seen it on the headed paper. *C. Cherry Lodge, Cinema (Odeon and Vue), Chinese Restaurant – Gerrard Street* – he had bracketed it *(very good)*, with a landline number and website address. *He's never taken me to that Chinese restaurant*, she thought bitterly, or any other restaurant in the last seven years, but Mark had clearly visited it often for the page was well-thumbed and he would never have merited it 'very good' if he hadn't eaten there a number of times, for Mark was a discerning food critic. Aisha continued over the page: *Children's school* – Oh, so you remembered you had children! *Chiropodist, Chauffeur-driven Cars, Car Hire, Christine*. She stopped. Christine. Christine. That name rang a bell.

She looked down again at Christine's details, her address in Pleasant Road was only a mile or so away, and the 10c probably meant it was a flat. Christine? Then sentences began to form and return from a long time ago and Aisha started to remember. Mark's voice, not the one that cursed and shouted at her but the cultured, softly spoken and charming voice of Mark that complimented her during their courtship: 'When my marriage to Angela ended,' she heard him say, 'I moved out. I lived in a bedsit … I really had reached rock bottom. Then I met Christine. She was the life and soul of the party … Within a few months we had set up home together. It was only then I found out …' Of course, Christine was the name of the alcoholic who had initially proved Mark's saving grace before the drink set in. Same person or a coincidence? There was no surname and she doubted she had ever known it anyway.

Aisha continued to look through the book, there were lots of women's names; as well as Christine, and Ann of www. annwright.co.uk, there was Jane, Marion Peters, Sue, and Yvette Walters, none of whom seemed to be work contacts. *So, is that where you were when you stayed out all night, or disappeared at weekends and took the car? Is that why you needed the insurance to cover any driver?* For it had occurred to Aisha that while she was relieved she hadn't been driving Mark's car illegally, without insurance, it raised the question as to why he had the additional cover. 'I wasn't allowed to drive your car so it wasn't for my benefit,' she said. 'More likely it was so you could have a decent bottle of wine with your meal at one of these expensive restaurants and let someone else drive.' Aisha remembered that Mark had been very particular about drink and driving during their courtship, and how impressed she'd been when he'd passed her his car keys at the end of one evening and said, 'Here, love, you drive, I've had a couple of drinks.' She also remembered how she'd sat proudly behind the wheel of his gleaming silver BMW while he'd watched her admiringly from the passenger seat and stroked her hair. A long long time ago – in the days when he told her how much he loved her and would do so forever.

Twenty-Six

With her eyes fixed and staring straight ahead, Aisha hurried along the pavement. Her coat was buttoned up to her neck and her hair, now completely loose, was flying out behind her in a tangled mane. She kept her gaze on some indistinct point straight in front, and ignored the stares of passers-by. Who cared what she looked like? Certainly not her. And she doubted the undertakers would pay much attention either; they must be used to people arriving bedraggled, overwhelmed by grief and unconcerned with their appearance.

Aisha hadn't realized that she would actually have to go to the undertaker, and straightaway. She had thought it was something that could be done over the phone, and more or less when she felt like it, which she hadn't, and certainly didn't now. It was her mother who had said that she needed to make the funeral arrangements when Aisha had phoned that morning to speak to the children. 'Haven't the hospital been in touch with the certificate of death?' her mother said.

'Yes.'

'Well, you need to get in contact with an undertaker, Aisha. You can't leave it any longer, it's been four days now.'

Which the woman at the undertakers had repeated when Aisha had phoned: 'We have a two o'clock appointment this afternoon, if that's convenient. We shouldn't really leave it much longer.' So Aisha had agreed, two o'clock was as convenient as any other time, if she really had to go. But it felt strange being out in the world after four days in the house. There was a distance, a light-headedness, an air of unreality in all she saw and heard. Though this could have been due to the lack of food, she thought, for apart from the last of her mother's *dhal* and mango squash, she'd had nothing but water. With the children away she really couldn't be bothered with buying food, cooking or eating.

Aisha paused to glance at her watch, but couldn't read the figures. The glass was shattered and cracks reached out from the centre like tentacles. She knew it was broken, so why it was still on her wrist she'd no idea. It had been like that since the accident, although she thought it had been broken in the garage when he'd brought her down – that was the only time she remembered hitting her arm. She stepped off the pavement to cross the road, then stopped quickly as a car screeched to a halt, its horn blaring. Aisha stared at the driver through his windscreen and then continued across. Before she reached the other side the driver tooted again and waved impatiently for her to hurry up. *Drivers could be so aggressive,* she thought; it was a wonder there weren't more accidents!

Continuing to the top of her road she turned left along the High Street, checking the shop numbers against the number she'd written on the scrap of paper she held in her hand. She must have passed the undertakers many times before when she'd gone to the small grocers with her handful of coins further up the High Street, but she couldn't remember seeing it. She supposed you didn't really take much notice of funeral parlours – they were like building societies and estate agents, you largely ignored them unless you required their services.

She counted down the shops to 158 and then looked up at the sign above the shop: 'H. Node, Funeral Director'. Wasn't a node a swelling, a painful lump that had to be checked for cancer? Strange name for an undertaker, she thought, or perhaps it wasn't. She'd chosen this undertaker from the plentiful lists in Yellow Pages simply because it was the nearest. Aisha studied the frosted glass door with its gold picture of a horse-drawn cortège. 'Est. 1820' it said in black lettering underneath. *Well, at least they would know what they were doing,* she thought, *which is more than I do.* But then again, did anyone her age know about funerals? How many people in their late thirties were proficient at burying the dead?

Aisha pushed open the door and a bell clanged from inside. A smartly dressed middle-aged woman in a grey two-piece suit appeared in reception. 'Mrs Williams?'

Aisha nodded.

'Come in, dear, I've been expecting you.' The woman smiled, a professional half-smile, which ignored Aisha's dishevelled appearance and offered sympathy.

'I hope I'm not late,' Aisha began. 'Only my watch isn't working and I dropped the one at home on the floor. It was his, you see, and I …'

The woman shook her head kindly. 'No, you're not. Come through to my office, we'll be quite comfortable in there.'

She showed Aisha through a door on the left and into a small red-carpeted room. Four brocade chairs were arranged around a long, low coffee table which had a vase of fresh flowers in the centre. *All very tasteful and low-key,* Aisha thought, and pretty much what she'd expected, if she'd expected anything at all. An oak filing cabinet was against one wall, and over it hung a gilt-framed portrait of an old man, who was very distinguished-looking with a long beard and fob watch dangling across the waistcoat of his pinstripe suit.

'Do sit down, dear, I'm Eileen Node, his great, great granddaughter,' she said nodding at the portrait. 'He was our founder.
We're a small family business. Can I get you something to drink?'

'No, thank you. I'd like to get this over as quickly as possible,
if you don't mind.'

'Yes, of course, dear. I do understand.' She tutted sympathetically. 'To be widowed so young and in such circumstances. Do
you not have parents, or a relative or friend who could help you?'

'My parents are looking after my children,' Aisha said blankly.

Eileen Node tutted again. 'I understand. Children ... poor little
mites.'

Aisha watched as Eileen went to the filing cabinet and took
out a ring-binder folder and a writing pad. She returned, and
sitting in the chair next to her, placed the folder on the table
between them, and the pad on her lap.

'Now, Mrs Williams, as I said on the phone, you mustn't
worry about any of the arrangements. We can take care of everything for you. There are a few decisions you will need to make,
but the rest we can see to. Have you brought the death certificate
with you?'

Aisha delved into her coat pocket and drew out the certificate;
with it came the monk's five-pound note, she tucked the money
back into her pocket.

Eileen looked at the certificate then up at her. 'This is the
certificate of the cause of death. We need the death certificate.
Have you been to the registry office and registered the death?'

'No,' Aisha said, confused.

'All right, there's no problem, but we need to do that as soon
as possible though. Would you like us to take you? We can't register the death for you, but we can send a car and accompany you.
I know how gruelling all this can be.'

Aisha nodded.

Eileen made a note on the pad in her lap. 'It must be done within five days of the date of death. We can collect you at nine thirty tomorrow – will that be all right?'

Aisha nodded again.

'I'll look after this certificate for you,' she said, tucking it into the back of her pad. 'The registrar will need it. If you have your husband's NHS medical number it's helpful, though not essential. You will find it on his medical card.'

Aisha sighed. 'I'll look for it. I don't know. There seems so much to remember.'

'Please don't worry,' Eileen said quickly. 'The only decisions you have to make now are about the type of funeral you would like. I'll talk you through it and explain everything. And if you wish to view your husband you will be able to do so here, from the day after tomorrow.'

Aisha stared at her, unable to believe what she had just heard. 'See him? Here? What, dead?'

'Yes, in our chapel of rest. It's a little room at the back.'

'No, I don't want to see him. He's not here now, is he?' she looked anxiously around the room.

'No, no, please don't upset yourself. The body is still at the hospital. You don't have to view it, dear; some people find it helpful but others do not. There is no compulsion.' She flickered her half-smile of reassurance again and patted Aisha's arm. 'There would be no sign of the accident though, if you did change your mind. Your husband would be just as you remember him.'

She was horrified. 'No, I wouldn't find it helpful, not at all,' Aisha said, agitated. 'Can we just get on with this, please; I'm really not feeling so well.'

'All right, dear, let's concentrate on the arrangements.' Eileen opened the folder and spread it on the table between them. She always found it was better to get straight down to arranging the funeral if the client was very distressed, it gave them something to focus on. Some liked to talk about the deceased, share their memories, but clearly that was not the case here.

'Now, all you have to do now is to make a few decisions about the type of funeral you would like – cremation or burial, the cars, music, and order of service. Some of this will depend on your budget, of course.' She glanced at Aisha. 'Did your husband have funeral insurance, do you know?'

'Insurance? I don't know. Probably not, I haven't found anything in his papers.'

'No, most people don't have funeral insurance so that's why we have an easy payment plan. I'll give you the details later. Now, you said on the phone you were thinking of a burial. Is that definite?'

Aisha nodded. 'If it's easier, yes.'

'Well, in terms of form-filling, yes, but it really depends on the wishes of the deceased and next of kin.' She looked at Aisha and waited.

Aisha felt the woman close beside her and thought how aptly her slow, measured movements fitted with her sombre line of work. She wondered if she had always been like that, or if it was a manner she had developed over time. Either way, Aisha wished she would just get on with it.

'So it's a burial then,' Eileen Nodes said, making a note on her pad. She opened the folder to the first page, and Aisha looked down at it. There were photographs of cars, lined up in a funeral procession, with a shiny black hearse leading gleaming black limousines.

'Do you know approximately how many will be attending the funeral, Mrs Williams?' Eileen asked.

'No, but I don't think it will be many. There are my parents, his family. I don't know about his friends or work.'

'It's just the immediate family I need to think about for the cars. Friends and work colleagues usually make their own way to the church and cemetery – unless you would prefer otherwise?'

Aisha shook her head.

'So, how many are there in your family?'

'Only my parents.'

'Are your children going?'

'I don't know, I really hadn't thought about it.'

'I'll allow for them, to be on the safe side. And your husband's family?'

'His parents and one brother. Maybe an aunt and uncle, I don't know. He wasn't close to his family, we hadn't seen them in years.'

Eileen wrote on her pad while Aisha looked at the photographs of the black cars and wondered how on earth she was going to cope: the funeral on top of everything else was too much; she couldn't start to get her mind round it.

'Now, let's take a look at the range of coffins,' Eileen said, turning the page to a double spread of photographed coffins with various linings and handles. 'This is our basic, economy one.' She pointed with a well-manicured and polished nail. 'It's veneered wood, with a simple cotton lining and imitation brass handles. Quite adequate, but obviously not as luxurious as this, or this.' Eileen ran her pink-glossed fingertip down and across the page. 'Our classic is made from oak, with a real silk lining and genuine brass finishings.'

259

Aisha gazed at the photographed coffins as Eileen continued with her commentary, outlining other 'finishings'. The catalogue reminded Aisha of the one she and her mother had chosen the invitations from when they'd planned her wedding a lifetime ago. But instead of the pages being laced with white and gold, these photographs were mounted on grey, with the pages trimmed in black. The hearse was in place of the white Rolls-Royce, and the wedding invitations were now order of service sheets, with examples of hymns and prayers. Bouquets and sprays were now wreaths or flowers crafted into a name – Mum, Dad, Sister, Uncle; in fact you could have anything you liked to remember the deceased, and Aisha wondered about 'Bastard'. But why did people go to all this trouble for someone who would never see the end result? she thought. Why spend all this time and money when they were dead? Unless there was a link between guilt and the amount you should spend on a funeral, in which case, she decided, she'd need a massive loan to send Mark off in style.

Eileen had stopped talking and was waiting for her response.

'They're very nice,' Aisha said, not realizing she was supposed to be making a choice. Something had started to trouble Aisha beyond all the talk of coffins and the disposal of the deceased's remains. An odd smell, a half-familiar perfume, seemed to have come into the room while Eileen had been talking, and was becoming quite uncomfortable. 'I'm sorry,' Aisha said, sniffing the air, 'that perfume you're wearing, it's familiar. What is it?'

Eileen smiled kindly. '*La Chaleur*. Smell can be a very poignant reminder, can't it? It's the most sensitive of all our senses, and also the last to leave us.' Eileen returned to the folder and started talking again, this time about the dispersion of the flowers after the funeral, and how they could be taken to a hospital or nursing home, so that others could enjoy them rather than just leaving them on the grave and to the elements.

Aisha sniffed the air again. *Poignant reminder indeed, too poignant by half*, she thought. The smell was growing stronger by the second and she doubted it was Eileen's *La Chaleur*. It was the same aroma that she smelt at home and it was just like Mark's aftershave when he'd finished spraying it in the bathroom and had left the door open. Perhaps she'd got some on her hands when she'd thrown out all his aerosols and bottles and knotted them in the black bag? Aisha tentatively raised her fingers to her nose and sniffed, but it was no stronger on her fingers. Then she sniffed the palms of her hands, but there was nothing beyond the faintest hint of lavender from the cheap soap in the bathroom at home. Yet a smell there definitely was, and it was quickly getting worse, filling the room, permeating the air, flooding into her lungs and turning her breath sour. She pressed her chin down towards her shoulder and sniffed the material of her coat, but it only smelt slightly damp, and anyway she hadn't been wearing her coat when she'd cleared out the bathroom cabinet. She looked at Eileen.

'Do you use embalming fluid?' Aisha asked, remembering she'd read it was something used by undertakers.

Eileen stopped in mid-sentence. 'Well, yes, normally. Unless there is a cultural concern?'

'No, but that smell, it's so strong. I'm sure it's not your perfume.'

Eileen frowned, concerned. 'The embalming fluid is odourless and colourless,' she said. 'And the embalming room is at the far end of the courtyard, at the rear. We have never had a complaint before.'

'And he's definitely not here?' Aisha said.

'Your husband? No, dear. We'll collect him from the morgue tomorrow. We need the death certificate first. Please, try not to worry, I'm sure it's nothing.' Eileen hesitated; then patting Aisha's arm reassuringly, returned to the folder. 'It's usual to give the mourners something to eat and drink after the funeral,' she continued. 'A light buffet is normally sufficient. This can be at home, or we can hire a hall if it's more convenient. We have used the same catering firm for many years. I'll give you a leaflet, they're quite reasonably priced and very discreet. Once we know the numbers I'll arrange it for you.'

The smell was overpowering now and more poignant than ever before. It was saturating the air, rushing into her throat each time she took a breath. Millions of tiny droplets of his musky aftershave, cloying her mouth and the lining of her nose, making it almost impossible to breathe or swallow. Like an asthma attack, Aisha thought although she'd never suffered from asthma even as a child. And the temperature was dropping now, like it did at home; for despite having turned up the thermostat and set the heating to constant, she had been permanently cold. Eileen seemed not to notice the fall in temperature and appeared comfortable in her thin open-neck blouse and light cotton suit. Aisha shivered and drew her coat closer around her. Eileen stopped and looked at her.

'Are you all right, dear?' She placed a reassuring hand on Aisha's arm again. 'Can I get you something? A glass of water? Cup of tea?'

'No, but I can't stay much longer, I have to go. You decide about the funeral. Whatever you think is suitable; just do it for me, please.'

Eileen looked surprised. 'Are you sure?'

'Yes, please, you must. I really have to go now. I can't stay any longer.'

Eileen took her hand from Aisha's arm. 'Well, if you're sure, I'll book the funeral for next Friday, that's the first free day. Would you prefer a morning or an afternoon?'

'I really don't mind,' Aisha said. 'You decide. Whatever you think, just do it. Phone if you need anything.' She stood and the room tilted. Eileen steadied her arm.

The smell was indescribable now, clogging her pores, putrefying the air and lodging in her stomach. She had to get out of this dreadful room before she was sick.

'We'll pick you up tomorrow then to register the death,' Eileen was saying. 'At nine thirty. You can give me the deposit and let me know about the numbers expected then.'

'Yes, yes.' Aisha turned and fled past her, through reception, and to the door; she pulled it open and the bell clanged behind her.

She was out on the pavement now, running, running up the High Street, gulping in the air, trying to get rid of the dreadful smell and taste. It was his aftershave, she was certain, now mingling with something even more unpleasant that could have been the smell of death. Mark had been there, she was sure, and not just because of the smell. She had sensed him, felt his presence as she did at home; when she saw a movement or shadow out of the corner of her eye and turned round to confront him, but found he had already gone. As she ran, her coat and hair flying out behind her, she glanced back over her shoulder, half-expecting to see him pursuing her. But there were only strangers who were staring at her.

She ran past the last of the shops on the High Street and turned into her road, gulping in the fresh air, breath after breath, taking it deep into her lungs, and trying to rid herself of the awful smell and taste. She checked over her shoulder again, and seeing it was still clear, slowed to a walking pace and tried to catch her breath. Her lungs felt as though they were about to explode, and her head and eyes throbbed. But worse was the noise, the street noise, which was now so loud it seemed to surround and engulf her. The bare branches of the trees overhead chaffed against each other like sandpaper on dry wood. The engines and wheel noise of the cars that passed were deafening, and seemed designed to pummel her into the ground. Then all the colours of everything she passed started jumping out at her, startlingly vivid, and blinding her with their brilliance: the red of the bus, the blue car, the yellow piece of paper blowing in the wind. Aisha screwed her eyes shut, opened them and tried to refocus, but it made no difference.

Concentrate on something, she told herself, *something still and silent that won't attack. That garden gate, the tree trunk, that discarded Coke can in the gutter.* A dog came towards her, its paws thundering along the pavement, its tongue lolling out. She could see the string of saliva hanging from its jaw, and could almost hear it stretching, then fall to the pavement with a mighty splash. She fled past it and up the road as everything seemed to conspire against her, trying to bring her down.

She made the last few steps to the house and flung open the gate, rushed up the path, and managed somehow to get her key into the lock. Stumbling in, she slammed the door behind her, then with one hand cupped over her mouth and nose to block out the smell, ran through the house, opening all the windows, upstairs and down. She knew he was here somewhere, she could feel his presence, smell his aftershave mingling with the warmth of his body as it had done on that first date, and then in the garage when she'd stood close to him. He was in here somewhere, hiding, waiting to pounce. He was angry, seething, and she knew it wasn't safe to stay inside, not with him in this mood, he would kill her for sure.

Running into the kitchen she unlocked the back door and then ran to the end of the garden, where she dropped down beside the shed. She drew her knees up to her chest and looped her arms around her legs, then rested her chin on top. She stared at the back of the house, and waited, watching for any sign of movement. Only when she was absolutely certain that he had gone, and she was finally free of him for good, would she dare to return inside.

Twenty-Seven

Run, run as fast as you can. You can't catch me, I'm the gingerbread man. The refrain ran through Aisha's head over and over again. It was from a story her father knew by heart and had narrated endlessly when she was a child. It was one of her favourites and she had begged him to tell her the story over and over again. 'Please, one more time,' she used to say as he tucked her into bed and said goodnight. But as the gingerbread man found out to his peril, you can't run for ever, at some point you get caught and will pay the price.

Still at the bottom of the garden, hunched forwards, with her arms around her knees, Aisha rocked back and forth in tune to the rhythm of the refrain. The sky was beginning to darken, late afternoon was turning into night. The clouds had rolled in and the lone bird that had accompanied her all afternoon had now stopped singing and had taken refuge for the night in some distant tree. *Run, run as fast as you can. You can't catch me, I'm the gingerbread man.* The plaintiff melody, which had confined and absorbed her thoughts while she waited by the shed, slowly petered out.

She shifted slightly, pulled her coat closer around her, and then moved her legs. They were numb from the cold and sitting in one position for so long. She flexed her toes and blew on her hands, then felt her fingers and toes start to tingle as the blood began to circulate. At some point she would have to stand and go

266

into the house. At some point, but not yet. In a while, she thought, when she was certain he had gone, for sometimes the house appeared to be empty, but then she would catch sight of his shadow, the briefest flicker of grey as he crossed behind one of the open windows. He was a crafty one, that was for sure, lying dormant for minutes on end and then trying to slip past her when he thought she wasn't looking – trying to catch her out. She looped her arms around her knees again and continued rocking. *Run, run as fast as you can.* There was a safety, a comfort in rocking, it soothed like a cradle or rocking chair, and took the edge off the pain.

Yet it was strange, Aisha had to admit, being conscious of what she was doing, and why. To be aware that she was sitting at the bottom of the garden in the middle of winter, rocking to the rhythm of a nursery rhyme, while waiting for the house to clear of a ghost. She could see herself doing it, almost objectively, as if in third person, and knew it was quite bizarre. She'd assumed madness crept up and took you by surprise, so that everyone else knew how oddly you were behaving, apart from you. Yet here she was quite lucidly observing herself, while being unable to alter what she saw. There was a type of voyeurism in watching yourself go mad – a fly-on-the-wall documentary, where you watched but couldn't act.

A few minutes more, she thought, then she would risk it, stand and go in. She drew back the sleeve of her coat to check her watch, and laughed out loud. 'You idiot! You knew it was broken. It's not likely to have fixed itself.' She looked up again at the back of the house. There hadn't been any movement at any of the windows for quite a while now. She ran her eyes from the kitchen to the lounge, then up to the bathroom, and across to the box room Mark used for storage; they were all still clear.

'On the count of three then,' she said, and placed her hands, palms down, either side ready to push herself up. *One, two, three,* and she was standing. Her head spun and she steadied herself on the shed. Dried twigs and muddy leaves clung to her coat and she bent down and brushed them off. She took a couple of steps and felt her legs wobble, then strengthen as she continued gingerly over the lawn and to the back door.

Reaching in, she tentatively switched on the light, and satisfied it was all clear, continued in, closing and locking the door behind her. She crossed to the sink, closed the window above, then poured a glass of water and drank it in one go. Pity there wasn't any more mango squash, she thought, she really fancied some of that now. Turning, she went through the archway that led to the lounge, switched on the light, paused, and sniffed the air. Good. There was no smell, and no movement. But what a mess! The light illuminated the contents of Mark's briefcase still in the middle of the floor.

Aisha waited again and listened some more, half-expecting to hear Mark to tell her to clear it up, but the room remained quiet and calm. Reassuring herself that the house was truly empty and therefore safe, Aisha continued across the lounge and closed the bay windows, then returned to the unruly heap of papers beside Mark's open briefcase. She knelt down and began rummaging through the papers until she found what she was looking for. She pulled out his address book. Aisha wanted to check on something, to see if she had remembered correctly. For while she'd been sitting in the garden, waiting and thinking, something had occurred to her – a realization, which had continued to poke and dig, chaffing her mind and making it sore.

She opened the address book, and flipping through the first few pages, stopped at C. Christine, yes, she thought so; she *had* remembered correctly. She wasn't so daft after all! She stared at Mark's neat fountain pen entry, the stylish slant of his words. It seemed to be speaking to her, sending out a message, a clue, if she was smart enough to see it, which she was now. For Mark's sleek black leather address book wasn't very old, only a year or so she thought, and yet Christine's address had been updated; which meant it was a recent move, and one that Mark had clearly been informed of.

So why, Aisha thought, savouring the wisdom of her insight, *why had he been told Christine's new address, if he hadn't seen her in ten years?* She didn't think it was for Christmas cards, although indeed he might have sent her one. But there was another, far more plausible explanation, obvious now, as it should have been years ago, if she'd had the wit and energy to see it. Quite clearly Mark had been seeing Christine, it was the only reason she could think of for him having updated her entry in his address book. The two of them had been carrying on behind her back, which meant, Aisha thought, Christine was as much to blame for her unhappiness as Mark had been. Her anger flared.

Aisha stood and kicked his briefcase hard, sending it flying across the room. 'Fuck you! The both of you!' she cried out loud. 'Especially you, Christine! I didn't stand a chance with you waiting in the wings! What sort of woman are you who has an affair with a man who beats his wife and neglects his children? You're despicable, that's what you are! How long has it been going on? Or perhaps it never stopped! Is that why he treated me as he did? Because I was always second best? Did he tell you about me, and how pathetic I was? I bet he did! I bet he told you between the sheets and you gave him sympathy. In many ways you're worse than him for without you he might have tried harder, but why should he, with you to run to? All those years of lies, deceit, and beatings! Did you savour your exalted position and laugh at my expense? I bet you did, you cow, you slut. The two of you have ruined my life, and while Mark has paid the price, you, Christine, his accomplice, have not!'

Aisha paused, and looked down at the address book, still open in her hand. But wait, just a minute ... now there's a thought: she knew where Christine lived. And 10c Pleasant Road wasn't so very far away, well within walking distance, if she fancied a walk ...

Which she did.

'I think it's time I paid you a visit, Christine, and found out what's really been going on.'

Aisha snapped shut the address book and dropped it on the bureau beside the photograph, then took off her coat, and leaving it on the hall stand, went upstairs and into the main bedroom. The smell had gone, and there was no shadow lurking in the corner. She closed the bedroom window and then stopped still. It was all very well thinking she was going to wash and change before she visited Christine but what exactly was she going to change into? No point in looking in her wardrobe; she went instead to the built-in cupboard and took down the old cardboard box containing her belongings from home. Carefully removing the china ornaments and school certificates, she took out the flat tissue-wrapped parcel beneath. She knew what was in it, she'd recognized it before when she'd been searching for her driving licence. Carefully unwrapping the tissue paper, she took out the only decent piece of clothing she possessed – specially made for her, and worn once at her graduation fifteen years before. It was her one and only sari.

She shook out the long piece of gaily printed blue silk. She remembered her mother saying that blue suited her, and her father had called it 'becoming'. Draping it over her arm, Aisha went to the small cabinet which contained her few clothes, and took out the cream bodice which went under the sari and which fortuitously she had kept, and a clean pair of pants. With her thoughts calmer and more focused than they had been in days, possibly years, she crossed the landing and entered the bath-room. It was cold, but there was no hint of his aftershave. She closed the window and laid the sari carefully on the toilet lid, then took off her old clothes and turned on the shower. Once the water had run hot, she stepped under the shower. It felt good, purifying, and she wondered why she hadn't done it sooner – with Mark gone she could have a hot shower whenever she wanted; she must remember that, she thought.

The steam rose around her and Aisha reached for the tablet of lavender soap and worked it into a lather between her palms. She ran it all over her body, once, twice, three times, then watched the jet of water carry the suds in a murky stream towards and down the plughole. There wasn't any shampoo, it had run out a long while ago and she'd never had the money to replace it. She had thrown away all Mark's shampoo, so she would have to use the soap, just as she did for the children's hair. But whereas Sarah's and James's hair was always well groomed and washed regularly, hers was now so greasy and matted she found it impos-sible to work it into a lather. She tried again and again, rubbing the soap directly into her hair, but while her scalp felt reasonably clean, when she tried to massage the lather though to the ends of her hair, her fingers caught in the knotted strands and wouldn't go any further than her shoulders. There was nothing else for it, she decided; she'd have to cut it.

Rinsing off the last of the soap, Aisha turned off the shower and stepped out. Using the one remaining towel, which had been hers and the children's, and was clean although threadbare, she dried herself, and then pulled on her pants and bodice. She turned to the wall cabinet and slid open the glass door and felt along the otherwise empty shelves for the scissors. She knew she'd kept the scissors because they were hers, given to her by her mother when she had left home. Although Mark had commandeered them, recognizing their quality, he had never used them so they were not tainted and could be kept. 'A good quality pair of scissors is essential,' her mother had said as she trimmed Aisha's hair when she'd been living at home.

Her fingers alighted on the cold metal and she took down the scissors, then flexed them open and shut a couple of times, watching the sharp metal blades clash together. Turning to the mirror over the sink, she rubbed the glass clear of mist with the towel and examined what she saw. How thin she was! She knew she had lost weight, her trousers were loose, but she hadn't realized just how much. Her ribs stuck out from under the cream bodice so much so she could count them. And her hip bones, once rounded, now jutted either side of her concave stomach, and were visible at the top of her pants. Nothing she could do about it now, she thought, it would take months to put the weight back on, and fortunately no one was going to see. 'Best get down to the job in hand,' she said stoically.

Aisha looked at her hair in the mirror. 'Now, where to cut? Here or here?' She ran the open blades up and down her straggling wet hair. 'Or we could be daring and go for a completely new style. Yes, why not? We'll have a neat bob like Belinda's, that will impress Christine.' And for a moment Aisha thought she should also blame Belinda – for bringing Mark and her together, but decided Mark was such a good liar he could have fooled anyone.

Aisha separated out a manageable clump of hair, and placing the open scissors at chin level, slowly closed the blades. A thick skein of long wet hair dropped to the floor and lay snake-like at her feet. She checked in the mirror. 'Not perfect, but it will do. After all, it's not the queen I'm going to visit, more a scheming bitch!'

Using her chin as a guideline, Aisha set about the rest, cutting as far as she could see round one side, and then going round the other. Snip. Snip. Snip. The hair rained down and formed a circle at her feet. *A magic circle,* she thought, *protecting me from evil.*

With both sides more or less the same length, all that remained was the clump at the very back. This was going to be more difficult as it was impossible to see that far round. 'What I could really do with is a friend to help me,' she said, 'but I haven't got any of those, have I? You saw to that!' She grabbed the final skein of hair, and drawing it up and forwards, over the top of her head, placed the open blades where it looked about right. An estimate, but preferable to leaving it looking like a Mohican with one long strand down her back. She made the cut and the skein came away in her hand: she threw it on the floor with the rest.

Aisha stared at the results in the mirror. One side appeared to be slightly longer than the other, but she couldn't do much about that without starting all over again, and making it shorter all round. *Once it's dry,* she thought, *it probably won't be so noticeable.* She gave her hair a good rub on the towel and shook her head, the hair fanned out and settled. Not bad, and it felt so much lighter, and made her feel lighter too. She picked up the sari, and pinching one end, held it to her waist, and began wrapping it round, then up and over her shoulder, as her mother had taught her as a child. She tucked the end into the waist and stood in front of the mirror, arms hanging loosely at her sides. Aisha barely recognized the Asian woman who stared back, her face thin, eyes wild, and determination set in her features.

Leaving the mirror, she stepped over the pile of clothes and hair and crossed the landing. Taking hold of the banister with her left hand and lifting up her sari with the right, she began slowly down. She wasn't used to wearing a sari, she hadn't worn one since she'd met Mark, and she was having to step very carefully to avoid catching her feet in the hem. Halfway down the stairs, she heard a ringing, and it took her a moment to realize that it was the phone on the hall table that was making all the noise. Who on earth could be phoning her? She had telephoned the children that morning, and wasn't expecting them to call back. In fact she wasn't expecting anyone to call, unless it was the undertakers? Or more likely someone for Mark who hadn't yet heard of his death.

Cautiously she picked it up. 'Hello?'

'Mrs Williams?' It was a deep male voice that seemed vaguely familiar.

'Yes?'

'Stan Calder.'

She said nothing, still unable to place the caller's voice.

'Inspector Calder,' he clarified.

'Oh, yes?'

'I hope I haven't disturbed you, Mrs Williams, but I thought you would like to know that our enquiries are complete. I have filed my report, and you won't be charged with dangerous driving. I'll return your licence and insurance in the post.'

She paused. 'Oh right, I see, thank you.' She hadn't even been aware he was thinking of charging her with dangerous driving. Had he told her? Possibly, she couldn't remember.

'Also, at some point, Mrs Williams, and there's no rush, you will need to make arrangements to collect and dispose of your husband's car and bike. They are in the police compound, forensics have finished with them. There will be a letter in the post, explaining what you have to do.'

'I see,' she said again. 'Thank you.'

'You're welcome. That's the end of my involvement then. Goodbye and take care.'

'Yes, and you. Goodbye, Inspector.'

The line went dead and Aisha stood for some moments listening to the tone, and then slowly replaced the handset.

Twenty-Eight

Aisha really didn't need that now, not exoneration. What she needed was to be blamed and punished. For who was she going to talk to now the inspector had gone and with it her lifeline of confession? All those nights since the accident when she'd sat alone in the chair, confessing, telling the inspector what had really happened and how she was to blame. To be let off now, absolved and pardoned, was more than she could bear. But if she wasn't to blame then someone else must be. Christine loomed, ever more the accomplice.

Grabbing her coat from the hall stand, Aisha went out of the front door and slammed it shut behind her. It was pitch dark now, with a biting cold wind, and she didn't relish the prospect of the thirty-minute walk to Christine's flat. With the monk's five-pound note still in her coat pocket, and her father's one hundred pounds untouched at home, she felt unprecedentedly rich, so she decided to take the bus. She vaguely remembered the area Pleasant Road was in, from having used a dentist there once when she'd first been married and had had toothache and was allowed to go to the dentist. She felt sure the number 32 bus would take her to just past the end of the road, and if not it would only be a short walk away.

Aisha sat in a near-side window seat and stared out through the glass, monitoring the bus's haltingly slow progress up the High Street. Every so often her eyes refocused on the glass and her unfamiliar profile with its chin-length hair. Aisha wondered where this stranger had come from, for it wasn't the person who'd had a life before Mark — who had studied and worked hard and achieved; but neither was it the person who'd come after, who had cowered in obedience and was beaten for her trouble. No, the person in the glass was someone new, someone who was in the middle of before and after, and who was frantically trying to find answers — to unravel the knot of pain in her head, and put logic where there was none.

The bus turned down by the old grammar school and past the playing fields attached to the college. Then it pulled into a bus stop and the automatic doors swished open with a sigh. Scooping up her sari, Aisha went down the steps and onto the pavement. She could see the end of Pleasant Road — it was where she had thought it was, although the corner shop had changed and was now selling electrical goods, its window full of lamps and dazzling chandeliers.

She began along the road, past numbers 4, 6 and 8, which were bungalows. Set further back was number 10, a small, modern, infill development of flats, with a short path, flanked by shrubs, leading to the main door. She went up to the door and studied the illuminated labelled bells on a metal grid on the wall: Flat 10a — D Sharpe, 10b — Tony Hyde, 10c — Christine Price, 10d — P Waterman. She gave the buzzer to 10c one long press and waited.

A female voice, distorted by the intercom, came through. 'Hello?'

Aisha leant towards the grill as she spoke. 'Is that Christine Price?'

A small hesitation, then, 'Yes. Who is this?'

There was no point in lying, she would find out soon enough. 'Aisha Williams,' she said evenly.

Another hesitation, then, 'Mark's widow?'

So she recognized her name, and knew he was dead; clearly news travelled fast in their close and doubtless select network of friends. 'Yes.'

'What do you want?'

'I'd like to talk to you.'

A longer pause, then, 'OK, come up. But I can't give you long – I'm going out in half an hour.'

Very trusting, Aisha thought, she doubted she would have let her in if she'd been Christine.

The front door clicked its release and Aisha pushed it open and went in; it shut automatically behind her. She stood for a moment and looked around the entrance hall with its immaculate inlaid wood floor free of scuffmarks, and spotless magnolia emulsion walls. A pine balustrade staircase rose elegantly before her. Doors to flats 10a and 10b led off either side of the hall, and outside 10a was a huge Chinese vase with a magnificent arrangement of dried flowers. *All very pleasant, like its road name,* Aisha thought bitingly. Doubtless Mark and Christine spent many a pleasant night in her flat.

Hitching up the hem of her sari, she took hold of the wooden handrail and began to climb the staircase. She heard a door above open and glanced up; a woman in a white toweling bathrobe with a matching towel wrapped turban-like around her head appeared on the landing and smiled. Aisha looked down again and concentrated on the stairs. As she completed the climb, Christine came forwards to shake hands. 'Hello Aisha, we meet at last.' She was softly spoken with a London accent and not at all embarrassed by meeting her.

Aisha would have liked to have ignored Christine's offered hand and slapped her face instead. But even now her upbringing told her it was unacceptably rude. 'Manners maketh the man,' her father used to say, and ridiculously Aisha remembered Mark saying it too. She took Christine's smooth, cool hand in hers and looked into her perfectly composed face. Her eyes were blue, almost the same shade as Mark's, and her delicate pale skin was flawless without any trace of make-up.

'Do excuse me,' Christine said. 'I was in the shower. I hope you don't mind talking while I get ready.' She dropped Aisha's hand and without waiting for a reply, turned and led the way into the flat.

Tall and slim, Christine exuded elegance and confidence, and Aisha could see only too clearly what Mark had seen in her. Time had obviously been kind to Christine, time and success, for there were none of the signs of the alcohol abuse that Mark had described – the coarse red features and heavily lined skin from years of heavy drinking. Christine must be older than Aisha, yet looked much younger. But what struck Aisha more than anything was that Christine didn't seem to be grieving for the death of her lover, but appeared incredibly composed and was actually getting ready to go out.

Aisha followed Christine down the short hall and into the very spacious lounge-cum-dining room. It was white, pure white, all of it, even the leather four-seater sofa was white.

'Do sit down,' Christine said lightly, waving to the sofa. 'I thought you might pay me a visit.'

'You did?' Aisha stayed where she was and stared at her, shocked. 'Why?'

Christine shrugged. 'It's what I would have done. Though I didn't think it would be now. It must be the funeral soon.'

Aisha held her gaze, flustered and uncertain. 'Yes, Friday, I think.'

'Don't you know?' she gave a little laugh. 'Can I get you a drink?'
Aisha shook her head.

'Well, sit down then and make yourself at home. You look like you could do with a rest. I'm just going to get a glass of water. I haven't been in long from work.'

Work – a career and a life, Aisha thought bitterly as Christine disappeared into the hall. She went to the sofa and perched at one end and looked at the room. How Mark must have loved it here, with its calm and uncluttered sophistication, a world away from what she could offer, with two children and no money.

'So, how did you find me?' Christine asked, returning with the glass of water and placing it on the marble mantelpiece. 'Mark surely didn't tell you?'

Taken aback by her directness, Aisha faltered. It was she who should be asking the questions and demanding answers, not Christine. 'I found it in his address book,' she said at last.

'I see. Before or after his death?'

'After, when I was clearing out. Why?'

Christine shrugged. 'Just curious.'

Aisha watched as Christine turned to the huge gilt-framed mirror over the mantelpiece, and unwinding the towel from her head, shook out her blonde shoulder-length hair. Taking a comb from the pocket of her bathrobe, she began running it through the professionally styled layers.

'So why didn't you come and see me before he died?' Christine asked after a moment.

Aisha stared at Christine's reflection in the mirror, confused. 'Why should I? There was no need until I found your address and realized he'd been seeing you.'

'No? Really?' Christine returned her gaze in the mirror and gave a small tight laugh. 'So the leopard has changed his spots? I don't think so. Not in my experience at least.' She picked up the glass of water and walked nonchalantly to the armchair opposite Aisha. She sat down, draping one long leg over the other. Aisha stared at her, and her anger flared – this woman who should have been apologizing but seemed one step ahead of her.

'Why couldn't you just leave us alone?' Aisha blurted angrily. 'You have so much. It could have worked without you. He might have tried harder if he hadn't had you to run to. You are to blame as much as he was!'

Christine tucked the comb into her robe and, unfazed, rested one arm along the chair. 'If that is what you really believe, Aisha, then you're a bigger fool than I thought. But you're not, are you? You know it's not that convenient. Mark came here yes, more than once, full of sob stories about how you didn't understand him and refused to have sex. He even thought you were having an affair.' Aisha gasped and opened her mouth to defend herself, but Christine raised her hand. 'Don't worry, I didn't believe him. Remember, I had lived with Mark too, and as I said a leopard doesn't change its spots. But I was curious. I wanted to hear how life was treating him. So I let him in, listened to him, gave him a drink, then sent him on his way, possibly back to you, or not – it wasn't any of my business.'

Their eyes met and locked. 'I don't believe you,' Aisha said.

'Suit yourself. I've learnt a lot, Aisha, and one of the things I've learned is that some men are dangerous – so dangerous they should carry a government health warning. I expect some women are too, but that's not the point. Here, let me show you something that might help you to understand.'

Christine stood and crossed to a bureau at the far end of the room. Aisha saw that the bureau was almost the same as the one she had at home – it had been Mark's before he had met her.

Picking up a framed photograph, she carried it back and placed it squarely in Aisha's lap.

'Familiar?' Christine said. 'My guess is you have an identical picture. Angela has. You know about her, I assume?'

Aisha stared at the photograph in her lap, and heard the name of Mark's first wife. She looked at the ten-by-eight photograph, unable to believe or understand what she was seeing. The couple sitting side by side on the bench beneath the oak tree – a couple so obviously in love; they had taken their eyes from each other just long enough to smile into the lens. Christine was right, it was a replica of the one she had on the bureau at home: the photograph Mark had asked a passer-by to take, then given to her framed as a token of his undying love. Only, instead of Mark and her it was a younger version of Christine and Mark. Aisha looked up, not knowing what to say, or think.

'Each of us has one,' Christine said matter-of-factly. 'First Angela, then me, and you too. We all had the life that went with it too. History repeated itself. True, I didn't have children, but it didn't make it any easier, believe me.' She stopped and sitting at the other end of the sofa lightly rested her head back.

Aisha looked at her. 'So are you going to tell me?'

She gave a faint nod. 'I thought I was pretty smart,' she said in a low, even voice. 'I thought I was streetwise when it came to men. I was in my late twenties, not a lovesick teenager, I thought I could read men like a book. And of course everything was perfect to begin with, I had a man who was the answer to every woman's prayers. Mark wooed me with his incredible charm and good manners just like he did Angela, and then later, you. I was completely won over and yearned to make him happy, to make up for the way his first wife had treated him. But by the end of our first year together I was a wreck and unrecognizable from the person I had once been. Yet still I tried to make it work because I was convinced it was my fault and I was to blame. So I tried harder and each time I got a harder beating for my efforts. I could never get it right. Then I turned to the bottle and tried to block out the pain by drinking. As a result, I lost my job and eventually, with no further to fall, got out.' Christine gave a small dry laugh. 'Ironically, it was Mark who allowed me the means to escape in the end. He gave me such a beating one night that I landed in hospital. It was while I was there, away from him and his control, and surrounded by so much kindness and attention from the nurses and doctors, that I was able to see what I had become. I left him with what I stood up in and didn't go back. No one can understand unless they have been in the same position. Abuse strips you of everything, bleeds you dry, so that you end up believing that you couldn't survive without the very person who is doing it to you.'

Christine stopped. Her words hung in the air and Aisha heard the truth in what she'd said. The account Christine had just given her – with all its detail – like the photograph, was an exact replica of her life with Mark.

'But if you knew,' Aisha said after some moments, her voice rising, 'why didn't you tell me? You could have said something, warned me. Why let me go through all that if you knew, and you knew it could happen again. You should have warned me!'

Christine turned to look at her, her delicate features sincere. 'Would it have made any difference if I had? Aisha, would you have believed me with all that was on offer? No, of course you wouldn't. I couldn't prove it and Mark was so charming when he wanted to be. You'd have dismissed me as the embittered ex, which is what I did with Angela, when she tried to tell me. And there was always the chance it could have worked out for you two. There was only Angela and me then, there wasn't an ex-wives club. I always thought that if you needed to know – if you were in trouble and history was repeating itself – then you would find me. I would have done what I could.'

Aisha looked from Christine to the photograph and had to admit she was right. Like Christine had done with Angela, she too would have rejected any suggestion that Mark was less than the person he appeared to be – she'd been too much in love and there'd been too much at stake.

'That tree is still there,' Christine said more lightly after a moment. 'I pass it on the way to work. It's seen a lot, that tree. It might have seen more, had you not stopped him. I admire what you did, Aisha. You've certainly got more guts than me.'

Aisha looked at her sharply. 'What do you mean?'

Christine met her gaze. 'I read the report of the accident in the paper. Didn't you see it?' Aisha shook her head. 'It was quite a large piece based on the cruel irony of a wife being responsible for the death of her husband. But I also read the unwritten story behind it, Aisha. Some men are dangerous, but not as dangerous as a desperate wife who's been beaten for years. And for you, coming from your background, there was probably no other way out. I guessed it was either kill him or yourself. Am I right?'

Aisha looked into the clear blue eyes which now echoed empathy and concern. The woman whom she'd come here to blame and vilify, now transformed into an ally with a common past. Aisha rested her head back and closed her eyes. The life drained from her, and the photograph trembled in her hand. 'Yes, I killed him,' she said softly, 'but I'm paying the price. I might just as well have killed myself for what I have left. You escaped, but I am still trapped. This will haunt me forever.'

Twenty-Nine

*D*ark. So very dark. It was impossible to see. The dark was packed tight around her, forming a wall as impenetrable as stone. No air, no light, no sound, just a thick black cowl. And hot, hotter than the raging fires of hell that melted her skin and turned her eyes to liquid so she couldn't see or feel. Aisha tossed and turned in delirium, fought against the constraints that seemed to bind her and held her in a torment of endless nights. Then on the edge, trying to break in, was a noise, a series of notes resonating down through the layers of darkness to the edge of her consciousness. 'A-ish-sha. A-ish-sha. A-ish sha.'

She shied away, withdrew back into the darkness, for although the black was crushing, it was also safe. But the sound continued, louder, clearer, more insistent. 'Aisha. Aisha. Can you hear me?' It was familiar now, reminding her of a time a long while ago that was safe.

Her mind and body began to rise, soaring up through the layers of darkness into a small void of gloomy light. Her eyes flickered and then opened. Shadows and images swirled in a moving pool of grey and she tried to focus. A room, dimly lit, a bedroom that had never held the dark. 'Aisha, love. Can you hear me? Are you awake?'

She turned her head towards the voice and saw the outline of her father sitting close beside her. He leaned towards her, his face

285

bathed in the soft glow of the lamp. 'It's all right. You're at our house. In your old bed. It's nearly midnight.'

She started, tried to pull herself up. 'Sarah? James?' The room tilted and swayed. He eased her back onto the pillow.

'Don't worry. They're safe. They're asleep in the spare room. Try to relax. There's nothing for you to worry about.' And this was enough for now – the knowledge that the children were safe, close by, and being looked after. Her eyes closed again, and she felt her father's cool hand on her forehead, soothing her as he had done when she was unwell as a child. Then other thoughts began to surface and she opened her eyes and looked at him again. 'Christine? I was at Christine's. How did I get here?'

'She phoned us, and then brought you here in her car.'

'And the funeral? Isn't the funeral today?'

'Yesterday. Today is Saturday. Your mother took the children. Don't worry. Everything went as it should, and I have settled the bill.'

She allowed her head to relax back again onto the pillow and moved her gaze from him, to look around the room. The contents were exactly as she had left them on the morning of her marriage all those years ago: the wardrobe, the chest of drawers, her desk and chair in the alcove as though expecting her at any moment to return and resume studying. She could smell the familiar scent of her mother's homemade potpourri, a combination of pine and jasmine. She looked at her father's tired, worn face, even older now, and her heart went out to him. 'I'm sorry, Father. I'm sorry I've caused you so much trouble. I'm sorry I've disappointed you and brought you so much shame. Will you ever be able to forgive me?'

His brow furrowed in pain and he took her hand from the duvet and enfolded it in his. 'Aisha, please don't. There is nothing to forgive. Not on your part, at least.'

She looked at him questioningly and he shook his head sadly. He had something to say, but Aisha could see it was difficult for him. He squeezed her hand and then gently returned it to the duvet and stood. She watched as he slowly crossed to the window and looked out through the parted curtains. She heard his intake of breath.

'Aisha, while the children have been staying with us they have been talking. They speak wisely, with voices far older than their years. They have told us many things, sad things, about their father, and the life you had together. It causes me much pain, Aisha, and I am very sorry you have suffered.'

'Father, there's nothing for you to be sorry for,' she said quickly. 'It's not your fault. It's mine. I have failed your expectations miserably. I didn't mean to. I so wanted you to be proud of me. You could never be to blame.'

'Exactly, Aisha. My expectations.' He straightened and looked up towards the night sky. 'Aisha, I brought you up as I would have done in my own country, strictly, compared to Western standards. I instilled in you a sense of obedience and duty – you were an obedient and dutiful daughter. Yes, I was proud of you, what father wouldn't have been? You took that sense of duty and honour into your marriage and became an obedient and dutiful wife. I can see now that it was that sense of duty that kept you in a marriage far longer than it should have done. I now know it was a bitter and cruel marriage, Aisha, and I think you stayed to protect me. That is why I am sorry.'

She looked at his profile, stooped and humbled by his admission. She wanted to cry out, tell him it wasn't his fault, that it could never ever be his fault, that she loved him dearly and she was solely to blame. But she had to admit there was a truth in what he said, that he had inadvertently made her what she was.

'You did what you thought was right,' she said quietly. 'Please don't blame yourself. I should have known you and Mother were always here for me. But I was so far down I couldn't see, I still can't. I wonder if I ever will.'

He was silent for some moments, his frame silhouetted between the curtains against the night sky. She heard the clock ticking as it had done when she was a child and had to get up early for school. Then he moved slightly, straightened his shoulders, and looked up again towards the heavens.

'While you have been sleeping these two days, Aisha, I have spent a lot of time standing here, thinking. I remembered the time we watched the eclipse together. I don't suppose you remember it, you were only three or four. You were very scared as the birds stopped singing and the day turned to night. I tried to explain that the sun hadn't gone forever and it would return. But you didn't believe me, not until it happened. Then as the sun slowly slid into view again and the light gradually returned, your little face was a picture. You were so happy. "We are alive," you cried. "There *is* a tomorrow." I will never forget it, Aisha.'

He turned and looked at her, sad and vulnerable from sharing his feelings. He crossed to the bed and sat again beside her. 'Aisha, my darling, an eclipse doesn't last forever. Although it may not seem so now, it will pass, I promise you. The light will return to your life and it will be brighter because of the darkness. And until it does we will be here to care for you.'

She held his gaze, saw the hope, the expectation that she could succeed in this as she had done in other things. To disappoint him again was too much. She turned her head away from him and closed her eyes. A single spotlamp on full beam flashed across her vision, and with it came the sound of breaking glass and shattering metal.

'Father,' she said without opening her eyes, 'sometimes we do things that change us forever. An eclipse passes, but what I have done will blot out the light for good.'

'No, Aisha, you're wrong. Trust me. I know what happened and I know it was not your fault. In time you will recover from this and I know I am right.'

Thirty

'Beautiful flowers for a beautiful lady.' He grinned roguishly as he placed the bouquet on top of the papers on which she was working.

Aisha touched the delicate array of pink blooms and moved them to one side. 'Thank you, David, but I wish you wouldn't. They must have cost a fortune in the middle of winter.'

He grinned again. 'You're worth it, as I keep telling you. Any chance of dinner tonight?'

She smiled apologetically. 'I'm sorry, but I have a pile of work to take home, and my daughter is bringing a friend to tea.'

David laughed good-humouredly. 'And what about this friend? When do I get a look in? I won't give up you know, Aisha. I'll pester you until you give in, or sack me on the spot.'

'I'd never sack you,' she laughed. 'I need you too much in the department. In fact, I couldn't manage without you.' Aisha threw him a smile and then returned to the letter, picking up her pen ready to sign.

He watched her as she wrote, her long neck with its trailing plait curved gracefully forwards like a beautiful swan reaching over the edge of a riverbank to drink. 'You know,' he said after a moment, 'despite us working together for nearly three years, I sometimes feel I don't know you at all. It's like the first day you walked in with a big notice saying "Keep out. Private. Trespassers will be prosecuted".'

She looked up and smiled questioningly.

He shrugged. 'Oh, I don't mean your rebuffs. I'm game for that. But there's something else, something I can't quite put my finger on. A sort of detachment, I suppose. A closed area …' He paused, searching for the right word. 'Oh, I don't know, but whatever it is, it makes you all the more appealing. Though I do wonder if anyone will ever get that close to you.'

Aisha gave a small dismissive laugh and, dropping the letter in the 'out tray', stood. 'The lure of the illusive woman?' she teased. 'You know I like to keep my private life separate, David. I always have done.'

'No, it's more than that,' he began again; then shrugged and let it go. 'Anyway, when you change your mind about dinner, which you will one day, I'll be waiting.' He winked and headed towards the door.

'Thanks again for the flowers,' she called after him. 'They're very much appreciated.'

'So are you! You're welcome. Enjoy!'

Aisha watched the door close behind him and then glanced at her watch. She would have to get a move on if she was going to stop off at the supermarket on the way home. She liked to make a special dessert when either of the children brought a friend home for tea. Chocolate gateaux or pavlova – Sarah loved meringue. Picking up the flowers and her briefcase, Aisha unhooked her coat from the stand and went out through the main office, calling goodbyes as she went. At least it wasn't far to home which was one of the reasons why she had accepted the position. She and the children left the house together in the morning and she could be back by five thirty when necessary.

Going down the steps at the rear of the building, she crossed the staff car park and flicked the central locking system on her car. She smiled to herself as she got in and laid the flowers on the passenger seat. How many bouquets was that now? She'd lost count, and all the little gifts David had left on her desk, or recently, more boldly, presented to her in person. The first had been a potted plant for the windowsill in her office with a note saying he hoped he wasn't being presumptuous. It must have been over a year ago. That had been followed with chocolates and perfume and then the huge bouquets tied with ribbon. And while initially Aisha had felt uncomfortable accepting the gifts, feeling she was in his debt, it had become a little harmless fun, where David joked he would eventually capture the heart of his boss and they would run off together into the sunset. He was her deputy, and she was the assistant claims manager at Medway Life Assurance Company.

Aisha turned on the heater in the car and pulled to the exit. Sam Griffiths, the sales director, tooted his horn as he drew up behind her and then gave a little wave. She waved back. They got on well. In fact she got on with most of the staff in the small and friendly office. It was a subsidiary of an American company and the directors liked their managers squeaky clean; and for them widowhood equalled dignity, with no skeletons in the cupboard. Aisha suspected the occasional wearing of her sari helped the company's political correctness. She made a point of wearing it if anyone from the New York head office paid a visit, and it hadn't gone unnoticed.

Making the detour via the shops, Aisha continued home and parked on the drive. As she got out, she paused to admire the front garden, for even in winter it had colour, with the carefully chosen evergreen shrubs and heathers. She and her father had worked on it all the previous summer, and like the house it now bore her stamp and no trace of Mark. Going in, she found James sprawled on the sofa, as usual, deaf to everything except the music coming from his MP3 player. Aisha ruffled his hair as she went by and he grinned, languidly raising one hand to acknowledge her. There was no sign of Sarah; she would be upstairs with her friend, poring over teenage magazines or trying out new hairstyles.

Aisha set the kettle to boil for a cup of tea and then arranged David's flowers in a vase. She vaguely wondered what he was doing at this moment. He had a teenage son living with him so perhaps his evening routine wasn't so very different from hers: preparing the evening meal, tiding, trying to initiate conversation; parents of teenagers who were needed, but not required. Sarah and James's generation were free spirits, she thought, unrestrained by tradition or the need to be seen to do the right thing.

Aisha glanced at the wall clock – it was nearly six o'clock. She would start the spaghetti bolognese just as soon as she'd paid her evening visit – the visit she made at six o'clock every evening.

Taking the key from under the tea towels in the kitchen drawer, Aisha silently unlocked the interconnecting door to the garage and went in. There was no need to lock it from the inside; the children knew not to disturb her at this time.

She stood for a moment, allowing her eyes to adjust – the only light came from the two candles on the floor, near the centre of the garage. The shadow on the wall opposite danced in the draft from the closing door, like a cave painting of a giant wildebeest on the run. Six o'clock, exactly the right time. She knew because the radio had been on. The six o'clock news coming from Magic, ringing in her ears and drowning out the sound of crunching metal and breaking glass. She stood silently as the shadow sleeked around the walls, then settled, the handlebars sticking out like the antlers of a beast ready to charge. It was the shadow of Mark's

293

motorbike, the bike returned to her by the police, now balanced on its stand in the centre of the garage, just like the evening she had first seen it. It wasn't complete, of course, the fenders and headlamps were missing, severed in the crash and swept up with the other debris. The framework was bent in places and the previously immaculate paint work had ugly gashes down both sides. But she'd had it collected from the police compound and kept it, and it had stood here for nearly five years, as a testament, a monument, lest she ever forget.

Aisha walked slowly to the centre of the garage as the shadow of the bike distorted and flickered around walls. Stopping at the side of the bike, she ran her hand over the length of the leather seat, just as Mark had done. Propped at the end of the seat was the framed photograph, partially illuminated by the candlelight. Aisha picked up the photograph and breathed on the glass, then rubbed it hard with the sleeve of her cardigan. The couple in love smiled back, assured and unrepentant. She breathed and rubbed again, then returned it to its position so that it looked out over the garage and kept watch. The candles had burned low and needed replacing; she replaced them every evening from a box kept full on the workbench beneath his tools. The garage was exactly as it had been on that fateful night – a shrine, a cenotaph, an acknowledgement to what she had done and that she was very sorry.

Aisha remained quiet for a few minutes, looking around, taking in the scene and remembering. But tonight, instead of fetching new candles from the box, she squatted down on her haunches and pinched out the last of the flames. The garage fell into darkness.

Memories pale, bitterness loses its edge, pain and humiliation fade. At some point we have to cloak the past in experience and move on, wiser, to the future. Aisha won't be replacing the candles tonight or ever again, for she has decided that five years is long enough to repent and be sorry. Tomorrow she will make arrangements to have the garage completely cleared – of the bike, his tools, the photograph, and everything. Then possibly the closed part of her that David had recognized might begin to open, and she might, just might, accept his dinner invitation. Her father had been right – an eclipse doesn't last forever – and there could and would be an even brighter future with a lifetime of tomorrows, just as soon as she told the inspector what really happened that night.